ᵛᵗₑ C

Victorian Values

Personalities and Perspectives in Nineteenth-Century Society

Second Edition

Edited by Gordon Marsden

LONGMAN
London and New York

Addison Wesley Longman Limited
Edinburgh Gate, Harlow,
Essex CM20 2JE, England
and Associated Companies throughout the world.

Published in the United States of America
by Longman Publishing, New York

Editorial matter © Gordon Marsden 1990, 1998
Articles © History Today 1987, 1989, 1996, 1997

First published 1990
Second Edition 1998

ISBN 0 582 29289 1

Visit Addison Wesley Longman on the world wide web at
http://www.awl-he.com

British Library Cataloguing in Publication Data
A catalogue record for this book is available from the
British Library

Library of Congress Cataloging in Publication Data
Victorian values : personalities and perspectives in Nineteenth-
century society / edited by Gordon Marsden. — 2nd ed.
     p.   cm.
  Includes biliographical references (p.   ) and index.
  ISBN 0-582-29289-1
  1. Great Britain—Social conditions—19th century. 2. Social
values—History—19th century. 3. Great Britain—History—Victoria,
1837–1901—Biography. 4. Great Britain—Biography. I. Marsden,
Gordon, 1953– .
HN385.V55   1998
306'.0941'09034 —dc21

98–4601
CIP

Set in 10/12pt Palatino

Transferred to digital print on demand, 2002

Printed and bound by Antony Rowe Ltd, Eastbourne

Contents

List of Illustrations

Foreword

Victorian values have hit the headlines several times during the last ten years. The Victorians might or might not have been pleased, but they would certainly have been occasionally amused. They were well aware of the divergence of precept and practice. Recent topical interest has thrown more light on our own society and culture – and on our economy – than on theirs.

Professional historians have long pointed out how difficult it is to generalise about Victorian values or, for that matter, anything else Victorian. Had not 'the good Queen' lived so long we would have divided the nineteenth century in a different way and no-one could have talked of Victorianism. As it is, we rightly distinguish between early, middle and late Victorian. We also note contrasts at any point in the long reign between perceptions in one part of the country and another part or between one class and another. The two were, of course, directly related. Because there were so many barriers of communication the mode of proclaiming and communicating values is a subject of great interest in itself.

In a period of continuing change there was never any full agreement about what Victorian values really were, and during the late-Victorian years there was a sustained, if usually unsuccessful, attack on those Victorian values which had been dominant during the mid-Victorian years.

Nonetheless, most articulate Victorians were concerned about values even when they were in disagreement about religion, a core subject to study, about economics, where recent, current and prospective changes were recognised to be far-reaching, and about politics, where much, though not all, of the development must be explained in terms other than those of values.

In reprinting this series of articles on Victorian values from *History Today*, we focus on Victorian experience in diverse forms. The questions raised cannot be answered glibly. Moreover, they cover all aspects of experience, not least double standards in relation to sex. The psychology cannot be left out, turning as it does on issues of character and will. Because the questions are often basic, it is doubtful whether they will ever be exhausted. Whatever the reasons for the topical interest in Victorian values, we are still not out of a society and culture which feels it necessary to appeal to them.

ASA BRIGGS

Acknowledgements

Special thanks are due to those who helped make both the History Today *Victorian Values* articles and the subsequent book project possible: Asa Briggs, for his initial enthusiasm for the series and subsequent advice and to my colleagues at *History Today*, particularly Marion Soldan, and Jacqueline Guy, whose tremendous experience and magpie eye garnered the wealth of illustrations for *Victorian Values* (of which the present book version can offer merely a representative sample). Thanks also to my parents and grandparents, who filtered through to me the best of those values, and to Richard, for looking to the future while putting up with the past.

GORDON MARSDEN

Queen Victoria
Woodcut by Sir William Nicholson, c. 1899. (HT Archives)

1
Introduction

Gordon Marsden

'The past is a foreign country,' remarks a character in L. P. Hartley's novel *The Go Between*, 'they do things differently there.' But did they? And should we? No period from the past has been more enthusiastically plundered to promote the present in the past fifteen years than the Victorian era. The supposed values and principles that underpinned its society have been rediscovered and recommended in that period by a motley mix of academics, journalists and politicians, including the prime minister of Great Britain who ended up attaching *her* name to a pivotal period of twentieth-century British history, thus emulating the great queen herself. (Would Victoria have been amused? Given her way with over-assertive chief ministers such as Gladstone, one suspects not.)

The way in which re-examinations of the Victorian period and explanations for Britain's supposed industrial decline were linked in the 1980s with a resurgence of enthusiasm for the enterprise culture on both sides of the Atlantic was most carefully charted at the time in a *Past and Present* (No 123) article by Simon Raven. His account of how this debate turned and progressed from influential academic works from historians such as Correlli Barnett, Martin Wiener and Harold Perkin centre-stage, to the political think-tanks and research institutes of British and North American industry, and finally to the front benches and cabinet offices of government, is a powerful if controversial underlining of the use (or misuse) of history for political polemic.

The political purpose underlying the propagation of Victorian values in the 1980s was in most cases transparent. If self-help, self-reliance, entrepreneurship, individual charity (rather than a state dole), law and order, family discipline and a stricter sexual morality were the principles that enabled the Victorians to make hitherto undreamed of progress, and were responsible in Britain's case for a 'golden age' of power and influence, were they not an endorsement for a similar philosophy of Mrs Thatcher's Britain? And if the values that made Britain great in the second half of the nineteenth century were essentially those of an imperialist ethos, was it not perhaps time for more confidence and less guilt about the latter's legacy, a confidence that had translated itself into that Gaullist assertiveness that was a hallmark of much of Mrs Thatcher's dealings with the rest of the world from Galtieri to the Common Market (and which seemed to have been emulated in President Reagan's way of seeing the world beyond America over the same period)?

Even if such a summary had been an adequate assessment of
the values of Victorian society, it would still be open to us to
reject them – as so many intellectuals and others enthusiastically
did in the years succeeding the Great War, notably Lytton Strachey
in his wicked sideswipe at the period's great figures, *Eminent
Victorians*. And, in addition, many were keen to challenge this
view of Victorian society – among them James Walvin in his
book on *Victorian Values*, produced to accompany the 1987 Gra-
nada Television series of the same name. The authors of the pieces
that make up our book cast their own light on this particular
debate while observing the caveat judiciously made by Professor
Asa Briggs in his Foreword, which introduced the original series
in *History Today*.

> Professional historians have long pointed out how difficult it is to gener-
> alise about Victorian values . . . had not 'the good Queen' lived so long
> we would have divided the nineteenth century in a different way and
> no-one could have talked of Victorianism. As it is we rightly distinguish
> between early, middle and late Victorian.

But beyond the narrower political polemic, there are very good
reasons why Victorian society should have come to hold so great
a fascination for us today, considerations that were strongly to
the fore when the original decision was made to commission for
History Today a series of articles to mark the 150th anniversary of
Victoria's accession. Chief among these has been the collapse of
confidence in many aspects of post-war society and culture, most
searingly in the areas of architecture and urban planning. This
revolt against the Modern Movement and its disciples has spread
from the grumblings of the man on the Clapham omnibus (a
splendidly Victorian artefact) to enlist the support of the chatter-
ing classes and finally enjoy the patronage of the heir to the
throne himself.

If parallels are to be sought between then and now, one of the
most intriguing that might be investigated is that between Prince
Charles and Prince Albert – both intelligent, sensitive men seeking to break out of the constitutional straitjackets imposed upon
them, and to establish for themselves a role as orchestrators of
vigorous social and cultural debate – and both attracting bitter
and snide opposition from entrenched establishments in doing so.

The parallel begins to break down, of course, when one com-
pares the uxorious bliss of Albert and Victoria with the marital
problems and breakdown that have dogged the Prince of Wales

in the past ten years, culminating in the trauma of the death of his former wife. The immediate royal reaction to this, to pull up the drawbridge at Balmoral – and the public dissatisfaction it provoked – has uncanny echoes with the premature death of Albert, when the grief-stricken withdrawal of Victoria from public life – often to that same gloomy, neo-Gothic royal refuge – provoked a severe crisis of confidence in the monarchy. Britain in the late 1860s came as close to a sentiment of republicanism as it has ever done – until, perhaps intriguingly, the present day.

It is perhaps too early to say whether the extraordinary public outpouring of grief at the death of Diana, Princess of Wales, and the criticism of the Royal Family that has followed in its wake, will indeed result in sweeping changes and responses similar to those that put the monarch – and the monarchy – back on the road to popularity in late-Victorian Britain. But even before the traumatic events of September 1997, the debate that had opened up about the future of the monarchy in Britain on the back of the break-up of Charles's and Diana's marriage had prompted historians to look more closely at the invention of tradition – both state and royal – in late-Victorian Britain. As historians such as David Cannadine and William Kuhn have argued in recent books, albeit from different perspectives, there is plenty of scope here to hold up Victorian values to illuminate today's clouded royal mirror.

Controversy about the separation of the public from the private, the presentation of the formal and the preservation of the informal, and the role of the monarchy in a changing British state, was as relevant in the 1860s and 1870s as they are in the late 1990s. Now, perhaps, a new British prime minister has in the wake of Diana's death gently encouraged the monarchy down the road of modernisation and less formality: Tony Blair's Victorian counterpart was another new prime minister, Benjamin Disraeli, who coaxed the widowed queen out of seclusion with a 'makeover' that went in the opposite direction, and a title 'Empress of India' that bestowed antiquity on a new global reality: the British Empire.

It is no coincidence that with the increasing interest (arguably accentuated by post-modernism) among historians in such questions as the invention of tradition and the construction of identity in Britain (to which Linda Colley's brilliant book on the forging of a British identity in the wake of the eighteenth-century Hanoverian settlement gave a strong boost) has come, particularly in the last ten years since the first 'Victorian Values' series was originally published in *History Today*, an ever-more lively debate about the relationship of Empire to those values.

The invention of monarchical tradition, the construction of British identity, the reflection of both in the construction of a popular ideology for an acquired empire – this holy trinity of historical relationships has come centre-stage into nineteenth- and early twentieth-century British studies. It has been stimulated as more and more of our contemporary debate has focused on the nature of a twenty-first-century British monarchy (if there is to be one) and on the future for Britishness and indeed for the Union, with pressures both from above – towards greater integration in the European Union – and from below, with devolution initiatives for Scotland, Wales and, potentially, the English regions.

Bernard Porter, in a perceptive 'Cross-Current' piece for *History Today* in August 1996, pointed out how many of the assumptions about the role of monarchy and the late-Victorian/Edwardian creation of a role for the state had been underpinned by the mechanisms of that Empire and by the *noblesse oblige* cast of mind that its administrators brought with them. Investigating how far that imperial ethos was a creation of or an impetus for the values of late-Victorian Britain has correspondingly been a magnet for historians.

Economic and commercial history has been prominent in this new research. Peter Cain and Tony Hopkins, with their two 1993 volumes *British Imperialism: Innovation and Expansion, 1688–1914* and *British Imperialism: Crisis and Destruction, 1914–1990*, brought to fruition more than a decade of careful argument and sustained analysis to challenge the idea that 'trade followed the flag'. In the first volume particularly they were at pains, as Theo Barker observed in his review of the books in *History Today*, 'to argue that the British empire grew in response to the needs of British commerce and the financial sources which supported it'. The packed seminar room I squeezed into at a subsequent American Historical Association session on the books and their implications was testimony to the intense interest generated on both sides of the Atlantic by their description of the network of connections between Britain and its informal as well as formal empire – the former particularly of interest to those seeking comparative clues to the rise and fall of the Pax Americana in a post-Vietnam world.

At the same time, the revival of narrative in historiography has found its echoes in studies of the makers of Victorian empire: number-crunching and tales of derring-do have been blended as strands in this 1990s coverage. Books like Edward Ingram's *Empire Building and Empire Builders*, Frank McLynn's controversial *Stanley: Sorcerer's Apprentice*, and the strong narrative thrust of Lawrence James's *Rise and Fall of the British Empire*, have been complemented by exploration of the explorers in other media – most recently with the Livingstone exhibition and accompanying essay/catalogue from the National Portrait Gallery in London and the BBC's television *magnum opus* on the life of Cecil Rhodes. The latter – although panned by the critics and a flop with the viewers – did, for all its flaws (far fewer in the accompanying book by Antony Thomas than in the series itself), at least attempt to tease out, via the life of one of the most extraordinary figures of Victorian imperialism, the strange amalgam of greed, low cunning, high cant, guilty nobility and lost idealism that seems to be emerging as historians reassess Victoria's 'empire-builders'.

The acceptance that this kaleidoscope of mixed motives could co-exist in such characters is a product perhaps of a coming of age in nineteenth-century imperial studies. Thesis, anti-thesis, synthesis: thus time after time history proceeds, and the study of Victorian imperialism has been no exception. Eulogised in British schools almost to the eve of Suez as the selfless discharging of the White Man's Burden (and articulated by teachers with maps of red in the manner so brilliantly captured by a playwright such as Dennis Potter), demonised in the wake of decolonisation by a generation of 1960s historians who sought to point out, quite rightly, the havoc wrought on traditional social and tribal structures, particularly in Africa, by the arbitrary boundaries of colonial administrators, it is perhaps only now, a generation removed from that 'wind of change', that we can assess the pluses and minuses of Empire more dispassionately.

The recent fiftieth anniversaries of Independence in the Indian subcontinent revealingly caught that new sense of distance's objectivity both in the response of academics (assessing a Raj which, though it covered in one form or another a period of nearly two centuries, was centrally a late-Victorian creation) and in the official and popular reflections and commemorations in India and Pakistan themselves.

Despite this move away from a black-and-white verdict in historiography on the values of Victorian empire, the area remains sensitive and controversial. Those who seek to become new guardians of the flame can be fiercely contested: anyone in any doubt of that needed only to look at Max Beloff's assault on the choice of the University of Texas as the editorial base for the new *Oxford History of the British Empire*, due to be published this year. Beloff's concern that its contributors would misunderstand the imperial ethos and reshape its history in line with fashionable American political correctness reverberated in the article he wrote reviewing the state of Imperial studies for the January 1996 issue of *History Today* and was subsequently elaborated on a BBC TV 'Newsnight' programme that took up the controversy. In a *Sunday Times* article reviewing the affair, Beloff drew support from Jan Morris, who in her own trilogy has been as influential a populariser of nineteenth-century imperial history as A. L. Rowse was on sixteenth-century Elizabethan England – 'of course the Empire was exploitative, but there were also administrators who did a lot of good.'

Inevitably historical trends reflect contemporary angst, a point well made by Gareth Stedman Jones in his commentary on the changing historiography of nineteenth-century Britain in a May 1991 article for *History Today*. But the truth is also that the angst was there at the time. One of the strengths of this Second Edition has been the ability to include a new article by Denis Judd which focuses on the cracks in the Imperial façade of self-confidence that were observed even at its zenith, the Diamond Jubilee of June 1897 (whose recent centenary has given further impetus to a *fin-de-siècle* obsession in popular Victorian studies). In focusing on the response to the Jubilee from the Empire's own bard, Rudyard Kipling, via his poem *Recessional*, Judd rightly identifies that angst: 'the lines are stirring yet disturbing, containing a series of measured and sober warnings against patriotic and imperial excess within a framework of thoughtful introspection . . . behind the bold, brash and frequently self-congratulatory front that the Diamond Jubilee celebrations presented to the world, lurked in almost unquantifiable measure, pessimism and insecurity'. Even as the global triumph of Victorian values was being hymned in London, there were intimations of the Last Post that the Great War would start to usher in.

The dismantling of Empire took less than a generation, the rejection of many of the values that sustained it arguably begun the generation before when Lytton Strachey penned his iconoclastic work, *Eminent Victorians*. But such was the power and pull of that lost world that nostalgia for it was not long emerging.

The handmaidens of the reaction against Modernism have been the heritage and conservation movements – and in Britain the spectacular growth in membership and influence of organisations like the National Trust, as well as of more specialist campaigning groups such as the Georgian Group and the Victorian Society itself, is a further example of the phenomenon.

Closely associated with the restoration of Victorian artefacts to popular esteem was an attack on the 1960s and its cultural and social legacies. Not every young (or old) fogey lovingly restoring a black-leaded fireplace with its Staffordshire figures or dusting off the antimacassar has been a denouncer of the decade and all its works; but in many cases the banishing of formica and conti-board has brought with it a soured reappraisal of some of the benefits of the permissive society. Whether condemned by the moral majority for their sexual mores or sneered at by their children for their naivety and lack of style, the 1960s generation was placed on the psychological defensive – and part of that process involved an apotheosis of Victoriana with which to dish them.

Other periods of history have been pressed into this service as well, of course. It is arguable that in the US, for example, the nostalgic appeal of the 1950s – the Eisenhower years, when the Pax Americana had been tarnished by neither Vietnam nor Watergate – or the wholesome tranquillity of small-town America between the wars (in so many ways the source of Ronald Reagan's philosophy, with an extraordinary appeal to ordinary Americans) – have provided a counterpart golden age to that of the Victorian era in Britain. But on both sides of the Atlantic, renewal and refurbishment of urban centres whose architectural hearts are often still Victorian, has acted as a reproach to the post-war grim concrete boxes and to walkways of estates that have become the repository of crime and built-in obsolescence.

It is also arguable that the *longue durée* of human genealogy and memory has combined with the factors above to give the Victorian period a peculiarly powerful appeal at the present time. It is a world far enough away to demand and receive a deepening historical perspective, distant enough to avoid the reflex rejection that those born in the first decades of the twentieth century bestowed upon the Victorian era, yet near enough to have many of its artefacts plentifully present, near enough to have its folk memories and family tales communicated by our parents and grandparents.

This, after all, is how Margaret Thatcher imbibed her draught of Victorian values, at the knee of Alderman Roberts in the corner shop at Grantham. It is a world whose pillar boxes, drinking fountains, Gothic revival churches, town halls and sewers (just) are still with us. Its china and apostle spoons still nestle as family heirlooms on our back shelves, and our bottom drawers still shelter samples of the heavy, pre-decimal, Victorian copper pennies. And now, newly burnished under the patina of revisionism, the Victorian world reaches out in a very real sense as a historical *heimat* – a homeland in which we can identify a repository of shared experience, and to which it is still possible to return in our style time-machine. This *heimat* is, of course, quintessentially a vision of the late-Victorian period (stretching to include an Edwardian one with those long, golden summers of innocence before 1914). But are the values currently being propagated from that period, or are they rather those of the early to middle years of Victoria's reign?

These then have perhaps been some of the factors behind the popular, instinctive revival of interest in Victorian society and Victorianism. Side by side with it – and pre-dating the debate about Victorian values – has been an explosion of interest in the period in the academic world and in school and university syllabuses. At the same time, a new impetus for the interdisciplinary study of history has enabled us to see far more lucidly the sum of the parts of Victorian society.

In so doing we are rediscovering the connections the Victorians themselves made between cultural manifestations and their religious and philosophical beliefs. This interdisciplinary approach, it must be pointed out, has long been more vigorous and innovative in North America – witness the publication of the quarterly journal *Victorian Studies* by Indiana University which has stressed these links. But Britain caught up fast, and here some of the most pioneering work has been done by the Open University, with path-breaking courses at various levels on Victorian religion and society as well as the more detailed investigation, utilising modern multi-media, including on-line and CD-Rom, of the significance of the 'history from below' that the censuses of late Victorian Britain, and other data, including the pioneering social science of Charles Booth, reveal. The work there of academics such as David Englander and Rosemary O'Day also underlines another important trend in Victorian studies – the restoration of religion to a central position in discussing the history of the period and the motivation of its prime movers. This shift from a deracinated view of the Victorian era was heralded by the publication of the massive Gladstone diaries, now complete, along with Colin Matthew's

commentaries and Roy Jenkins's biography, both of which empha-
sise the centrality of religion to understanding one of the central
political figures of the age. The broad-brush canvasses such as
Edward Norman's *The English Catholic Church in the Nineteenth
Century* and Peter Gay's *magnum opus* – *The Bourgeois Experience:
Victoria to Freud* have been supplemented by a clutch of detailed
studies – Richard Brant's *Liberal Anglican Politics*, J. P. Parry's
Democracy and Religion: Gladstone and the Liberal Party, and Boyd
Hilton's *The Age of Atonement: the Influence of Evangelicalism on
Social and Economic Thought, 1750–1865* are three examples that
spring to mind. The age's key religious and philosophical think-
ers have also been subjected to penetrating biographical analysis.
Alongside Ian Kerr's massive study of Newman, there have been
other works exploring the tensions between private belief and
public policy, such as the collection of essays edited by Bernard
Lightman on *Victorian Faith in Crisis*, Stefan Collini's *Public Moral-
ists: Political Thought and Intellectual Life in Britain, 1850–1930*, and
José Harris's *Private Lives, Public Spirit: A Social History of Britain,
1870–1914*. At the same time, some of the newer contributions
from women's studies on both sides of the Atlantic – Colleen
McDannell's *The Christian Home in Victorian America, 1840–1900*,
Gail Malmgreen's *Religion in the Lives of English Women, 1760–
1930*, Deborah Valenze's *Prophetic Sons and Daughters* and, most
recently, Anne Summers's *Angels & Citizens: British Women as Military Nurses, 1854–1914*, Lynda Nead's *Myths of Sexuality: Representations of Women in Victorian Britain* and Leonore Davidoff and
Catherine Hall's *Family Fortunes: Men and Women in the English
Middle Class, 1780–1850* – have integrated religious motivation and
experience into a discussion of the rising self-consciousness of
women and their role in Victorian society.

The new emphasis on religion's role inevitably has included a
new emphasis on two of the powerful revivers of religion in
Victorian Britain, Evangelicalism and Anglo-Catholicism; on the
continuing central role of Nonconformity; and on the sharpening
effect of the challenge from science. The importance of the conjunction is one that Gerald Parsons comments on (in his introduction to the fourth volume of accompanying text to the Open
University course on *Religion in Victorian Britain*):

. . . it was the coincidence of on the one hand that religious revival, and
on the other hand the rise of a secular intellectual elite seeking to present
a new and post-Christian intellectual synthesis, which gave rise to much
of the intensity of the religious controversy of the Victorian age.

It was a debate immeasurably sharpened, of course, by the controversy over the origin of the species and its implications for the
Genesis creation myth, that finds expression in Robert Browning's
cerebral but poignant discussion 'Unfaith and Faith':

> Why first, you don't believe, you don't and can't . . .
> In any revelation called divine;
> No dogmas nail your faith; and what remains
> But say so, like the honest man you are.

But that conjunction also reminds us how essentially Janus-faced
Victorian society was. It looked forward to the triumph of science
and technology and a better and brighter future – and a world
that knows AIDS, acid rain, the greenhouse effect and Chernobyl
might reasonably indulge in nostalgia for the technological self-
confidence that drove a Stephenson, a Brunel, a Stanford or a
Carnegie. But it also looked back – to an idealised medieval world
with imagined harmony between church and state, to a time when
the arts conspired *ad majorem Dei gloriam*, and when there was a
general acceptance of a *noblesse oblige* order of society. Victorian
society craved novelty and innovation, but it also took comfort
from tradition. Where necessary, it also invented it, as remarked
previously.

Perhaps the greatest invention of Victorian popular culture was
that of Christmas. Puritan hostility and Enlightenment cynicism
had all but extinguished Christmas as a popular phenomenon,
and it is entirely appropriate that the figure responsible almost
single-handed for breathing life back into the medieval feast should
have been the literary giant who is most synonymous in our
minds with the Victorian period: Charles Dickens. It was G. K.
Chesterton who, in his essay on Dickens's *A Christmas Carol*,
pointed out the paradox of this utilitarian friend of progress having come to the rescue of what in other contexts he might have
seen as a backward Catholic superstition. The paradox is still a
striking one today, and one which received further attention with
Geoffrey Rowell's 'Dickens and the Construction of Christmas' in
the December 1993 issue of *History Today*, where he linked the
festival's revival with Victorian fears about social cohesion and
shared values – a foreboding that again is occupying centre-stage
in many of the discussions of British society in the 1990s.

Paradox, indeed, is the predominant characteristic observed the
more one peers into the workings of the Victorian world. It is a
recurring theme in the essays presented here. The arch-progenitor

of imperialist sentiment and protectionism in late-Victorian Britain, Joseph Chamberlain, was also the man regarded as a dangerous gas and water socialist for his work in municipalising Birmingham's private supply companies. His brand of radical populism advocating education, church and land reform in the 1880s made him appear as a wild man of the left to Gladstone and his more temperate Liberal allies. By contrast, Gladstone himself, embodiment of the conscience of a largely Nonconformist party, was a devoted High Anglican, mistrustful of jingoism and imperial adventure. The values that Nonconformity taught could also be doubled-edged in their effects: sobriety, deference, honest toil and modesty may have been one side of the coin, but on the other was the assertion of solidarity in working-class communities, and the self-confidence of the self-helped that led men from the pulpit to the strike meeting and eventually to the political platform. Hence the dictum that the moral and organisational roots of the British Labour Party owe far more to Methodism than to Marx.

Such a kaleidoscope of attitudes should make even the boldest of editors pause for thought before commissioning a series of articles on Victorian values. The vast majority of the pieces which appear here take as their starting-point some of the colourful individuals who left their mark on Victorian society – partly because the biographical route is always a vivid way of harnessing the general reader to the past, and partly because the contradictions and conflicting pressures within those individuals offer a useful way in to an analysis of the movements and attitudes with which they were associated. Fourteen of the twenty pieces in this revised and expanded Second Edition appeared originally, with Asa Briggs's introduction, under the series title 'Victorian Values' in *History Today* between March and September 1987. The original version of Dea Birkett's profile of Mary Kingsley and West Africa appeared independently in the May 1987 issue, and Anne Summers's examination of Victorian nursing and social reform in the February 1989 number of *History Today*. These have been joined in this Second Edition by a quartet of 'Victorian Values Mark II' articles that appeared in the magazine between May 1996 and June 1997, designed to add two key individuals – William Morris and Rudyard Kipling – whom it had not been possible to include in the original survey, as well as to strengthen the coverage of Victorian popular culture which has become so important and dynamic a part of historical study of the period. John Tosh's intriguing piece on the changing face of 'Masculinity' in nineteenth-century Britain is an example of how we have tried to give conscious weight to some of the new types of work that have broken the mould of traditional ways of looking at the Victorian period. Janet Wolff and Caroline Arscott's illuminating exposé of the myth of the philistine northern businessman is a striking example – where there was muck there was apparently not only money but a great deal of fine patronage of the latest pre-Raphaelite painting. To it could and should be added the late Stephen Jones's lucid survey of the powerful impact of aestheticism and Robert Young's untangling of the web of 'inevitable progress' propagated by *Vanity Fair*'s wild-eyed Professor, Herbert Spencer.

Great names – Gladstone, Smiles, Chamberlain, Salt and Dickens – have not been neglected, but we have found time to consider others – like Stewart Headlam and George Godwin who, though lesser-known today, illuminate key movements and groupings in the Victorian era. And in the coverage of the better-known names we have tried to bring out their lesser-known perspectives – Lovett as the universal educator rather than the Chartist agitator, Smiles not as a simplistic apostle of *laissez-faire* but as the scourge of the 'terrible Nobody' that other exponents of untrammelled capitalism had excused for the bad food, cholera or crime that afflicted Victorian society.

If there is a commentary here on the claims made for Victorian values in our own time, it is a natural and not a forced one. We have perhaps forgotten how relentless the Victorian establishment could be in criticising and regulating itself by using the apparatus of the state. A Fry or a Shaftesbury might awaken individual consciences but it was government, central or local, that often had to take the decisive steps via legislation or regulation.

Surprises abound – our respectable forebears did not always do or say what we would expect of them. Queen Victoria's Britain was as much the target then as Colonel Gadaffi's Libya or post-Revolutionary Iran was in recent years for failing to expel *émigrés* and would-be traitors opposed to a variety of European regimes. Lord Palmerston, approving in 1850 of the mob of London draymen who had jostled the notoriously repressive Austrian general Haynau, with the remark they should have 'tossed him in a blanket, rolled him in the kennel and then sent him home in a cab', is not the most likely proponent of diplomatic decorum and the rights of foreign emissaries ever to have occupied the British Foreign Office. And the tale here told by Ian Bradley of the 'enlightened entrepreneur' Titus Salt – self-effacing, humble, 'whose one personal indulgence was to buy a gold watch when his savings reached £1,000' – hardly sits comfortably as a role model beside some of the 'greed is good' excesses of the 1980s that now find less favour at the end of the century. 'Tracts for the Times' have an unpleasant habit of twisting the moral – and the reader may find these essays no exception to that rule. On the other hand, the obsession with 'sleaze' and impropriety that dominated British politics in the run-up to the 1997 General Election and had its echo in controversies not just on the other side of the Atlantic but also in scandals in continental Europe has its counterpart in the excesses of entrepreneurial laissez-faire in Victorian values as well, as James Foreman-Peck reminded *History Today* readers in a glimpse of the railway scandals of mid-nineteenth-century Britain in an August 1995 article.

There is perhaps one final way in which this book may contribute to revising some conventional nostrums. That is in the very sharp perspective it gives of a galaxy of characters and views from the end of the era reflecting what one can only describe as anti-Victorian values. If it is argued that the Victorian period saw the origin of many of those late-twentieth-century vices that contemporary commentators have railed against, then the period post-1880 is the one where they may most fruitfully be sought out.

There is inevitably a cut-off problem here – the articles by Paul Rich, Sheila Rowbotham and to a lesser extent Edward Norman tilt over into the Edwardian era – but, I would argue, they have their essential thrust and genesis in the Victorian one, justifying their appearance in this volume. This is the period in which the balance visibly begins to turn from praising individual endeavour to orchestrating state involvement, in which the costs as well as the benefits of Victorian Britain's mechanisms begin to be counted, the period of the poverty surveys of Rowntree and the Webbs. It is a world whose conscience, or at least sense of balance, begins to express itself, as exemplified in Churchill's acid comment, 'I see little glory in an empire which can rule the waves and is unable to flush the sewers' – a remark that adds perspective to the debate there has been about private affluence and public squalor in both Britain and the US, and which has dominated attempts to devise post-Reagan and post-Thatcher strategies that will square that circle without returning to the New Deal or old-style interventionist politics of Britain's post-war Welfare State.

It is intriguing to note, for those who are devotees of the theories of cyclical history, that many of the New Age attitudes and sentiments that have come to the fore in the 1990s in a revolt against the heartless style of yuppiedom, find an 1890s echo in the back-to-nature groups of artists, intellectuals and political activists who clustered around men like William Morris and Edward Carpenter. Morris's manifesto *News from Nowhere*, the Arts and Crafts movement, Carpenter's homoerotic market garden commune at Millthorpe, Havelock Ellis's Fellowship of the New Life, and the small groups of self-conscious and often socialist feminists who in due course contributed importantly to the suffragette movement – all underline the vigour of alternative models in late-Victorian England. It is mischievous but interesting to speculate whether it would have been the massed ranks of Middle England wearing fabrics with his designs and paying homage at the recent V & A anniversary exhibition devoted to him that William Morris would have identified with – or Swampy and his bond of eco-warriors taking direct action to protest at the motorway bypass and runway extensions of 1990s Britain.

When taken with the quest for Englishness that Paul Rich describes – a search for 'an indigenous Merrie England' myth which embraced both a moral critique of capitalist industrialism and a search into England's distant past – it is easy to see why the supposed vices of the 1960s as well as the supposed virtues of the 1980s can claim an ancestry from the Victorian era.

Paul Rich describes *News from Nowhere* as 'an alternative land of adventure which sought to avoid the rapacious exploits of Victorian imperialism'. The latter is very much a product of the late-Victorian period, and though there is no one essay in the collection here that focuses narrowly on its inspirations and impact, its backwash can be observed in several of them.

I wrote in the original Introduction to the First Edition of these essays that Imperialism and its cultural manifestations are undoubtedly one of the great growth industries of Victorian studies, and cited the *Studies in Imperialism* series produced by Manchester University Press under its general editor John MacKenzie as well as the profusion of books examining the impact of the public school ethos on the psychology of empire – with authors such as Michael Rosanthal, J. A. Morgan, John Chandos, James Walvin and Peter Parker.

It is important here to add a word about the choice of illustrations for the book. *History Today* has always prided itself on both the range and profusion of the illustrations accompanying its articles, but considerations both of space and also of expense – particularly in view of the publishers' objective that this book should reach a wide general audience – have meant that only a small proportion of the original illustrations that accompanied the series could be reproduced here. In making the choice we have tried to be guided by the dictum that the pictures should complement rather than merely simplistically illustrate the text, and have paid particular emphasis to those pieces – Stephen Jones on Leighton and Janet Wolff and Caroline Arscott on 'cultivated capital', for example – where the visual element seemed particularly crucial to advancing the author's argument.

No-one could hope within the covers of one book to look at all the virtuosos whose lives shed light on the complexities of the Victorian world. But we have done our best, and the inclusion of Kipling in this Second Edition via Denis Judd's article has strengthened the analysis of one of those major hallmarks of the period.

> The tumult and the shouting dies
> The Captains and the Kings depart . . .
> Lord God of Hosts, be with us yet,
> Lest we forget – lest we forget!

Much will be required of those to whom much is given – Kipling's lines from his Diamond Jubilee poem *Recessional* echo the parable of the talents, which was perhaps the most penetrating of all the moral texts weighing heavily on the Victorian establishment; and though it is an easy task to guy their moral earnestness or denounce the hypocrisy into which it could so often shade, it has still, at its best, a power to move even the weary cynics of late-twentieth-century society.

In the Introduction to the First Edition of *Victorian Values* I yoked Kipling with Tennyson as perceptive commentators on the Zeitgeist of the Victorians. I am happy still to do so – not least because in the best of his work there is that oscillation between energy and optimism and raw vulnerability that, when all the superficial vogue for things Victorian is burnt away, will still sustain our fascination with a world whose achievements and blunders alike have made us what we are. Let us leave Tennyson some final words on Victorian values:

> O yet we trust that somehow good
> Will be the final goal of ill . . .

That nothing walks with aimless feet;
That not one life shall be destroyed
Or cast as rubbish to the void,
When God hath made the pile complete . . .

So runs my dream: but what am I?
An infant crying in the night;
An infant crying for the light;
And with no language but a cry.

FREE EVENING CLASS AT LOUTH, TAUGHT BY MR. COLAM.

"TO DO GOOD, AND TO COMMUNICATE, FORGET NOT."

2

'Kindness and Reason'
William Lovett and Education

Brian Harrison

Opposite: a free evening class for agricultural labourers at Louth, Lincolnshire, 1862. Lovett saw adult education as making good the gaps in elementary education. (Mansell Collection)

THE IDIOSYNCRASIES of individual Victorian men and women inevitably complicate simplistic attempts to align their views completely with the groups and causes they fought for. So does their longevity – the radical of thirty-five may be the crusty conservative of sixty-five. The career of William Lovett (1800–77) is a case in point.

His contribution to history is usually associated umbilically with the phenomenon of Chartism, that great mass movement of the 1830s and 1840s demanding a broader franchise, annual Parliament, greater freedoms of press and public assembly and embodying the hopes of articulate artisans among the working class. The great Chartist demonstration of 1848 drew 100,000 to Kennington Common and seemed for a time as if it might be the harbinger of revolution similar to those which broke out that same year all over the continent of Europe.

By 1848, however, Lovett had parted company with the demagoguery of Chartism and his leading rival in the movement, Fergus O'Connor. Here Brian Harrison argues that his significance for us today rests much more with the other, less revered Victorian values that Lovett espoused, wrote about and was an active advocate of, for the last forty years of his life: a passion for the self-improvement, respectability, and improved opportunity of the virtuous workers and an unswerving belief in 'progress'.

Just across the road from Karl Marx in Highgate cemetery, William Lovett lies buried. Yet his grave has few visitors; indeed, until last autumn its inscription was indecipherable – obscured by a century's neglect, lichen and weathering. Yet he is far more representative than Marx of nineteenth-century British working-class politics, was far better known in his day, and was much more accurate in his predictions about British social trends.

Most people, if they've heard of Lovett at all, know of him as a Chartist – as the high-minded secretary of the London Working Men's Association which gave birth to Chartism, and as the courageous champion of 'moral force' methods against the 'physical force' methods of the rival Chartist leader Feargus O'Connor. Yet this is misleading, for it locates Lovett in the pre-Victorian context of class conflict that died away in the mid-1840s, and sees his career as ending prematurely; 'as far as it influenced history', writes G. D. H. Cole, his career 'was over before he was forty: the rest of his life was merely an epilogue of dogged, disillusioned faith'.

In reality, Lovett epitomises Victorian values. Though born in 1800, he was no has-been in 1840, the year he began writing his autobiography; indeed, he continued adding to it right up to 1874, devoted over a third of it to the post-Chartist years after 1842, and published it in 1876, the year before he died. The book is thoroughly Victorian in tone, and like so many in its genre, does not see the world in terms of class conflict; on the contrary – respectability, class harmony, and education will ensure mankind's steady progress towards prosperity and peace. The world will progress the more his readers mould themselves in his own image – hence the book's somewhat sermonising tone, with its concluding injunctions against gambling, drinking and race-going. It takes its place securely beside the antimacassar and the pressed flowers as a scrapbook which does double duty as guard-book for interesting documents and as repository for Lovett's passing thoughts.

It is Victorian also in its passion for education as the key to self-fulfilment and enriched opportunity – a passion now found only in underdeveloped countries, but which fuelled both Lovett's Chartist zeal and his decision in 1840 to leave the movement. Lovett belongs in the humane, participatory and libertarian tradition that the Victorians inherited from the eighteenth-century Enlightenment: an aroused public opinion and a widened franchise will uphold the Englishman's liberties against the arrogance of executive power, and render powerless its armies and police.

Education is a major theme in Lovett's life; he educated himself, and then set about instructing others through promoting educational movements, writing textbooks, founding schools and himself teaching in them. The Victorians' belief in the transforming power of education led them into a vast and spontaneous school-building programme, at first with only minimal aid from the state. But whereas many Victorian schools aimed to inculcate discipline and respect for authority, Lovett saw them as aids to self-liberation, as weapons against 'Gothic' superstition, and as a profoundly radical influence girding up the individual to resist tyranny and superstition. So education will dominate this portrait, and Lovett would have liked it that way.

His autobiography's aim is itself educational:

. . . if the following pages may in any way serve to stimulate younger and wiser men to continue the contest, earnestly but discreetly, till the victory is won over political injustice, social oppression, ignorance and wrong, I shall not have written them in vain.

Autobiography teaches by example. Here it reveals the posthumous son of a sea-captain becoming a lifelong enthusiast for self-improvement with the aid of his strictly-disciplined Cornish Methodist upbringing. Arriving in London to seek his fortune in 1821, he eventually got work as a cabinet-maker.

Fascinated by science, Lovett went without food to buy books, and soon began moving in working-class radical circles. A gallery of villains now haunted his humane and liberal mind: corrupt placemen sponging on the taxpayer, haughty aristocrats sporting their stars and ribbons, hypocritical bishops promoting superstition and division among Christ's poor, military men whose pride and bombast foster false authoritarian values and sow dissension between peace-loving peoples. Salvation lies through applying co-operative methods to trade and industry, widening the electorate and above all fostering liberty at home and abroad – in the press, in religious belief and in political structure.

Literate, reliable and upright working men were rarities in those days, and Lovett soon became indispensable to the radical working-class movements of the 1830s – campaigning for Owenite co-operative associations, a free press and a wider franchise. Leading figures from several of these causes coalesced into the London Working Men's Association, formed in 1836; with Lovett as secretary, it drew together working men ardent for the self-improvement of their class.

Industriously scribbling his manifestos and declarations of principle, Lovett saw politics throughout his life as an educational and moralistic crusade; discover the facts, publicise correct principles and truth will always, 'like the sun of heaven . . . find its way through some cranny'. Public opinion is 'the great tribunal of justice, to which the poor and the oppressed appeal.' He was deeply conscious of British libertarian traditions and courageously exploited them – most notably in two great trial scenes. In 1832 he was acquitted when prosecuted for organising public disrespect for the National Fast Day, which had been mounted to ward off cholera; still more memorable was his trial of 1839, which grew out of his Chartist commitment.

As the LWMA lecturers spread out from London after 1836, provincial enthusiasm drove them to launch a national movement for the People's Charter that they had never envisaged, and by 1839 Lovett was acting as the overworked and unpaid secretary of its National Convention of delegates in London. For Lovett, truth would inevitably prevail, so there was no need for secrecy or conspiracy. He therefore often seemed less radical in his short-term methods than his more populist and flamboyant colleagues, though in his long-term aims he was far more radical than they. Prison denied Chartism his restraining influence and rescued him from the embarrassment of being drawn into demagogic company. He was arrested at Birmingham, to which the Convention had recently moved, for protesting when the police disrupted a Chartist meeting; his uncompromising and learned speech in his own defence did not save him from a year's imprisonment.

It was a turning-point in Lovett's life. So far the Enlightenment's rationalistic radicalism had led him to promote what are now seen as the Victorian values of respectability, political participation and liberty. But after 1839 he was free to concentrate more fully on education. On leaving prison in 1840 he founded the National Association to restore the LWMA's moral and educational priorities, but O'Connor denounced it as a 'new move', its adherents were persecuted by his disciples, and the Association never came to very much.

Lovett's stormy relationship with O'Connor is too often portrayed as a contest between Lovett's advocacy of 'moral' force and O'Connor's of 'physical' force. In reality, moral and physical force were uppermost in the minds of both. For Lovett, violent change was always the ultimate possibility if all else failed: the dreaded abyss that would open up if his alternative – moral reform in the masses – failed to get enough middle- and working-class support. It was also the ultimate sanction of a morally aroused people if the government dared to spurn them. O'Connor, too, wanted moral reform, but he knew it was too long-term a remedy for the aroused industrial populations of the North of England, Scotland and Ireland: they wanted quick action. So O'Connor used physical force as a threat that would push politicians into short-term concession, and so stave off the violence he too wished to avoid.

Lovett's moralistic aims entailed repudiating leadership, whether from kings, aristocrats, the middle classes or radical orators; a self-reliant working people will spurn the deference the demagogue demands. A Chartist triumph without moral reform will merely supplant one tyranny by another, for the vote will not produce emancipation of its own accord; electors must be trained to use it effectively. Hence Lovett's assault on O'Connor, populist hero of so many great Chartist open-air meetings in the north, as 'the great "I AM" of politics', beating the big drum of his own vanity. This gulf opened up very early on in Chartist history, for

Lovett detested the way his demagoguery fostered irrational loyalties, intolerant persecutions, diversions from rational self-improvement, encouragements to 'animal propensities'. The bitterness of his attacks on O'Connor reflects the breadth of the hopes he had placed in the LWMA, now superseded by events.

Once out of prison, Lovett's attacks on 'the blight of democracy from the first moment he opened his mouth as its *professed advocate*', became scorching. The contrast between Lovett's humane, peace-loving temperament and his public scorn for those who seemed to be frustrating his ideals did not go unnoticed: his tediously detailed rejoinders, excoriating the sins of his enemies, must have pained his more sensitive admirers. They probably seemed merely hypocritical to O'Connor's disciples – especially when accompanied by disclaimers of personal malice.

Whenever his ideals were challenged, Lovett's temper was precarious. He always expected too much of human nature, and when colleagues repeatedly fell by the wayside, his gloom deepened; Francis Place, the radical tailor, saw him as 'a man of melancholy temperament, soured with the perplexities of the world'. Not only was he too principled a man for practical success in politics and business: he was also unrealistic in thinking so huge a movement as Chartism could ever be controlled by leaders who could offer only well-intentioned exhortations to moral self-development and appeals to reason. In G. D. H. Cole's sympathetic portrait, Lovett is 'the born secretary' who finds 'no president with whom he could work in harmony'.

The little book on *Chartism* that he wrote in prison with John Collins (though the ideas and much of the writing seem to be Lovett's alone) puts mass education once more firmly on the agenda. Its proposals reflect the contemporary context, whereby meeting places available to ordinary people were multiplying in the early 1840s – nonconformist chapels, temperance halls, mechanics' institutes, schools and Owenite halls of science. But Cole detected a 'massive simplicity' in its hopes of raising huge sums for educational 'district halls' through funds reclaimed from the pothouse. The book dwells lovingly on the smallest details of the proposed schools, with their circular swings in the playgrounds and an individual peg for the hat of each pupil – but it never faces the practical difficulties involved in organisation and fund-raising. Lovett set up a 'National Hall' in Holborn, but it never got its day-school established, survived only to 1857, and found no imitators.

The irrationalities of a popular agitation are only the first of the nine giants of unreason that Lovett confronts; the others are superstition, ignorance, religious and party sectarianism, drink, deliberate professional mystification, war and class hatred. His autobiography aims to slay them all, and we can now follow up each dimension of a rationalistic campaign pursued consistently throughout his adult life. He argues working men to remember that 'ignorance and superstition are the two chief crutches which prop up and support every species of despotism, corruption, and error in every part of the world'. He describes the Cornish fear of ghosts and boggarts as 'the curse of my boyhood', and deplores the impact on his mother of her gloomy Methodist preoccupation with sin. He sees education as the cure for superstition as well as ignorance; in language which is no doubt his, the LWMA denounced 'the hawks and owls of society' who tried to prevent the people from getting it.

Viewed as a revelation of personality, his autobiography is a very curious document, for Lovett is interested neither in himself, nor in his own contribution to working-class politics, except insofar as his own story will inspire others; he says all too little about his personal circumstances and feelings. The book is a weapon in the war against ignorance; his aim is to make converts, and he reprints at length the high-flown appeals to fellow radicals he had drafted in middle age. 'Brothers in Political Bondage . . .', they begin: 'Citizens of the American Republic . . .'. It is not clear how many people heard the message at the time, but his autobiography proudly reprints them thirty years later; they occupy well over half the space he allots to the period between 1829 and 1842, and not so very much less in the period from 1842 to 1874.

His educational ideas owe much to the phrenologist George Combe, whose book, *The Constitution of Man* explained how the individual with forethought and self-discipline could nurture his independence. 'Whatever little good I have been able to achieve I am widely indebted to yourself', Lovett told Combe in 1849; Combe's book had enabled him to attain a balance between passion, intellect and morality. 'I know of no man whose good opinion I esteem more than your own', he added. No doubt Lovett was pleased when Combe publicly pronounced his little book on *Social and Political Morality* (1853) 'calculated to advance the great cause of human improvement which you and I have both at heart.'

Lovett's ideas on education illustrate the rich diversity of the Victorian legacy, for they are not at all repressive: progressive in their day, they are progressive still, reflecting his quest for educational innovation and his practical experience of teaching. He strongly attacks rote-learning, opposes competition within the classroom, and argues that '*kindness* and *reason* should always be employed to urge [children] to their duties, coercion and anger never'. Education is the key to unlock humanity's huge unrealised potential. The schoolroom should become 'a little world of love, of lively and interesting enjoyments', and promote both physical health and aesthetic appreciation. As late as 1872, educational knowledge remained for him 'the great essential, the grand panacea, of our social and political salvation'. For R. H. Tawney, Lovett was 'the first and greatest of working-class educationists'; G. D. H. Cole saw him as anticipating the twentieth-century work of the Workers' Educational Association.

The teacher's role was to simplify, and Lovett reserves his favourite insult 'Gothic' for the antiquated medievalism so rampant in British public life. He criticises the obscure learning promoted in the ancient universities, and in both classroom and textbook he challenges the deliberate obscurantism of the professions – especially from lawyers and doctors. He wants to bridge the conventional boundaries between academic subjects: to play down classics and divinity while playing up science, modern languages, geography and what we now call 'social studies'. The 'social science' in Lovett's ideal curriculum is less concerned with academic study than with ensuring that people bring their personal conduct into harmony with the laws of science. Its highly prescriptive amalgam of economics, politics and ethics is fully displayed in Lovett's neglected 'ABC of Social Science', whose twenty instalments were published in the trade unionists' periodical the *Bee-Hive* during 1868.

The way must be made plain for ordinary people, so that they can gain control over their own lives; syllabuses must be practical. Lovett and Collins deplored the nation's 'aristocratic contempt for all useful labour', and in the laboratory and workshop within their proposed district halls, senior pupils will be taught the '*first principles of the most useful trades and occupations*'. Like Bentham, Lovett yearned to codify and clarify British law; in his trials of 1832 and 1839, he deplored the labyrinth lawyers had created, while simultaneously demonstrating that an intelligent and persevering working man could find his way through it.

He was equally impatient with doctors, and when he could find no schoolteacher qualified to give instruction in medicine, he set about writing his *Elementary Anatomy and Physiology*. Lacking medical qualifications, he pored painstakingly though medical manuals whose Latin terminology, he says, 'at first gave me the headache and the heartache'. 'I almost began to despair of even understanding the subject', he goes on 'much less of being able to teach it'. Yet his textbook appeared in 1851 and went into a second edition two years later.

Working people must be emancipated from the doctor as well as from the clergyman and the lawyer, so his textbook laces its anatomy and physiology with guidance on diet, intoxicants and tobacco. Readers are reassured that many diseases once attributed to supernatural influences really stem from 'the neglect or infringement of some of the great physical and moral laws of the universe'; pupils in their daily conduct must follow physiology's laws, and must remember *'that the exercise of our own moderate abilities to prevent disease, is far better than the exalted wisdom of others to cure it'*.

How influential were Lovett's educational views? He himself ran only one school, though he taught in others. His influence on working-class movements was considerable, though in the largest of them, Chartism, his influence soon succumbed before leaders who promised more immediate gratification. The *Lancet* praised his medical textbook, but it went into only two editions, and his *Social and Political Morality* never achieved more than one. He made little money from his publications, and could find no publisher at all for his last textbook, *Zoology for Schools*, 'a work of immense labour' which took 'the best portion of my time for . . . six years'. It is in fact less as a direct educational influence than as a representative and symbolic educational figure that Lovett claims our attention today.

The sharpness and persistence of his quarrels with religion stem partly from distaste for superstition and ceremonial. Yet he also dissents from organised religion in its more progressive aspects, for he thought he could have used the clergyman's resources so much more effectively, and hated seeing his prized practical 'great religion of duty' being driven out of the classroom by sectarian squabbles and unintelligible theology. Sectarian divisions – between Whig and Tory – produced irrationalism in politics, too. Periodic bursts of political excitement and controversy were no substitute for the steady and continuous pursuit of progress for which he longed.

He showed a lifelong impatience with what he saw as self-interested and incompetent aristocratic politicians; they seemed to spend so much time quarrelling in public, so little time co-operating on an agreed programme of reform, and he wanted them to take a qualifying examination before getting nominated. There is a hint in Lovett's autobiography that Gladstone won his respect in later life, but no clear recognition that old Chartists now belonged in the Gladstonian Liberal Party, for Lovett did not believe in party. Confined to his room by bronchitis towards the end of his life, he whiled away the time making a model of his beloved district hall which, with its 'self-registering ballot box', would attain his dream of purifying the political process.

Drink was for him the major fount of unreason, and public houses were 'the greatest of all enemies to the intellectual and moral, as well as the social and political, progress of our people'. His district halls aimed to counteract the pub by providing some of its more harmless recreations. A pioneer prohibitionist, he sometimes wrote articles for the prohibitionist *Alliance News*. Drink could usually be found in association with Lovett's other bugbears – corrupt elections and the recruiting of low-grade army recruits. Like many respectable Victorian working men, he deplored the low social level and mindless training of the typical army recruit, and feared the army's authoritarian mood; Cornwall's fear of the press-gang during the Napoleonic wars was, he says, 'deeply engraven on the memory of my boyhood'.

Most of all, he hated war as the ultimate irrationality, and deplored 'the high-swelling cant of "individual glory" and "national honour", the din and dazzle of warlike preparation' which seduce the unreflecting. As with the middle-class spokesman Richard Cobden, empire provides 'resting-places for aristocratical fledglings', war is 'the sport and hobby of kings', trade is 'one of the greatest civilisers of the world', and internationalism must gain from the progress of democracy. Lovett too wanted an international law code, and in 1844 suggested a representative 'conference of nations' to settle all national disputes through arbitration. He thought war loaded the people with taxes, threatened parliamentary government and distracted attention from social reform.

Fear of aristocracy shapes Lovett's outlook on class; America is his ideal – free, prosperous and unsullied by aristocratic idlers, a refuge for the destitute of all nations. Like the LWMA in 1837 he deplored the 'gothic ignorance' that surrounded the new queen with ceremonial and 'such absurdities as dress-swords, coats, and wigs', thus warding off her humbler subjects. For him, aristocratic cunning lurks everywhere: in war, recreation, drink, politics and charity. All charity is potentially demeaning, he thinks: except for the aged and the sick, it 'may be said to be misapplied' whenever 'it has not for its object *the prevention of future charity*'. Still more lowering is the racecourse, whose 'saturnian revels' bring aristocrats and working people together in a corrupting atmosphere of drink, gambling, 'slangy sportsmen, showy courtesans, and fighting, roaring, and rampant brutality'.

In combating the last great source of unreason – class conflict – Lovett's outlook grows naturally out of a society where it was difficult for intelligent working men to rise out of their class. Such men were often reconciled to their status in Victorian Britain provided that they were not insulted by being denied the vote, and provided that national legislation did not affront their respectable values. But if only the LWMA could draw 'into one bond of *unity* the *intelligent* and *influential* portion of the working classes in town and country', middle- and working-class respectability might erode both social extremes and democracy might at last arrive.

The respectable working-class élite was small in Lovett's day, and the LWMA itself admitted only 279 members between 1836 and 1839; but Lovett rightly predicted the rapid growth of 'the honest, sober, and reflecting portion of every town and village . . . setting an example of propriety to their neighbours'. Cleanliness and punctuality could remove class distinctions, 'unwashed faces, unshorn chins, and dirty habits', he warned working men in 1845 (in a dig at O'Connor), 'will in nowise prepare you for political or social equality with the decent portion of your brethren'. In protesting to parliament at their treatment in Warwick gaol, Lovett and Collins expressed horror that they had been obliged to strip on admission, wash in the same water as prisoners 'some of whom were in a filthy state', and dry themselves on the same towel; it is no accident that their district halls were each equipped with hot and cold baths.

Respectability required new patterns of domestic life. In 1836 the LWMA urged its members to 'read . . . talk, and politically and morally instruct your wives and children; let them . . . share in your pleasures', and in his autobiography Lovett urges working men to keep their wives at home so that the children can be properly brought up. He certainly practised what he preached, and in old age movingly described his wife as 'a second self; always my best adviser and truest friend; ever interesting herself, and sympathising with me in all my pursuits, toils and troubles'. Not least among the causes for praise in the inscription on the obelisk over his grave is the fact that 'he was an affectionate husband' and 'a fond father' as well as 'a true citizen'.

He was disappointed when his daughter Mary became an actress; 'I would much rather she had devoted herself to her home', he wrote, and her daughter Kezia spent much of her childhood with her grandparents. Respectability required the wife to be a good housekeeper, and in his articles of 1868 Lovett warned working men against tallymen, the 'social spiders' who encouraged their wives to overspend by extending them credit. He denounced parents who produced swarms of children they could not support, and thought respectable parents should shield their children against the bad language, temptations and squalor of slum life.

In 1842 a close observer at a reformers' conference saw Lovett as 'a tall, gentlemanly-looking man with a high and ample forehead, a pale, contemplative cast of countenance, dark-brown hair, and . . . a very prepossessing exterior, in manner quiet, modest and unassuming'; he spoke seldom, and his voice was not powerful, yet his words commanded instant attention. A working man of this type was likely to find middle-class allies. Lovett had always resisted sectarian working-class policies that seemed likely to alienate them.

Several influential middle-class sympathisers were reaching out across the class divide. John Stuart Mill praised the respectability of Chartist leaders and wanted to see some of them in parliament; and Joseph Sturge's Complete Suffrage Union tried to unite the two classes behind a campaign for franchise extension. 'I think Lovett a very fine man in every way', John Bright told Cobden in 1842. Ten years later Cobden read Lovett's *Social and Political Morality*, and (according to his published testimonial) could 'scarcely find a sentiment in which I do not concur'.

Yet self-help did not invariably lead to middle-class alliance. The Complete Suffrage Union eventually foundered, partly because at the crucial moment Lovett refused to go along with the Union's middle-class supporters and desert the People's Charter.

It is this upstanding defence of working-class dignity that leads the present-day Labour Party to claim him as one of their own; throughout his life Lovett wanted working people to participate fully in the political process, with trade unions to safeguard working-class living standards. Labour would also echo his distaste for 'the present state of society, with its mere money-getting and sensual aspirations . . . its mass of squalid misery'. In his autobiography he thought it 'surely time to put an end to this social strife in the work of production, and not to allow of a state of things . . . when all the great capitalists will swallow up all the little ones'. He was puzzled and saddened that 'after all my struggles, all my industry, and . . . all my temperance and frugality, I cannot earn or live upon my own bread in my old age.'

Yet this did not lead him towards socialist remedies. *Social and Political Morality* attacks the sort of strike that ignores market forces and so is doomed to failure, and in the 1860s Lovett hoped that co-operative production and profit-sharing would moderate industrial conflict. His approach to economics lay through what he called 'social economy', which assumed that personal morality in the thrifty artisan, the conscientious employer and the serious-minded politician 'formed the basis of our social and political arrangements'. At the Chartists' famous Palace Yard meeting of 1838 he firmly declared that 'capital was as necessary for labour, as air was for the existence of man', and though at the end of his life he admitted that capital had sometimes been unjustly accumulated, he rejected 'foolish threats of confiscation'. He came to doubt whether human beings were good enough to operate Owenite socialism successfully, and opposed nationalisation of the land.

Some explain Lovett's non-socialist ideas by saying that, in Tawney's words, he 'did not know or understand the north'. Others blame an intellect too weak to challenge the political economy that was fashionable in his day. True, he had little direct experience of the industrial areas, but he corresponded much with those who knew more about them, and no Chartist could be unaware of their problems. As for Lovett's intellect, he was no narrow devotee of cheap government and *laissez faire*. In his articles of 1868 he wants the rates equalised between rich and poor localities and government loans to improve working-class housing. He wants firm health regulations on house-design, and blames crime on governments that allow their citizens to grow up as 'social savages'. In reality, the conventional political economy was capable of quite broad extension into welfare measures, and already in the 1860s Lovett was travelling along that road.

Besides, the socialist critique of mid-Victorian political economy stems more from value-judgement than from intellect. Lovett recognised the problems caused by industrialisation, but he did not want a remedy worse than the disease. So the Labour Party's claim upon him as a precursor will never go unchallenged. He profoundly distrusted government, and his related belief in individual freedom made him a keen critic of slavery. Socialism 'would produce a kind of social despotism far worse than any that now exists', he thought, whereas invention and improvement stem from 'the hope of wealth, fame, or station, *keeping up man's energies to the tension point*'. His reasons for opposing land nationalisation are interesting: the need for compensation would not only cause this reform to inflate the national debt – it would concentrate too much power and patronage in central government. He therefore preferred the more gradualist Liberal policies of reforming the legal arrangements for land transfer.

Lovett's *Social and Political Morality*, with its acknowledgements to J. S. Mill, Bentham, Combe and Perronet Thompson breathes liberal principles at every turn. Liberty is championed – in trade, in knowledge and elsewhere – as essential to the morality that must lie at the foundation of society. The book is a sort of expanded but secularised Ten Commandments, recommending sobriety, industry, honesty, kindness, economy, chastity and self-education. Individual property is seen as 'the best safeguard for the liberty and independence of a country, as those who have their own little estates to defend would be interested in promoting peace, liberty, and security'.

A fear of what he called 'irresponsible power' informs Lovett's entire political outlook; the concentration of power risks cramping experiment, diversity and local energy. Even his thirst for education does not lead him to press for state aid on any scale. He always wanted the state to encourage education, but he wanted it funded from the rates, with control vested in teachers and in locally-elected school committees; a Prussian centralisation, however efficient, is anathema. Free institutions enable 'the passions of the multitude' to act when necessary as 'God's messenger to teach their oppressors justice'.

'Remember my dear Sir that I am still a *moral force* Chartist', Lovett told Combe in 1849, 'and have faith to believe that at no distant period the principles of the Peoples' Charter will be the law of England'. In all important respects Lovett's prediction was correct, but this biographical sketch shows that if Chartist leaders went underground after the 1840s, this was not because they rejected Victorianism. It was at first a surprise to find, at the base of Lovett's obelisk at Highgate, a thoroughly Victorian motto:

Man's true worth is the good he does in this world. When he dies mortals will ask what property has he left behind him. Angels will inquire what good deeds hast thou sent before thee.

Yet, on reflection, the motto is not at all surprising. Liberty, thrift, enterprise, respectability, political participation and above all education filled Lovett's horizon, and ensured that – for posterity as well as for his contemporaries – he would seem a thoroughly representative Victorian.

For Further Reading:

The best introduction to Lovett is his autobiography, published in 1876. R. H. Tawney published a good essay on him in his *The Radical Tradition* (Pelican, 1966), and G. D. H. Cole's study in his *Chartist Portraits* (Macmillan, 1941) is useful. For context, see David Goodway's *London Chartism, 1838–1848* (Cambridge University Press, 1982). The latest study of the Chartist movement is Dorothy Thompson's *The Chartists* (Wildwood House, 1984).

3

'Cultivated Capital'

Patronage and Art in Nineteenth-Century Manchester and Leeds

Janet Wolff and Caroline Arscott

Opposite: Urban reality: all the variety and vitality of city living is crammed into Ford Madox Brown's 'Work', commissioned by the Leeds stockbroker, Thomas Plint. (Manchester City Art Galleries)

THE FOUNDATION OF PROSPERITY in nineteenth-century Britain (and of many of the other characteristics which Victorian society exhibited) was the manufacturing wealth produced above all in the new industrial cities of the north and midlands. 'Britain's bread hangs by Lancashire's thread' was the way one adage put it. The image of such centres as the 'workshop of the world', turning out goods that underpinned trade and empire overseas, was linked with others of pragmatism, primitivism and philistinism among the new class of largely self-made men who were the Victorian captains of industry. It was an attitude to life caricatured in the immortal phrase 'where there's muck, there's money'.

But though this character-sketch of northern middle-class society was widely believed at the time and has continued to be propagated by many historians and art critics since, it was very far from the truth. Recent research is increasingly showing that the industrialists and businessmen of the north were frequently in the vanguard of patronising and propagating new cultural forms, particularly in the visual arts. Janet Wolff and Caroline Arscott discuss here the enthusiasm for culture among the urban middle classes of Manchester and Leeds.

'What in the world do you want with Art in Manchester? Why can't you stick to your cotton spinning?' This remark was made by a nobleman, on being asked to lend pictures from his collection to the Art Treasures Exhibition held in Manchester in 1857. This belief in the incompatibility of culture and industry, and in the fundamental philistinism of the northern middle class, was one which was widely held, and which went back to earlier decades. A reviewer of a book of poems published in Manchester claimed to be 'absolutely astounded' by this phenomenon, saying of that city:

There is something in the very name itself which puts to flight all poetical associations. Only couple, for instance, in your mind the ideas of Manchester and Wordsworth, and see if, by any mental process, you can introduce them into any sort of union. The genius of that great man would have been absolutely clouded for ever by one week's residence in the fogs of Manchester.

Moreover, this image of the new industrial cities and of their inhabitants has persisted to the present day. Contemporary historians refer to the supposed ignorance of the industrialists and manufacturers with regard to the arts, and their tendency to buy forgeries on the assumption that they were Old Masters. Although it is well known and accepted that many of these people were important patrons of the Pre-Raphaelites in the mid-nineteenth century, Quentin Bell has recently explained this exercise in taste as one based precisely on lack of knowledge:

These painters found their market among those whom contemporaries would have considered an ignorant and philistine clientèle, the 'self-made' men and manufacturers of the North . . . The advantage from the Pre-Raphaelite point of view, of this kind of client, was that he would have been relatively uneducated. He would not have known enough to know that for a cultivated public, Pre-Raphaelite painting was full of faults.

The stereotype of the northern businessmen and manufacturers has not progressed far from the figures of Mr Gradgrind and Mr Bounderby in Dickens' *Hard Times*.

However, a study of the urban middle class of Manchester and Leeds exposes this stereotype as a myth, and reveals an extensive involvement in, and understanding of, the arts on the part of bankers, merchants, manufacturers and industrialists. The Art Treasures Exhibition of 1857 in Manchester itself was an important example of this. This was the first national exhibition ever to be devoted entirely to art (though its inspiration came partly from the Great Exhibition of 1851 in London). It enjoyed royal patronage, and was held in a specially built palace at Old Trafford, Manchester. The enormous number of works shown ranged from Old Masters to contemporary paintings and photography. Over a million people visited the exhibition. The motivation behind this event, as well as its planning and organisation, came from a group of merchants and manufacturers in Manchester, and notably Thomas Fairbairn, partner in a local engineering firm. But it was not only the 'second-generation' manufacturers who were active in the cultural life of their city. Fairbairn's own father, William Fairbairn, founder of the firm and a self-made and self-taught man, had been involved in the setting up of the Mechanics' Institute in 1824, was a patron of artists (for example, Benjamin Haydon), and was also involved in founding the School of Design in Manchester (the first outside London) in 1838.

The participation of industrialists, financiers and professional men in culture and the arts took numerous forms. They were always central to initiatives for exhibitions and other cultural events. They were also active patrons and supporters of local and other contemporary artists (often along with members of the gentry). And they were active in forming new cultural institutions in the cities – institutions like the Literary and Philosophical Society (1781 in Manchester; 1819 in Leeds, where it was called the Philosophical and Literary Society), the Royal Manchester Institution (1823), The Mechanics' Institutes (1824 in both cities), the Schools of Design (1838 in Manchester; 1846 in Leeds), and the public libraries. They were clearly prepared to devote their time as well as their money to such initiatives. (Edmund Potter, the Manchester calico printer, complained that he had spent almost the whole of two years of his life organising the Art Treasures Exhibition.) In addition, the middle classes (in this case including professionals and others, as well as the 'high bourgeoisie' of commercial and industrial entrepreneurs) provided the basis for cultural and musical life in the two cities. In Manchester it was their support which kept going the Gentlemen's Concerts, and which brought Charles Hallé to that city in 1848; the calico printer, Hermann Leo, was instrumental in this. In Leeds, as well as supporting subscription concerts, bourgeois families began a society for musical soirées in 1848, in which music was played and enjoyed in members' homes. There is no doubt, then, that the cultural life of the middle class was lively and sophisticated. It is worth looking in a little more detail at the specific activities of these people in the visual arts in the first half of the nineteenth century.

As direct patrons of art, the bourgeoisie had a most important part to play. We have already referred to the particular case of the support of some members of this group for the Pre-Raphaelites; it is generally agreed that this willingness to take risks with new (and so far unpopular) work was crucial to the fortunes of that particular group of painters. But the buying practices of the industrialists and men of commerce were far more wide-ranging than is usually assumed. William Hardman, a prosperous drysalter in Manchester, had a major collection of art at the turn of the century, including, reportedly, works by Titian, Canaletto, Veronese, Ruisdael, Rembrandt, Wilson, Wright and Fuseli. Edward Loyd, a partner in a Manchester banking firm, had a collection specialising particularly in Dutch art (Cuyp, Hobbema, Ruisdael, Steen, de Hooch). Other local collectors had begun to patronise contemporary artists. Henry McConnel, partner in a Manchester cotton mill, owned several Turners and also works by lesser-known English artists, including local ones. Samuel and Thomas Ashton, of a Manchester family of cotton manufacturers, included in their collection works by Constable, Turner, Collins, Holman Hunt, Egg and Leighton. Leeds manufacturers were equally involved in building picture collections. Several of them loaned pictures for the three Polytechnic Exhibitions of 1839, 1843 and 1845.

A common way of buying paintings was to purchase them from the walls of the Royal Academy or from some exhibiting society. But painters would also take their prospective buyers into account in their work. It was also common for direct commissions to be agreed. Thomas Plint, a Leeds stockbroker, was an enthusiastic patron of the artist, William Mulready. He also commissioned Ford Madox Brown's now famous painting, Work (1852–65).

The commission for this painting provides an unusually clear example of the buyer specifying to the artist how he wanted the work done. (This practice, which was usual in earlier centuries, when patrons might specify how much gold or ultramarine paint the artist should use, or even how the painting should look and what it should contain, had retreated, as a conception developed of the artist as 'genius', expressing him- or herself in the work). Having seen the preliminary sketches for Work, Plint wrote to the artist, asking him to 'change one of the four fashionable young ladies into a quiet, earnest, holy-looking one, with a book or two and tracts', adding 'I want this put in, for I am much interested in this work myself, and know those who are'. The artist complied with this request, even modelling the 'holy-looking' lady on Plint's own wife. The two figures on the right of the painting represent Thomas Carlyle and F. D. Maurice; Plint's request here had been for representations of Carlyle and Charles Kingsley. This case, though an unusual one, does draw out attention to the fact that the meaning of paintings is likely to be related in some (no doubt complex) way to the patron's values and ideas.

Another interesting example of patronage is the case of the commission of William Holman Hunt's The Awakening Conscience (see front cover) by Thomas Fairbairn, the Manchester industrialist mentioned earlier in connection with the 1857 Exhibition. In 1853, Fairbairn approached Hunt with the general offer of a commission; this eventually became a commission for this particular work, begun in 1853. Before Fairbairn took possession of the painting, Hunt exhibited it at the Royal Academy Exhibition of 1854, where it attracted adverse criticism. Two years later, Fairbairn asked Hunt to repaint the expression on the face of the young woman, as he found it too painful to live with.

Again, what is interesting about this commission is the relationship between patron, artist and work itself. Fairbairn's interest in the painting makes sense when we understand more about his social and economic position, and his views about politics and family life. He was one of Manchester's leading industrialists, and had emerged as a spokesman for a particular group of large engineering firms who had taken on and beaten the engineering trade union in a dispute in 1852–3. His social position in Manchester was enhanced by the fact that he had spent eight years living in London, where manners and habits were more advanced than in the provinces, and by the fact that he had married a southerner in Greenwich. He had already started collecting pictures, and owned genre scenes, allegorical works and a number of family portraits by modern British artists. He was a respectable public figure and a family man, who used the notion of the purifying effects of the home and of a wife's influence in letters he wrote to *The Times*, attacking the striking engineering workers. His commission of *The Awakening Conscience* can be seen as consistent with the position and views that he·held. It was a painting of a man visiting his kept mistress. He is playing a tune at the piano, with the woman sitting on his knee. The picture shows the moment when the woman suddenly realises the sinfulness of her situation. The scene is the opposite of a virtuous home, and as such it may have appealed to Thomas Fairbairn; the graphic depiction of one extreme reinforced the importance of its opposite – of wholesome domesticity and of the virtuous married woman.

Far from being cultural deserts, the developing northern industrial cities contained thriving art markets and growing populations of artists, many of them, clearly, able to make a decent living through portraiture and other sales. In 1821, one source lists only six portraitists and one landscape painter in Manchester; by 1825, Baines' directory lists twenty-one professional artists. The 1851 census lists 156 painters in the town, and the 1861 census lists 181 (in 1851 the third largest population of professional painters in England, and in 1861 the second largest after London). The art dealers, Agnews and Grundys, were thriving in Manchester by the mid-nineteenth century. In Leeds, booksellers like Thomas Fenteman, and carvers and gliders, operated as art dealers in the expanding markets.

There were also a number of cultural institutions, founded as part of the activities of the new middle classes engaged in forging a collective and distinct identity. The Royal Manchester Institution is a good example of this. It was initiated in 1823 by a group of artists, who wanted to ensure regular exhibition of their works, but it was soon taken over by the town's governing class, who had been approached for their patronage. The first committee, set up in October 1823, included no artists among its twenty-eight members, but it did include several major cotton manufacturers (H. H. Birley, R. H. Greg, David Holt), various prosperous merchants, bankers, doctors and lawyers, and the President, Vice-President, Treasurer and several directors of the Manchester Chamber of Commerce. The Royal Manchester Institute continued to run art exhibitions, offered prizes (funded originally by the banker, Benjamin Heywood) and from an early date built its own collection from the works on display. (This collection formed the basis of what is now the City of Manchester Art Gallery's collection, where the premises and works of the Institution were transferred to Manchester Corporation in 1882).

One important role for the Royal Manchester Institution was in bringing about more social cohesion among the rather disparate sections of the town's middle class, helping to bridge differences of occupation, residence, religion and even politics. It also served the purpose of enhancing the image of the town. G. W. Wood, a partner in the Philips' hat-making business, who drafted the proposal for establishing the Institution in 1823, was quite explicit about this aspect:

The candid and reflecting will not deny that an exclusive interest in the pursuit of gain has a very unfavourable influence on taste and manners.

He pointed out that:

An alliance between Commerce and the Liberal Arts is at once natural and salutary . . . [The Arts] provide a counter-acting influence to the gross and sordid spirit, which is too often the result of an undivided attention to mercenary pursuits.

The way in which involvement in cultural institutions and activities served the crucial secondary purpose of producing a common class identity was paralleled in Leeds with regard to the three Polytechnic Exhibitions. These were large miscellaneous exhibitions, organised by voluntary committees to raise money for such projects as a new hall for the Mechanics' Institution or for the building of public baths. Each included a large art section where paintings were on show, lent by up to ninety local collectors. The exhibitions were commented on at the time as being exceptional in bringing together members of different religious and political factions of the middle classes. Tories and Liberals, Anglicans and Dissenters, who would normally have had a very little contact with each other, co-operated for months on the committees. An analysis of the lists of people who loaned pictures also shows participation across the entire spectrum of middle-class Leeds.

The cultural pursuits of members of the new middle class were complex in their motivations and effects. On the one hand, as we have suggested, they served the purpose of forging a class identity across the various fragments of the bourgeoisie. In this process, too, a specifically urban bourgeois identity was contrasted with the culture, politics and life-style of the gentry – the older ruling class (although the attitude of the industrial capitalists, bankers and merchants was always an ambivalent one, combining elements of emulation of gentry ways of life with vigorous rejection of other of its aspects). On the other hand, this cultural class identity was part of the efforts of this group to clarify its relationship with the lower strata. Culture operated both to control working-class activities and to educate workers into what were perceived to be appropriate values. On the occasion of the Art Treasures Exhibition in Manchester in 1857, for example, a fund was set up to enable children from poor districts to attend, and many employers sent train-loads of their employees to visit it. The entrance fees on Saturday afternoons were reduced to sixpence to encourage working people to attend. The Polytechnic Exhibitions in Leeds were also attended by large numbers of working people, encouraged by the organisers and other members of the Leeds bourgeoisie. Employers bought tickets for their employees, and gave them the day off to attend. There was a specially reduced penny rate for children from charity schools. Here, too, we see a combination of paternalistic benevolence and social control.

In general, class formation and class identity seem to be inextricably linked with cultural and artistic activities in mid-Victorian England. In relation to the visual arts, it is worth looking, finally, at one or two of the paintings themselves. Here, it is possible to interpret the ways in which the meaning of particular works, or types of work, is a central part of these processes. As we have already indicated with regard to the Plint and Fairbairn commissions, style and content of the works is entirely relevant to the way in which patrons and viewers 'use' the

works. 'Subject' pictures like *Work* and *The Awakening Conscience*
presented their chosen topic in a particular way, but the same can
be said of apparently neutral genres of painting, like portraiture
and city views. When Thomas Fairbairn commissioned a family
portrait from William Holman Hunt, ten years after buying *The
Awakening Conscience*, with its theme of the sinful woman and the
wicked ménage, he acquired a picture in which the opposite situation was represented.

The Children's Holiday is not just a realistic portrayal of his wife,
Allison, and their five youngest children, but is a representation
of a virtuous wife and a happy home. Mrs Fairbairn is shown as
strong and pivotal in her proper domestic sphere. The shape of
her body, tightly waisted in her gleaming silk dress, is broadened
across the upper half by the fringed paisley shawl that she wears,
so that she takes on the form both of the ancient oak tree above
her on the right of the picture, and of the elegant tea urn on the
left. The associations of nature, permanence, strength and
English virtue which carry over to her from the oak tree are
tempered by the associations of culture, classical art and learning,
and the taste and appreciation of fine modern workmanship,
which are conveyed by the tea urn. The picture is set outside
rather than inside a house, but all the more strongly are the essential features of home seen to be evident in the person of the
wife and mother. The comfort and repose of the leather-
upholstered armchair and the oriental carpet, and the refreshment
and nourishment promised by the tea table, are attached, by the
composition of the picture, to the figure of the woman. They are
literally butted up against her skirts, so that they take on the
character, not just of elements of her environment, but of her own
self. They can then be understood as spiritual as well as physical
benefits offered by the woman to her family.

In these ways, the portrait conveys a whole set of ideas about
the proper role of woman, and her proper sphere of operation.
Her position is seen as central and essential in the home, among
her children, but nonetheless the painting indicates the presence,
outside the picture, of her husband. She is submissive and
obedient to a master, just as the spaniel in the picture is to its
young master. In fact, the picture divides the figures into pairs:

---

*Opposite: Little women? The stereotypes of the Victorian middle-class wife and
mother embodied in Holman Hunt's 'The Children's Holiday'. (Torre Abbey
Collection, Torbay Borough Council)*

two deer, brother and little sister, elder sister and baby, boy and spaniel, and, finally, the figure of the husband outside the picture partners the wife and completes the set. In each pair, one figure is larger, and is protecting and controlling the smaller and weaker one. The portrait shows the limitations and dependence of women, as well as showing the positive virtues ascribed to women. The ideology of the family, and the social and economic relationships within the bourgeois family, are articulated very fully by this group portrait.

Similarly, a picture such as *Leeds from the Meadows* by Joseph Rhodes is something more than just a topographical view of a town. The picture dates from the 1820s, when Leeds was a rapidly growing industrial city, at the forefront of the development of wool- and flax-manufacturing technology. The way the city is shown in the painting is interesting at a time when industrialisation and the evils or benefits of city life were a subject of fierce controversy, and at a time when there was an economic and political struggle for influence within the city, as the traditional exercise of power by a merchant élite was disturbed. The part of the picture devoted to the city is just one narrow strip in what is otherwise a landscape showing trees, bushes, fields, a river, cows and two rustic figures. The city is, in this sense, safely contained in, and partly neutralised by, the countryside. The features of the city that occupy the skyline are not smoking chimneys, but mainly church towers and spires.

Nonetheless, the city is not completely de-industrialised in the way it is represented, because on the horizon at the right we can pick out a very large and prominent factory, and in front of it a modern bridge. The building is the four-storey main mill of the Park Mills woollen factory, owned by Benjamin Gott, and the bridge is Wellington Bridge, which he took the initiative in having built in 1818–19. The picture therefore finds a way of presenting Leeds as a city where innovation and factory production take their place without disturbing the idyllic peace of the countryside, and without disrupting the patterns of authority implied by a town, which is basically a cluster of houses round a few churches, and surrounded by fields.

The manufacturers and industrialists of the north, then, were not the 'ignorant and philistine' group Quentin Bell describes. They were very much involved in the arts, often in an extremely well-informed and sophisticated way. They were also central to most of the major cultural initiatives in industrial cities like Leeds and Manchester, whether temporary events like the Polytechnic Exhibitions in Leeds or the Art Treasures Exhibition in Manchester, or permanent institutions like the RMI or the Literary and Philosophical Societies. And, as we have suggested, the involvement of these members of the middle classes in patronage of the visual arts manifested itself in many of the paintings themselves. Occasionally this was the result of direct influence (as in the case of Plint); more generally, it is possible to read the paintings in terms of the cultural values and meanings of their prospective and actual buyers and viewers. The relationship of class, culture and art in nineteenth-century England is a complex and fascinating one, which will repay a good deal of further research.

For Further Reading:

The issues raised in this article are discussed in much greater detail in Janet Wolff and John Seed (eds.), *The Culture of Capital: Art, Power and the Nineteenth-Century Middle Class* (Manchester University Press, 1987). Related texts are John H. G. Archer (ed.), *Art and Architecture in Victorian Manchester* (Manchester University Press, 1985); R. J. Morris, 'Middle-class culture, 1700–1914', in Derek Fraser (ed.), *A History of Modern Leeds* (Manchester University Press, 1980); C. P. Darcy, *The Encouragement of the Fine Arts in Lancashire 1760–1860* (Manchester University Press, 1976); Trevor Fawcett, *The Rise of English Provincial Art: 1800–1830* (Clarendon Press, Oxford, 1974).

The research on which this article is based was funded by the Economic and Social Research Council. The authors would like to acknowledge the research by John Seed which has informed this article.

4
Dickens and his Readers

Philip Collins

THE EMPTY CHAIR.

FOR MANY PEOPLE, Charles Dickens (1812–70) *is* the Victorian era. The enormous success and public profile he enjoyed from the time of his first novel *The Pickwick Papers* to his last *The Mystery of Edwin Drood* and the sustaining and expansion of his reputation posthumously to generations of readers worldwide make him perhaps the most valuable literary touchstone when attempting to identify 'Victorian Values'. He touched all classes of Victorian society, from the Queen to the road-sweeper.

The serialised publication of many of his novels attracted the same sort of public fascination and interest in his characters as many of today's TV 'soap operas' – despite Oscar Wilde's acid remark that it would be a hard-hearted man indeed who could read about the death of Little Nell without laughing. The visual and dramatic power of his creations remain compelling – witness the success of film versions of this century of *Oliver Twist* and *Great Expectations* and most recently the stage shows of *Nicholas Nickleby*. But what did Dickens' writing reflect and what did his readers expect? Philip Collins considers the middle-brow persona that cloaked Dickens' moral purposes as well as the practical considerations implicit in the deceptively modest credo, 'we hope to do some solid good, and we mean to be as cheery and pleasant as we can'.

To understand a man, suggested that doyen of Victorian studies, G. M. Young, consider what was happening, what ideas were in the air, when he was around twenty, 'because what sixteen to twenty-four is talking about, twenty-four to sixty-four will usually write, or think, or do. Those are the charging years' (*The Victorian Noon-time*). Young's tip fits Dickens almost embarrassingly well: he became twenty in 1832, and was indeed a press-gallery reporter when the Reform Bill was passing through Parliament. When he was sixteen its major constitutional predecessors were enacted, the Repeal of the Test and Corporation Acts. In his twenty-fourth year he published his first book, *Sketches by Boz: Illustrative of Everyday Life and Everyday People*, and began writing and serialising his first novel, *Pickwick Papers* (1836–7); other books of that year included Pugin's *Contrasts* (which quickened the Gothic Revival) and the first instalment of G. W. Porter's *The Progress of the Nation* and of Robert Owen's *Book of the New Moral World*.

As many contemporaries recognised, Dickens was a man formed by the ideals and disappointments of the reformist 1830s – what George Eliot, looking back in the Finale to *Middlemarch* (1872), finely described as 'those times when reforms were begun with a young hopefulness of immediate good which has been much checked in our days'. He was the 'representative man', the 'characteristic Avatar', of the reform era (as Fitzjames Stephen, who disapproved, remarked), the spokesman of the 'sentimental' version of that radicalism which was 'the most instructive political characteristic of the years from 1825 to 1845' (said Walter Bagehot, who was in two minds about it). Or, to cite the more enthusiastic account by the future Poet Laureate, Alfred Austin, in an obituary appreciation (1870):

Happy was the genius of Dickens, being such as it was, in that he reached his majority at the precise time he did. The hour and the man arrived together. A change had come over the national dream . . . He was . . . the man of his epoch, and had the time-spirit throbbing within him.

'This is no fiction', interjects the narrator of *Pickwick* after its hero has been incarcerated in the Fleet Prison and the reader has been told how much better 'the sturdy felon' is treated in gaol than 'the penniless debtor'. A youthfully crude narrative device: but, from the start, Dickens' fictional works contained much topical and non-fictional material, much 'everyday life'. Even *Pickwick*, devised from a broadly comical scenario provided by its publishers, was manoeuvred into the grimness of the Fleet scenes and such explicit social protests as this – but by the time that episode was being serialised (Chapter 42, July 1837), Dickens had long been serialising alongside it *Oliver Twist* (1837–9), which opened in a workhouse and was virtually to end in the condemned cell at Newgate.

It was to be characteristic of Dickens, and part of his wisdom in apprehending and commenting upon his society, that his characters are so often seen, not just in their personal and occupational interaction with one another, but also in relation to the major institutions of their society – the legal system culminating in the prison and the scaffold, the governmental system (national and local), the churches and other supposedly moral forces, schools (and the absence of schools), the money market, the factory system, and much else. His career – always at the top, from *Pickwick* onwards – spanned almost exactly the middle third of the century; as Humphry House remarked, it 'coincided almost exactly with the rule of the Ten-Pound Householders' (1832–67), or, to quote G. M. Young's judgement, 'The political satire of Dickens is tedious and ignorant. But it registers . . . the disillusionment which followed on the hopes of 1830'.

Dickens' first story appeared in 1833 and he was still writing *Edwin Drood* when he died in 1870. These decades saw great political, social and institutional changes, to many of which he was very alert, realising that in modern urbanised society much of people's felicity or misery depended on the adequacy, efficiency, justice and humanity of institutions. Besides being the dominant and most popular novelist of the period, he had other means of persuasion and expression available: he was a much-admired public speaker, an active philanthropist, briefly the founder-editor of the Liberal *Daily News* in 1846 and, more significantly, the editor of a popular weekly (*Household Words*, later *All the Year Round*) from 1850 till his death.

Dickens was very visibly, as well as ideologically, a man of his times: but, though generally reformist and radical, he by no means approved of all the reforms of the 1830s. *Oliver Twist* began his attacks on the New Poor Law, which remain rigorous in his last completed novel *Our Mutual Friend* (1864–5). He was not a joiner nor an ideologue. '*Isms!* Oh Heaven for a world without an ism', he exclaimed in a letter (27 April 1844) referring to a favourite topic, the education of the untaught poor. 'In politics, he took no side', wrote his obituarist in *Fraser's Magazine* (well, he was never pro-Conservative, contemptuous though he was of such opponents of theirs as Palmerston, and indeed of politics and Parliament generally), 'but perhaps', continued *Fraser's* less contentiously, he:

. . . might be described as a practical, not at all a speculative, Radical, who desired to get rid of humbug and inefficiency in all departments, and to extend – not patronage, which he loathed, but – national justice and brotherly help to all honest working men, to secure them fair wages, fit leisure, good shelter, good drainage, good amusement, and good education for their children.

These were aims which commanded widespread sympathy and were increasingly being realised; thus, Forster's Education Bill was being debated when Dickens died. Anthony Trollope had dubbed him 'Mr Popular Sentiment' (in *The Warden*, 1855). He was more than that, but the title was not wholly undeserved. More than most authors, he was the common man writ large – though, of course, able to write brilliantly.

The American critic, Edmund Wilson, asserted in his very influential essay 'Dickens: The Two Scrooges' (1941) that 'Of all the great Victorian writers, he was probably the most antagonistic to

the Victorian age itself'. This was a promising way of recommending, in 1941, an author then undervalued, but Wilson's readers
should have spotted the implausibility of such vast popularity as
Dickens enjoyed co-existing with an antagonism to the ethos of
the age. In 1844, when he was still only thirty-two, he was the
subject of the first and longest chapter of R. H. Horne's *The New
Spirit of the Age*: he was, Horne concluded, 'manifestly the product
of his age. He is a genuine emanation from its aggregate and entire spirit . . . His influence upon his age is extensive – pleasurable,
instructive, healthy, reformatory'. A few years later, a social
worker, hoping to interest Dickens in her charitable activity,
remarked that 'he has so completely the confidence of the lower
classes (who all read his books if they can read at all) that . . . it
would be an immense step gained'. At the other end of the social
scale, Queen Victoria – who had recently met Dickens, and found
herself in agreement with him – wrote, cn his death:

He is a very great loss. He had a large loving mind and the strongest
sympathy with the poorer classes. He felt sure that a better feeling, and
much greater union of classes, would take place in time. And I pray
earnestly it may.

A costermonger's girl in Drury Lane, that day, exclaimed: 'Dickens dead? Then will Father Christmas die too?' – even she knew
of him, and rightly associated him with Christmas. 'Ah, sir!', said
a cabby, picking up one of Dickens' sons around this time, 'Mr
Dickens was the gentleman who looked after the poor man. We
cabmen were hoping he would give us a turn next'.

He was not only the great entertainer, the abundant humorist,
the exciting narrator who like his own Fat Boy could 'make your
flesh creep' very agreeably: he was also the critic and the conscience of his age, though rather as a member of a Loyal
Opposition to widely-acknowledged evils and shortcomings than
as a fundamental antagonist. As the above quotations indicate, he
commanded widespread assent besides enjoying – in both senses
of the word – 'that particular relation (personally affectionate and
like no other man's) which subsists between me and the public',
as he immodestly but accurately put it. He cherished this relationship and was careful not to endanger it – not that he often had
to scheme, or suppress, or pull his punches, to do so.

This may be seen in his handling of sexual matters. 'In England
nowadays,' wrote a *Spectator* critic in 1857, 'novels are written for
families; in France, they are written for men.' Dickens made fun

of his chauvinistic character Mr Podsnap, for whom 'Not English!' was the ultimate dismissal and whose 'question about everything was, would it bring a blush to the cheek of a young person?'. But there was a touch of Podsnap in Dickens himself; he never wrote, or as editor published, anything blushworthy. Some of his contemporaries, such as Thackeray, and immediate successors, such as Hardy, chafed against such restrictions, and his young friend and colleague Wilkie Collins sneered about the public's 'canting "national morality", and their blustering "purity of hearths and homes" '.

Not so Dickens (of whom maybe Collins was thinking): not for nothing was his weekly magazine entitled *Household Words,* and in the 'Preliminary Word' in its first issue (30 March 1850) he – 'the hand that writes these faltering lines' – proclaimed:

We have considered what an ambition it is to be admitted into many homes with affection and confidence; to be regarded as a friend by children and old people . . . and to be associated with the harmless laughter and the gentle tears of many hearths. We know the great responsibility of such a privilege . . .

and one thing meant by 'responsibility' is evident when he continues by attacking the mildly erotic periodicals edited by G. M. W. Reynolds and others ('Panders to the basest passions of the lowest natures'). As for that alleged 'antagonism' to the age, he promises here that the magazine will be concerned with 'the stirring world around us', and its 'many social wonders, good and evil' in ways 'not calculated to render any of us . . . less faithful in the progress of mankind, less thankful for the privilege of living in the summer-dawn of time'.

He belonged to what was later ironically called the Great Moral Majority, and did so by instinct and from principle, not by way of pretence. As a friend recalled:

Dickens was eminently pure-minded. His books speak for themselves in this respect, and in the course of a long and intimate friendship of many years [they were fellow-clubmen at the Garrick] I never heard him say a word which might not have been spoken in the society of ladies.

The 'purity' of his novels was much praised: it met and reflected the taste of its time and place, as was well remarked by the French critic of English literature and observer of English life, Hippolyte Taine, in 1856. After analysing the main features of Dickens' imagination, he commented:

Plant this talent on English soil; the literary opinion of the country will direct its growth and explain its fruits. For this public opinion is its private opinion; it does not submit to it as an external constraint, but feels it inwardly as an inner persuasion . . . The counsels of this public taste are somewhat like this . . . Be moral. All your novels must be such as may be read by young girls . . . We believe in family life, and we would not have literature paint the passions which would attack family life.

And Taine, joining in that then-favourite game of making cross-Channel comparisons, remarks that public opinion enjoins: 'Beware of resembling in this respect the most illustrious of our neighbours. Love is the hero of all George Sand's novels . . . George Sand makes us desire to be in love; do you make us desire to be married'. (A characteristic Gallic distinction, many of Dickens' fellow countrymen would have remarked, though recently it was delightfully endorsed by Peter Bruinvels, MP, commenting on the television lady's announcement of her unmarried pregnancy: she has had her bit of fun, said Mr Bruinvels, but now she should get married.)

Another example Taine gives of how 'the exigencies of morality mar the idea of the book' is the ending of *Dombey and Son*: under the pressure for happy endings, Dickens implausibly rescues Mr Dombey from his isolation and mental breakdown. As Taine tartly put it, 'he becomes the best of fathers, and spoils a fine novel'. The only time Dickens did alter an intended ending was after advance proofsheets of *Great Expectations* had been seen by his fellow novelist Bulwer Lytton: the hero, Pip, was to have ended the novel unmarried but Lytton urged that this was too bleak. 'I have no doubt the story will be more acceptable through the alteration', wrote Dickens, having indicated, in the published text, much happier prospects for Pip. This was a rare artistic retreat. Usually, as Taine perceived, he was inwardly consonant with public taste and expectations on such matters.

'In many of Mr Dickens' letters', wrote Percy Fitzgerald, one of the most prolific contributors to his journals, 'will be found admirable counsels to the novelist; one special one – avoid painful and disagreeable endings. The public likes everything pleasant.' Fitzgerald was not a sophisticated author, and what Dickens bespoke for his magazines did not wholly correspond to his deepest artistic intuitions; still, there was a large overlap and it is instructive to observe his editorial plans and injunctions. 'We hope to do some solid good, and we mean to be as cheery and pleasant as we can', he told prospective contributors; the journal's 'general mind and purpose' would be 'the raising up of those that are down, and the general improvement of our social condition'; and he particularly sought items touching on 'all social evils, and all home affections and associations'.

This reformism was very much in the air, as we noted above. The *Economist* welcoming *The Chimes* (here 'the *Economist* meets Dickens as a brother, and hails his work as a real light in our now darkened paths'), put this Christmas book in its political and cultural context:

One of the most remarkable circumstances of the day is the passion – we call it so designedly – which prevails to improve the condition of the working classes . . . Under the influence of this passion, all the so-called *light* writers, who catch their inspiration from the prevailing events, have turned political philosophers, perhaps without knowing it . . . Mr Dickens shares this national feeling . . . (18 January 1845)

So, in the 1840s, did the future Poet Laureate, who, though more conservative by temperament, overlaps with Dickens in many areas of conviction and sentiment. The two great social questions impending in England, said Tennyson, were 'the housing and education of the poor man before making him our master, and the higher education of women'. In 1847 Tennyson published *The Princess* – his first long poem – on the latter topic. Here Dickens did not share Tennyson's preoccupations: but he wrote much and effectively about 'the poor man', as Tennyson never did nor could, though it was characteristic of the unique cultural situation of their age that in 1865 he could publish, serially, a selection of his poems dedicated to the Working Men of England and could receive his monarch's thanks for doing so.

The poet and the novelist overlapped in that concern with 'home affections and associations'. As Taine and other foreign visitors remarked, and as scholars lately have pondered, the Victorians set an extraordinarily high value on domestic married bliss, hearth and home. The title of Coventry Patmore's popular narrative poem *The Angel in the House*, 1854–62, neatly encapsulates this widespread sentiment; *The Times* in 1888 wrote of 'what may be called the religion of the family throughout England'. Tennyson, remarks the Canadian scholar William E. Fredeman, is 'the domestic poet *par excellence* in English. His preoccupation with domestic themes and subjects . . . is central to any informed understanding of his poetry'. *The Times*, announcing Tennyson's death (7 October 1892), spoke of him indeed in the 'family' terms so familiar in references to Dickens: 'his name has long been a charmed household word around the hearths and in the hearts of admiring countrymen'. Similarly an obituarist wrote of Dickens:

His sympathy with the affections of hearth and home knows no bounds, and it is within this sphere that I confess I know of no other writer – in poetry or prose, amongst ourselves or other nations — to compare with him.

'Who ever understood children better than he?' this obituarist continues. It was in line with his feeling for family and home that Dickens effectively introduced childhood as a major topic in English fiction (and his was an age that saw a large expansion in legislative and philanthropical concern for children). These preoccupations with the family and childhood, together with much else that is central to Dickens' genius, come together in another topic which he made very much his own, Christmas. The Cratchits' Christmas dinner, and the prominence of the crippled Tiny Tim, are reminders of this aspect of his work. With *A Christmas Carol* (1843) he invented the Christmas story, as in his weeklies he inaugurated the Special Christmas Number – and again it is noteworthy that much of our 'traditional' Christmas is an early-Victorian development. It hardly seems coincidental that, in the weeks when Dickens was writing the *Carol*, elsewhere in London Henry Cole was inventing the Christmas card.

Dickens was temperamentally fitted to give classic expression to these contemporary preoccupations. 'No man was so inclined naturally to derive his happiness from home concerns', wrote his biographer John Forster; Christmas was the dearest time of the year to him, he was always then at his best, his children recalled. He was a sincere, never a calculating, author. *Fraser's Magazine*, trying as so many did to account for his unprecedented popularity, mentions several of the characteristics discussed above and adds other important features. It existed, said the reviewer:

. . . because of his kindly, all-pervading charity . . . because of his genial humour and exquisite comprehension of the national character and manners, because of his tenderness, because of his purity, and, above all, because of his deep reverence for the household sanctities, his enthusiastic worship of the household gods . . . Moreover, he is so thoroughly English. [December 1859]

An early reviewer had greeted him as 'a truly national author – English to the backbone'; even before he became a novelist, a reviewer had recommended *Sketches by Boz* to the Americans as better than any guidebook ('a perfect picture of the morals, manners, habits of a great portion of English society'). Again, the man and the novelist cohered. Foreign visitors and acquaintances remarked that he was 'essentially an Englishman in appearance' (exhibiting for instance that national characteristic, an 'exceedingly poor taste in the matter of dress'). Even when dining *en famille*, a French friend noted, he always wore evening dress – 'Superlatively English!'. He was, remarked an English colleague, 'strongly conservative in a good many social matters', and no modern author, except perhaps Cobbett, was 'a more thoroughly typical example of the plain, downright Englishman', as was evidenced not only by various personal and literary virtues but also by tendencies to chauvinism and a bluff philistinism and 'an ample stock of the soundest of old John Bull prejudices'. As Humphry House observed, 'In nothing is Dickens so much of an elementary John Bull as in his hatred of Roman Catholicism and of the Puseyites whom he regarded as the deluded apes of Rome'.

The 'tenderness' which *Fraser's* noted was, as many early commentators remarked, as important as his humour and benevolence in establishing that 'personally affectionate' relationship with a large public: and the greatest of English humorists surprised a friend by saying that 'he preferred the power of making the world cry, rather than laugh. So, he did not care for *Pickwick!*'. Often this pathos centres on a child – lost, oppressed, unfortunate, sick or dying – and it was generally found deeply moving at the time. Little Paul's death in *Dombey and Son* (1847) was said 'with hardly exaggeration', writes Forster, to have 'thrown a whole nation into mourning', while the death of the cross-sweeper boy Jo in *Bleak House* (1853) 'has made perhaps as deep an impression as anything for Dickens', and Forster quotes Dean Ramsay of Edinburgh as maintaining that nothing in English fiction surpassed this episode. Dickens' first major effect in this area came in *The Old Curiosity Shop* (1841), a story, writers Forster, 'which was to add largely to his popularity [and] more than any other of his works to make the bond between himself and his readers one of personal attachment'. At the first banquet given to Dickens in America (Boston, 1 February 1842), Josiah Quincy, Jr, in the chair, referred to the death of Little Nell, and Dickens took up this theme of the 'friendship' fostered by author's and readers' mourning over her fate:

At every act of kindness on your part, I say to myself 'That's for Oliver; I should not wonder if that was meant for Smike; I have no doubt that is intended for Nell' . . .

It was a time when 'friendly' relations between novelist and the public were common; serialisation encouraged this, by extending the relationship over, often, eighteen months for one novel, much as, today, viewers develop a special feeling for the characters in soap-opera (though not for their authors). As that *Fraser's* reviewer remarked:

The very mention of [Dickens'] 'last number' in any social gathering, is sure to be the signal for a chorus of eager admiration. Go where you will, it is the same. There is not a fireside in the kingdom where the cunning fellow has not contrived to secure a corner for himself, as one of the dearest, and, by this time, one of the oldest friends of the family.

Again one notes the family and fireside as the recipients, besides being a major topic, of the novels.

Little Nell 'died' in February 1841; Tennyson's May Queen, another moribund maiden often linked with her in later attacks on 'Victorian sentimentality', did so in *Poems* (May 1842), a volume which quickly became 'very favourite reading' with Dickens. 'BLAST years 1837 to 1900 . . . BLAST their weeping whiskers,' ran the opening manifesto of Wyndham Lewis' *Blast* (20 June 1914). Lewis' expression is more eloquent than strictly accurate; Victoria died in 1901, but anyway her reign had not been sixty-odd gloriously wet years. A reaction began against Dickens' and similar pathos in the mid-1850s: the *Saturday Review*, established in 1856, was a leader in this reaction, and thus we find George Eliot in 1861 confessing, 'I am afraid I have what *The Saturday Review* would call "a morbid delight in deathbeds" – not having reached that lofty superiority which considers it bad taste to allude to them'. It was perhaps a sign of Dickens' responsiveness to changing public sensibility that Jo's death in *Bleak House* in 1853 is his last major effort in this kind. This new cult of the 'stiff upper lip' appears in a *Spectator* article of 1869 which not only accuses Dickens of 'the most mawkish and unreal sentimentalism' but also contains the only Victorian allegation known to me that he was, in Podsnappian terminology, 'Not English!' – 'His picture of the domestic affections . . . seems to us very defective in simplicity and reserve. It is not really English, and tends to modify English family feeling in the direction of theatric tenderness and an impulsiveness wholly wanting in self-control'.

Maybe the reviewer should have said that, by 1869, some of Dickens' domestic sentiment was beginning to look old-fashioned, and maybe it was a sign of the times that in his last completed novel, *Our Mutual Friend* (1864–5), the heroine Bella Wilfer, instead of being of the modest, domestic type, often with religiose associations, favoured in most of the previous novels, is faulty and spirited (more like the controversial new-style 'Girl of the Period') and, when eventually she improves and gets married, she announces to her husband: 'I want to be something so much worthier than the doll in the doll's house'. G. M. Young comments: 'In the profusion of Dickens, the phrase might pass unnoticed. But Ibsen remembered it.' It must be admitted, however, that Bella's effort to become un-doll-like goes little further than reading the newspaper so that she can converse rationally with her John (not, apparently, because women too might be rational and interested in the news).

Like *Hamlet*, as the schoolboy said, this essay has been full of quotations, though not in the way the schoolboy meant. To see how Dickens' contemporaries regarded him and his work, and what they specially valued in it, is a way of indicating how much he expressed their mind and sentiments, and why therefore he could be mourned, in the *Daily News* obituary, as 'emphatically the novelist of the age . . . the one writer everybody read and everybody liked . . . More than any other writer he has been the home favourite. People who never read any novels, read Mr Dickens'.

He did not please all the people all the time, of course; that reaction against his pathos, among the more sophisticated (or 'loftily superior') critics coincided with a growing impatience among some critics with his 'darker' and more mordantly Radical tone. They wanted more *Pickwicks* from him, and particularly resented *Little Dorrit* (1855–7); part of Dickens' reply, in his Preface to that novel, was to proclaim that he had never had so many readers, and several reviewers of what proved to be his last novel, *Edwin Drood*, remarked on the extraordinary phenomenon of his having maintained his popularity, unbroken, for well over thirty years. He had abundant literary gifts – inexhaustible powers of comic creation, strong suits in the 'tender', the grotesque and the macabre, a vigorous narrative impetus, an attractive narratorial persona, a mastery of serialisation, the most intense and inventive prose style of any English novelist to date, and an unprecedented capacity for being able to dramatise topical concerns effectively.

His popularity did not depend primarily upon his embodying in his fictions – and sincerely too – widely congenial ideas, attitudes and sentiments, but the unique popularity he enjoyed could not have arisen or been sustained without his doing so.

He belonged to that Pantheon which Lytton Strachey, four years after *Blast*, was to present ironically as 'Eminent Victorians'. Many memoirs around the turn of the century look back on that generation of Great Men revered more widely and intensely – and in Dickens' case more affectionately too – than any comparable later figures. 'How tremendously it had been laid upon young persons of our generation', recalled Henry James (born 1843), 'to feel Dickens, down to the soles of our shoes, no more modern instance I might try to muster would give, I think, the least measure of . . There has been since his extinction no corresponding case'. Justin McCarthy (born 1830) similarly notes: 'No one born in the younger generation can easily understand, from any illustration that later years can give him, the immensity of the popular homage which Dickens then [in the 1850s] enjoyed'. But the same word was used about Tennyson, in the year when he published that Working Men's selection from his poems: 'Tennyson,' wrote Anthony Trollope, 'has received and is receiving a homage more devoted than was perhaps ever paid to a living poet' (and, one might add, he and Dickens were also paid more cash than any earlier English poet or novelist had received).

The age liked having its sages and masters, and rewarded them well. Dickens, as a voice of that age, had some advantages over Tennyson: he was writing in the dominant and most popular literary form; he was by birth more a 'man of the people' than Tennyson, who came from a professional and gentry family; though highly intelligent, he was not an intellectual (he was indifferent to the scientific and ideological developments which moved Tennyson and George Eliot); in an urbanised age, he was essentially, by residence and in his preferred fictional setting, a Londoner, unlike the country-born and country-living Tennyson. 'It needs an extraordinary combination of intellectual and moral qualities', wrote *The Times* obituarist,

. . . to gain the hearts of the public as Dickens has gained them. Extraordinary and very original genius must be united to good sense, consummate skill, a well-balanced mind, and proofs of a noble and affectionate disposition before the world will consent to enthrone a man as their unassailable and enduring favourite . . . He was made to be popular.

In 1855 Dickens was dining àt Lord John Russell's , and expressed himself vehemently (it 'was like bringing a Sebastopol battery among the polite society') about a grievance of the poor. The composer Meyerbeer was present, and later said to Dickens: '*Ah, mon ami illustre! Que c'est noble de vous entendre parler d' haute voix morale, à la table d'un ministre!*'

Not that, at Lord John's, Dickens was expressing highly revolutionary sentiments. He was giving the company 'a little bit of truth about Sunday' – presumably, that is, remarking on the current controversy about whether bands should be allowed to play in the parks on the Sabbath. This was in July 1855, and around this time he further expressed his views on Sunday amusements for the poor in a journalistic article, a public speech, and in the third chapter of *Little Dorrit*. His was not a lone voice: not only were *Punch* and *The Times* saying the same thing but so was his socially most illustrious admirer. The Queen informed her Prime Minister on 7 August 1855, that she much approved of, and sanctioned at Windsor and in the royal parks, this Sunday music, and elsewhere she expressed her annoyance over parliamentary opposition to the Sunday opening of museums – 'perfect cruelty', she said, for the working class who had no opportunity to visit them during the week. Not everybody agreed, however, with Dickens and his monarch; he could not please all the people all the time, even when he had such powerful allies or fellow-thinkers. In 1855 bands were allowed to play on Sundays, but a year later the Archbishop of Canterbury protested to Lord Palmerston, and the government, threatened with a vote of censure, withdrew permission.

To return to Meyerbeer's comment: a foreigner *would* be surprised and impressed, many Victorians would have commented. In their England, a 'high moral tone' was an expected element in the equipment of a major author – and Dickens commanded many other registers, too, as a voice of his age.

For Further Reading:

Humphry House, *The Dickens World* (Oxford University Press, 1941, revised 1942); Philip Collins, *Dickens and Crime* (Macmillan, 1962); K. J. Fielding, *Charles Dickens: a Critical Introduction* (Longman, 1965); Alexander Welsh, *The City of Dickens* (Oxford,

Clarendon Press, 1971); Philip Collins (ed.), *Dickens: the Critical Heritage* (Routledge, 1971); Robert L. Patten, *Charles Dickens and his Publishers* (Oxford, Clarendon Press, 1978); Malcolm Andrews, *Dickens on England and the English* (Harvester Press, 1979); Michael Slater, *Dickens and Women* (Dent, 1983).

5

Pugin and the Medieval Dream

Nigel Yates

CONTRASTED RESIDENCES FOR THE POOR

NOSTALGIA for the imagined harmony of the lost society of the Middle Ages had begun to manifest itself before the arrival of Victorian England. Horace Walpole's 'Gothick' villa at Strawberry Hill and the novels of Sir Walter Scott had started to make medievalism chic even while the styles of Georgian classicism and the Regency were still in full flood. But the accession of the young queen and her German consort gave a new impetus to romantic conceptions of feudal chivalry; Victoria and Albert were painted in medievalesque garb and in 1839 came the Eglington Tournament, a self-conscious revival of derring-do with Victorian gentlemen in period costume.

The medieval revival fed, however, on deeper concerns than mere aesthetics and style. Many Victorian intellectuals looked to the Middle Ages to provide models of faith, stability and aesthetic unity for a century increasingly marked – some would say afflicted –by the questioning and often ugly process of the Industrial Revolution. The appeal of that 'golden age' and the way in which social, religious and aesthetic reaction could come together is powerfully illustrated by the life and career of Augustus Pugin (1812–52). Nigel Yates argues that Pugin's architectural achievements and writings set the agenda for medieval renewal in church by the Oxford Movement and in society by the Young England group, to which among others Disraeli belonged.

There is a tendency to think of Britain in the Victorian era as a country in which the 'forces of reform' gradually persuaded the 'forces of reaction' to concede 'moderate progress' in the areas that mattered most: democracy, education, social conditions and the overall standard of living. There is, of course, some element of truth behind the popular images, but Victorian society was as complex as those that preceded and succeeded it. And one very important underlying trend within Victorian society was the appeal to a past golden age, in this case Christian Europe in the thirteenth and fourteenth centuries.

Appeals to the past are a common theme in history, and we are not exempt from them today. However, within the present century, such appeals have generally been linked with those considered eccentric and obscurantist. Within Victorian society these appeals were much more serious and mainstream and had a direct impact not merely upon aesthetic values in architecture, art and literature, but on politics, religion and social reform.

Victorian medievalism was not the creation of one person or a small group of people. It had its roots embedded very deeply in a strand of romanticism that had been present within English intellectual circles since at least the mid-eighteenth century – although there was a significant outburst of medievalism in the 1830s and 1840s, the impact of which lasted through the rest of the century. If one name can be connected with that outburst it is that of Augustus Welby Northmore Pugin (1812–52).

Pugin was an unlikely founder for any movement. In probably any other century his highly eccentric, idealist and unrealistic views would have been generally disregarded. But in the 1830s and 1840s they managed to catch the mood of the moment, to appear relevant to those concerned about current developments in politics and religion, and apparently to provide an answer to the perceived ills of contemporary society. Pugin was the son of a French émigré who was both an artist and bookseller with a strong interest in architecture. The son developed his father's ideas and became a practising architect. However, although he designed more than a hundred buildings in a career of less than twenty years, Pugin's principal contribution to Victorian architecture and Victorian medievalism were his writings. His books and articles were both academic and polemical, challenging what he regarded as the materialist and pagan attitudes of his fellow countrymen.

In 1835, at the age of twenty-three, Pugin became a Roman Catholic. It was an entirely intellectual conversion, or 'perversion' as contemporaries preferred to describe it. Aesthetically Pugin had little in common with the majority of his co-religionists who could understand neither his buildings nor his writings, and who initially had no sympathy with his medievalist outlook. However, he found sufficient financial support in the patronage of a few wealthy Roman Catholics, moral and religious support from the future Cardinal Wiseman, and enthusiastic adulation from medievally-minded Anglicans. Pugin was flattered to receive support from those he described simply as Protestants and, in turn, treated their buildings and writings with a degree of patronising respect.

The origins of Victorian medievalism are to be found in the romantic movement of the late eighteenth and early nineteenth centuries. Even further back the disruption caused by the English Civil War had led to an interest in what was perceived to be a more stable society, and to those pioneering collections of documents still so useful to medieval historians: Dugdale's *Monasticon Anglicanum*, le Neve's *Fasti Ecclesiae Anglicanae*, Rymer's *Foedera*,

Wharton's *Anglia Sacra* and Wilkins' *Concilia*. Various societies were established in the early eighteenth century, both local and national, for the study of antiquities, though nothing on the scale of the enormous flowering of such societies in the middle years of the nineteenth century. Gentlemen antiquaries began to preserve and adapt ancient ruins on their estates and to rebuild houses and churches in a strange pastiche of the Gothic style.

Gothic buildings were followed by Gothic literature, and indeed brought together by Horace Walpole, who rebuilt his house at Strawberry Hill in the Gothic style and who published an early Gothic novel, *The Castle of Otranto*, in 1765. In the same year Bishop Percy published his *Reliques of Ancient English Poetry*, and there followed a whole spate of mock medieval poetry and novels full of gloomy castles and mysterious inhabitants, works later satirised by Jane Austen and Thomas Love Peacock. In Wales there was a revival of *eisteddfodau*, and one of the leading lights in this movement, Iolo Morganwg, invented the Gorsedd of Bards, designed their druidical robes and forged a whole corpus of medieval Welsh literature, accepted as genuine by scholars until the 1920s.

The medievalism of Pugin and his disciples was wholly different from this sort of romantic medievalism, of which he strongly disapproved, though his own was equally unreal. It was also a reaction against other trends in comtemporary society of which he similarly disapproved: growing industrialisation, the increasing power of Protestant dissent, political reform, classicism in art and architecture. It is important to remember that Pugin's medieval dream was a double reaction against what he regarded as a decadent society on the one hand and meaningless romanticism on the other. Pugin's medievalism may have been unreal but it was meant to be practical. What Pugin advocated was the revival of 'Christian' architecture as the first stage in the creation of a truly 'Christian' society. He was not alone. Within the Church of England there was a growing body of opinion among the clergy that the bishops had become little more than government spokesmen on religious issues and that the church was in danger of losing its spiritual integrity. There was profound disquiet at the likely effects of the legislation gradually removing the political and social disabilities imposed on Roman Catholics and Protestant dissenters. The younger Tories were unhappy with the way in which the Whigs had seized the political initiative over the reform issue and their perception that their own leaders had no alternative coherent political philosophy to offer the electors. Thus it was that in the 1830s England was ripe for a medieval revival, for an appeal to the past.

The most obvious effect of the new medieval revival, and the one which can be seen all around us at the present time, was that on art and architecture. As already stated, it was not wholly new. In a sense Gothic architecture had never died. Throughout the sixteenth, seventeenth and early eighteenth centuries some churches continued to be built or repaired in a strange Gothic manner which was a logical continuation of the late perpendicular style. From the late eighteenth century the number of Gothic buildings, not just churches, but houses, castles and follies, increased rapidly, though with little attention to stylistic accuracy in either fabric or fittings. The 1830s, and Pugin in particular, changed that approach completely. The younger architects studied the surviving buildings of medieval England and Europe, and formulated firm guidelines according to which Gothic buildings, and especially churches, should be constructed. Within the Church of England, the Camden Society, founded at Cambridge in 1839, took the lead in drawing up rules for the design and fitting up of new buildings and the restoration of old ones. The comfortable and cushioned box pews, the high pulpits and reading desks, which had evolved to meet the liturgical and practical requirements of the Book of Common Prayer, were denounced as abhorrent. Young and enthusiastic new incumbents led the campaign for their removal with the result that by end of the century only a handful of churches were left 'unrestored'.

Similar alterations took place in due course not just among the Roman Catholics, but among Protestant dissenters as well. It became artistically unacceptable to design a church in any style but Gothic, though there was a short-lived Romanesque revival in the 1840s. Even within the Gothic style it was the buildings of the thirteenth and fourteenth centuries that were particularly favoured. In fact 'medieval' churches were not particularly suitable for the type of worship favoured by any religious group in the nineteenth century except perhaps some very high Anglicans. It was a classic example of the victory of style over practicality, as subsequent liturgical reformers have discovered.

Too frequently Victorian Gothic buildings were as artistically unimaginative as they were impractical. But there were exceptions, especially among some of the later Victorian architects such as Bodley and Burges, Pearson and Street. Burges designed some remarkably innovative buildings in which the evocation of the Middle Ages, whilst totally unrealistic, is nevertheless both amazing and charming: his Yorkshire churches at Skelton and Studley Royal, his Anglican Cathedral in Cork, his romantic castles for the Marquess of Bute at Cardiff and Castell Coch. Thirty years earlier Pugin had shown a similar imagination in his fittings for the new Houses of Parliament.

Victorian Gothic architecture, together with the medievalist art and literature which complemented it, were escapist, yet they affected social attitudes just as much as the escapism of Hollywood affected English-speaking society in the 1930s. The novels of Sir Walter Scott upheld the ideals of medieval chivalry. Surely this was what was wrong with nineteenth-century society? Obligation and stability, the essential hallmarks of medieval feudal society, were entirely missing from a society for which the interests of capital, industry and trade were predominant. So at least ran the argument of the Victorian medievalists. What people read in books about the past made them think about the implications of the present.

There is no doubt that, both in creative literature and in some historical scholarship, the writers of the early nineteenth century romanticised the past. Myths were created of a nation that once existed containing a substantially free, property-owning peasantry, dependent on their lords but protected by them. It was a very easy step to contrast this with the poverty of the rural peasantry since the enclosure movement and the exploitation of the urban proletariat by the factory owners. It was a line taken by William Cobbett in his *History of the Protestant Reformation* and in *Rural Rides*, and it was a view which rapidly gained credence in intellectual circles in the 1820s and 1830s.

Pugin adapted this position to great effect in his *Contrasts*, published in 1836. Although the principal purpose of this volume was to show 'a parallel between the Noble Edifices of the Middle Ages and the corresponding buildings of the Present Day, showing the Present Decay of Taste', it also contained in its illustrations the type of social comment with which Cobbett had harangued his own readers. The modern industrial city, choked with filth and grime, was contrasted with the spacious medieval town dominated by its churches and monasteries. In the medieval town a well-dressed youth drinks from a Gothic fountain; in the modern city a shabby urchin is being kept away from a padlocked pump by a constable brandishing a whip. The most telling 'contrast' is that between the relief of poverty in the Middle Ages and the modern provision for the poor. The noble monastic buildings are replaced by a utilitarian workhouse; a diet of beef, mutton, bread and ale by one of bread and gruel; the poor person in his quasi-monastic habit by a beggar in rags; the master dispensing charity by a master wielding whips and chains; decent Christian burial by the dispatch of the corpse for dissection by medical student; and the discipline of an edifying sermon by that of a public flogging.

Comparisons of this type between medieval and Victorian society were clearly unfair. They both exaggerated existing evils and romanticised the Middle Ages, during which examples of cruelty and poverty were not hard to find. Nevertheless they did serve to highlight the inequalities and abuses of contemporary society and they were not therefore without impact. For Pugin, and for others, the essential difference between medieval and Victorian society was that the former was subject to the beneficent influence of religion. Pugin regarded this as impossible to achieve without the conversion of England to Roman Catholicism, since Protestantism provided no adequate role for the church in the government of society.

There were many Protestants who would have disagreed. It was not the Reformation that had brought this about. They could point to the role of the Anglican bishop in the early seventeenth century and allege that it was the Church of England itself that had surrendered its proper role as the spiritual leader of society and allowed itself to become a servant of the secular state. These allegations too were exaggerated but they struck a popular chord among the clergy, who stood to benefit from an ecclesiastical revival.

The Oxford Movement of the 1830s, whose catalyst was Keble and Newman's *Tracts for the Times*, aimed to restore the influence of the Church of England within the governmental structure of society and at the same time to give the Church a greater impact on the lives of individuals. Again, there was a feeling that the Church was out of touch with working people, that it had opted for far too close an alliance with the aristocracy and gentry. Recent research is beginning to show that the Church of England between the later seventeenth and the early nineteenth centuries was less out of touch than its critics had alleged. The Anglican establishment, however, had relatively few public defenders, either within its own ranks or outside in the 1830s. It was felt to

be tainted with the worst manifestations of rationalism, indolence and careerism.

Initially the participants within the Oxford Movement identified themselves closely with the Anglican divines of the early seventeenth century. However, their contacts with those in the field of architecture, art and literature who were idolising the Middle Ages brought about a fairly speedy shift of emphasis. The Oxford Movement became one of the principal contributors to growing medievalism. Its priorities changed from the theological to the liturgical and aesthetic, its worship adapted to suit the new and restored Gothic buildings. Initially the enthusiastic and mostly young high churchmen who propounded the principles of the movement most energetically had to face charges of popery in a society where Protestant reactions to Roman Catholicism were much the same as they are today in Northern Ireland. Gradually, the 'no popery' drum was banged less loudly, and by the 1870s virtually the whole Church of England was infected with a rampant medievalism not seriously challenged until the 1930s. Attempts by the more extreme Anglo-Catholics after 1870 to react against what they termed 'British Museum Religion' in favour of the contemporary excesses of German Baroque ornamentation were almost entirely unsuccessful.

Implementing the medieval dream, and in particular giving it a political reality, showed how shallow and unreal much of it was. It was easy to condemn the shortcomings of Victorian society and to admire an age of perceived order and stability. The difficulties began when one started to analyse the essential nature of medieval society. Although men like Carlyle and Cobbett, Morris and Ruskin, Pugin and Pusey, might all agree that medieval society formed a model for the reform of Victorian society, their perceptions of that model were vastly different.

Politically the two extremes could be found in the Young England group of Tories in the 1840s, and later in the Socialism of William Morris and some of his contemporaries. After 1830 the Tory Party became strongly split with the majority faction under Peel anxious to accept the Whig principles of economic and political reform in order to increase their support among the urban

---

Opposite: 'To the greater glory of God'. Victorian nostalgia for the divine craftsmanship of the Middle Ages manifested itself in forms such as Rossetti's evocation of St Catherine in a fifteenth-century studio – the model complete with her wheel of martyrdom. (The Tate Gallery, Bridgeman Art Gallery)

middle classes. The older group within the Tory Party, repre-
senting the interests of the country landowner, had little to offer
in opposition to the reformers. An alternative view of Toryism
was offered by the Young England group led by Lord John Manners, later Duke of Rutland, and counting Disraeli among its
adherents. The group supported, as had Pugin, the alleviation of
poverty and improvements in social conditions but allied these to
increasing the power of the throne, the Church and the land-
owners. What they effectively advocated was a new and caring
feudalism.

It was a view supported by many churchmen, both Anglicans
such as Pusey, or Roman Catholics such as Pugin. Most of those
clergy attracted to work among the poor in the later nineteenth
century, including the majority of ritualist slum priests, were
Tories and not Socialists, and saw no conflict whatsoever between
their Toryism and their passionate concern for the improvement
of social conditions. Interestingly enough, when some members
of the present Conservative Party make an appeal for the restoration of Victorian values, one suspects that their sympathies
politically lie far less with the Toryism of the Young England
group and Disraeli, than with the *laissez-faire* ideals then cherished
by the non-radical wing of the Liberal Party.

However, just as neo-medievalism could find a home among
the Tories, it led others to advocate socialism. It is likely that the
influence of medievalist socialism has been exaggerated, and that
it never attracted more than a few middle- and upper-class intellectuals. Nevertheless it was a formative influence in the creation
of the modern Labour Party. Whereas the Young England group
had tried to demonstrate the virtues of feudalism, medievalist
socialists based their political and social attitudes on the concepts
of a free peasantry, the surviving vestiges of which Morris claimed
to find in a visit to Iceland in 1871. The real enemy was not poverty but inequality. This could not be solved by the sort of
benevolent oligarchy favoured by the Young England group.
What was required was a truly classless society and this meant
either the overthrow, or at least the subjugation, of capitalism. An
alliance between the doctrines of Marx and medieval idealism
seems a strange one, but Morris and his friends found no incon-
sistency in such an alliance. Indeed they found their models in
the leaders of the Peasants' Revolt and other revolutionary figures
of the fourteenth and fifteenth centuries. Half a century later
Morris' ecclesiastical heir, Conrad Noel, was to eventually 'beatify'

John Ball and fit out a chapel to his memory over the porch of the parish Church of Thaxted. The early leaders of the Labour Party included Anglican high churchmen influenced by the writings of Morris as well as those from a radical Liberal and non-conformist background.

There was virtuality no area of Victorian society untouched by the appeal to the past, especially the medieval past, that the buildings and writings of Pugin had done so much to popularise. It was a constant underlying theme in any debate, political, religious or social. It shaped men's attitudes and it gave a historical perspective to their opinions. It also, eventually, brought about a more analytical approach to the study of the Middle Ages. Whereas Pugin or Corbett or Morris had used the medieval world as a quarry from which to construct their own dreams of an ideal society, it was historians like Freeman, Green and Stubbs who laid the foundations for the modern study of the Middle Ages, and the many local archaeological, historical and record-publishing societies founded in the later nineteenth century that enabled these researches to reach a far wider audience. It should, however, be pointed out that it was medieval idealism that had created the need for such societies and had attracted the initial members and subscribers.

One important aspect of Victorian medievalism was the strong personal links between its various manifestations, artistic, religious and political. Prominent churchmen might also be architects, artists or writers. Art and literature were linked by groups such as the Pre-Raphaelite Brotherhood. Many of those prominent in politics or social reform were also well-known as churchmen, artists or writers. One can trace without difficulty the impact that the writings of one medievalist made on the thoughts, and writings, of another, even if their final visions of the ideal society might turn out to be rather different.

Although the principal impact of Victorian medievalism was in the realm of ideas, and its influence on those trying to alter contemporary attitudes or improve the quality of contemporary life, the movement had its practical consequences. Much of Victorian art and literature was influenced, to some extent at least, by medieval themes. Victorian architecture was completely dominated by a medieval revival in building and furnishing styles. Religious attitudes, particularly (though not exclusively) within the Church of England, were transformed and, to a large extent, fossilised for several generations by the medievalist outlook of

Tractarian theologians and Camdenian liturgists. In politics and social reform the influence of medievalist ideas made a major contribution towards the criticism of uncontrolled capitalism or utilitarian attitudes towards the alleviation of poverty. It led to the development of both social conservatism and radical socialism. Could one even argue the case that, in the long run, the influence of medievalism on political and social thinking was a contributory cause to the eventual eclipse of the Liberal Party and the realignment of British politics in the 1920s? Perhaps this is going too far. Pugin, however, would have been delighted with the notion. For him political liberalism was a root cause of the decadence he saw all around him.

The appeal to the past, resulting in vibrant medievalism, was an important antidote to those other Victorian values, perhaps better known, that one usually sees in terms of 'progress'. At one level it offered an escape from the harsh realities of the present, at another it postulated a better society to which the modern world might attain. Victorian medievalism, though built on the romanticism of the eighteenth century, rejected this as shallow and unreal. Yet the new images it created were equally unreal, despite the popularity of their appeal. What is perhaps surprising is that so many people were prepared to overlook these unrealities, and for this the medievalists could thank Pugin, whose powerful prose and imaginative buildings converted all but the most aggressively hostile.

For Further Reading

Phoebe Stanton, *Pugin* (Thames and Hudson, 1971) is excellent. There is no general study of Victorian medievalism, but there is much useful material in the following: Alice Chandler, *A Dream of Order* (Routledge and Kegan Paul, 1971); Kenneth Clark, *The Gothic Revival* (John Murray, 1962); Philippa Levine, *The Amateur and the Professional* (Cambridge University Press, 1986); R. J. Smith, *The Gothic Bequest* (Cambridge University Press, 1987); James White, *The Cambridge Movement* (Cambridge University Press, 1962). Charles Eastlake's *History of the Gothic Revival* has been reprinted with an introduction by J. M. Crook (Leicester University Press, 1978).

TO THE
QUEEN'S PRIVATE APARTMENTS

THE QUEEN AND PRINCE ALBERT AT HOME.

6

New Men?
The Bourgeois Cult of Home

John Tosh

Opposite: The creation of the Royal 'Family' – with its implications for exalting domestic and bourgeois values – was engineered by Prince Albert (seen in games with the royal children in this charming 1840s lithograph) – so unlike the home life of Victoria's Regency uncles. (The Royal Collection © Her Majesty Queen Elizabeth II)

THE VICTORIAN PERIOD is often thought of as one where the looser morals and conventions of the Regency period (exemplified by the private vices and extravagances of the sons of George III, above all of the Prince Regent himself, which had left the monarchy in low public esteem) was succeeded by a much greater priority being given to bourgeois morality and the image of a cosy paterfamilias giving priority to domestic virtues, exemplified par excellence by a 'First Family' – Victoria and Albert.

But this image can be oversimplified. For one thing, though consciousness of the exploitation of children as 'little adults' was becoming more acute, with the agitation for a Ten-Hour Day and other liberalising movements, there was still ample exploitation, with the continuing atomisation of industrial society, to sear the pens of Dickens and other writers. In addition, the promotion of family values and the new man that went with it was by no means universal.

As John Tosh outlines here, the Victorian period proposed other models of masculinity – both chauvinist and homosocial – which jostled in acute tension with those of domesticity, both in fiction and social comment. The tensions this set up in elites and classes and across society are ones that still resonate today.

In 1831 John Ruskin's father, a wine merchant, wrote home from a business visit to Carlisle, 'Oh! how dull and dreary is the best society I fall into compared with the circle of my own Fire Side with my Love sitting opposite irradiating all around her, and my most extraordinary boy . . .' His sentiments were echoed with an incoherent intensity by Joshua Pritchard, a Methodist excise officer, in a letter to his wife a few years later: 'I have comfortable lodgings but yet Home, sweet Home, & Home is sweet & sweet is Home . . .'

The Victorian cult of the home tends to evoke largely female associations. Indeed the popular image of Victorian domesticity is so focused on women and children that it is hard to avoid the conclusion that their needs were its governing rationale. Recent historical scholarship has been largely concerned with whether domesticity should be interpreted as empowering or repressive of women. This emphasis certainly corresponds with many of the ways in which home was represented at the time. The new domestic advice literature on childcare, household management and the direction of servants was addressed exclusively to women.

The presiding image of a Victorian family Christmas was the Virgin and Child. 'Home Sweet Home', first performed in 1823 and later immortalised by Jenny Lind and Adelina Patti, was drawn from an opera about the abduction of a girl from her village home. In this world men can easily appear to be little more than worshippers on the edge of the charmed circle. Yet even at the cultural level appearances are deceptive. The theme of 'Home Sweet Home' was actually exile from home – a much more routine experience for men than for women, as Joshua Pritchard's effusion suggests. (John Howard Payne, the American librettist, had also led a notably peripatetic existence.) The hugely popular poet, Felicia Hemans, played on the meaning of home in the breast of the dying soldier or the distant wanderer. As for Christmas, the message became more ambiguous over time: little could be made of the figure of Joseph, no doubt, but the gendered character of the Christmas story was certainly modified by the rise of Father Christmas in the second half of the century.

In fact the triumph of domesticity in Victorian middle-class life answered primarily to the needs of men, in response to the gathering pace of urbanisation and industrialisation. Prior to the nineteenth century men had spent much of their leisure-time in the saddle, the street, the tavern and the coffee-house. What had kept them in touch with home was work, since the home was usually their place of business. Farming, artisanal production and professional life were all carried out from the home, and many middle-class Victorian men could recall a childhood spent in a working atmosphere, in a mill-house or over a shop; the basis for their family's livelihood was plain to see, and as children they had materially contributed to it. John Heaton, a prosperous doctor in mid-century Leeds, recalled his upbringing next door to his father's bookshop, with the second-hand stock crammed into storage space above the family apartment.

At the root of the new evaluation of domesticity was the separation of home from work. From the Industrial Revolution onwards, the work of middle-class men was increasingly performed in specialist business premises like the factory and the office. Family life was something that happened elsewhere, at first within walking distance, but then increasingly a railway journey away. This could have led to the virtual removal of men from the home – as certainly happened in the USA. But in England that outcome was stalled by the elevation of home to be not only the hallowed sphere of wife and children, but the refuge of the breadwinner as well. The distinctive hallmark of British domesticity was that it permeated the lives of men too – as husbands, as fathers, and as upholders of fireside virtues.

Of course Victorian society had its share of workaholics: in the 1850s the Bradford mill-owner, Isaac Holden, pleaded his affection for the 'dear old combing machines' and the need to 'keep close to the Business' in mitigation of his neglect of Sarah Holden, but these excuses cut much less ice than they would have done fifty years earlier. Domestic affections were almost *de rigueur* for the reputation of a virtuous public man, like W. E. Gladstone or John Bright; they even enhanced a military reputation, General Havelock (of Indian Mutiny fame) being the most celebrated example. The blameless (and very bourgeois) home of the Royal Family was essentially the Prince Consort's achievement; as Victoria herself recalled (skirting round her own dislike of babies), 'Dear Papa always directed our nursery and I believe that none was ever better'. Foreign visitors like Ralph Waldo Emerson from America and Hippolyte Taine from France were emphatic that in England domesticity was more than piety: it was lived as well as imagined by middle-class men.

The separation of home and work had far-reaching implications. A man who conducted his business away from home had much less reason to offer board and lodging to his employees, so apprentices soon disappeared from the middle-class home. The same process was going on in the countryside: here, even though the total separation of home from work was patently impossible, farmers dispensed with live-in labourers, replacing them with day labourers who boarded elsewhere. The home became a place for family only, with servants accommodated as discreetly as possible. The traditional patriarchal ideal of a husband-and-wife working partnership was almost gone. One can see its vestige in the lingering tendency for men to marry wives from the same occupational group as themselves, and sometimes to gain a useful source of independent professional advice – as Isaac Holden did in marrying the hard-headed sister of his fellow-woollen master, Jonas Sugden, in 1850. But by this time a much more typical 'partnership' was the marriage between a husband who commuted to a job in commerce, and a wife who knew little about his office life and regarded the home as the centre of her existence. It was women of this kind whom Sarah Ellis primarily addressed in her widely read advice manuals of the late 'thirties and 'forties.

By the 1830s the key elements of Victorian domesticity were in place. Not only marriage for love but marriage *as* love was the expectation. Both men and women continued to marry for money and social advantage, but these were supposed to be secondary

considerations. Marriage ought to be romantic, which is one reason why the sexual frustration of many marriages was so keenly
felt. The child, and above all the child at home, was now securely
established at the heart of middle-class sensibility – and the masculine sensibility in particular, since it was here that the Romantic view of the child entailed the sharpest break with the past.
Perhaps most important of all, the city and the market-place were
now perceived to be alienating and amoral, and the home came
into sharper focus as the emotional mooring of *homo economicus* –
the place where, as James Anthony Froude put it, 'we fall again
into our most human relations'.

Much of this turning away from the world to the home was
expressed in the most powerful religious language of the day –
that of Evangelicalism, in its Nonconformist as well as its Anglican variants. For very many Evangelicals the religious disciplines
of the home, presided over by the stern but loving *paterfamilias*,
were credited with greater moral power than the public forms of
worship in church or chapel; William Wilberforce was only the
best-known case of a godly and home-loving layman who enjoyed more religious prestige than any minister.

The Evangelicals certainly believed in masculine authority. The
household head was not only accountable for the religious welfare of his family, but stood in place of God to them – a position
one finds maintained by the Independent minister, John Angell
James, as well as the Broad Church Anglican, Edward Benson.
Family prayers – a practice which had fallen into disuse since the
seventeenth century – were now revived; in many households
they were quite explicitly used as a form of discipline, by means
of homilies about good conduct and public naming of errant
individuals. This pattern of domestic authority was, of course,
entirely consistent with traditional notions of patriarchy. By this
way of thinking, a man's first domestic duty was to exercise rule
over all his dependents – wife, children and servants – not least
because efficient household production required it. Domestic dis-
obedience and disorder exposed a man to community ridicule, as
being a slur on his masculinity. The growing separation of home
from productive work removed much of the rationale for this
position, but it was still enshrined in common law, with no significant modification by statute before the 1870s. It was taken for
granted that wife and daughters be at the husband's beck and
call, to attend to his little wants and bolster his self-esteem in what
was effectively a protected zone for the exercise of masculine

authority. Evangelical doctrines of the family can, in part, be seen as a means of shoring up patriarchy at a time when its traditional material foundations were crumbling.

But cutting across the traditional masculine investment in private patriarchy was the desire for companionship. The comforting image of men at the fireside was about intimacy, not authority. John Stuart Mill overstated the case when he told the House of Commons in 1867, 'women and men are, for the first time in history, really each others' companions'. But the aspiration for companionate marriage was widespread, a legacy of the rise of 'sensibility' since the late eighteenth century. Of course married Englishmen continued to attend clubs, conduct a public life in the community, and (though this has been exaggerated) visit prostitutes. But they spent comparatively little time on these pursuits, regarding the companionship of a wife as preferable to the pleasures of male conviviality. Mill himself was much exercised as to whether this companionship was an improving one. He knew that it had been so in the case of his marriage to Harriet Taylor, but then Harriet was exceptionally gifted, as he never tired of pointing out. In the generality of cases Mill was inclined to doubt the improving effect of marriage, partly because women's education still trailed so badly behind men's, and partly because men had been brought up to expect subservience from women. A concern with authority did not coexist comfortably with affection. As A. James Hammerton has pointed out, the consequence of men spending more time at home than in the past was often constant demarcation disputes between spouses, and this was certainly reflected in the rising incidence of divorce suits after the 1857 Divorce Act. The preference which so many Victorian husbands exercised for wives much younger than themselves is a good indication of the value they continued to set on securing unquestioned authority in the home. Edward Benson, for example, proposed to his cousin Mary Sidgwick when she was twelve and he was twenty-four; they married in 1859 when she was just eighteen and he already enjoyed the power and prestige of a public school headmaster.

Patriarchy was also undermined by the newly won moral prestige of the wife as mother. She was not only nurse for his children (though the comparatively new vogue for breastfeeding enhanced this role too); she was their moral guide, the moulder of their characters. The valorisation of the home and the new focus on the needs of children projected the wife into the pivotal domestic position, whatever traditional wisdom might say about the husband being master in his own home. Evangelicalism itself spoke with a divided voice, dignifying the household authority of the *paterfamilias*, while at the same time treating the woman as keeper of her husband's conscience and controller of her children's moral destiny.

This divided location of authority raised considerable difficulties with regard to parenting. The Victorian father is often taken to have been an unsmiling patriarch lording it over submissive wife and cowed children. But this is little more than a negative stereotype foisted on posterity by the first generation of angry post-Victorians (notably the Bloomsbury Group). Oppressive fatherhood was far from being the norm, and it was often a symptom of weakness, a clumsy attempt to regain moral ground lost to the Angel Mother. And for every despot there was an involved and playful father, like the Lincolnshire farmer, Cornelius Stovin, chasing his two-year-old round the dining-room, or the Unitarian minister, William Gaskell, sharing his daughters' holiday pranks. Stovin and Gaskell both worked from home. For other fathers, time spent with children in play or nurture was a vital dimension of the healing power of home in a harshly entrepreneurial world. That power might continue to be exercised by a favourite daughter for many years, often until the father died.

The most acute difficulties arose in the parenting of sons. The aspect of fatherhood least likely to be jettisoned was overseeing the passage of boys into manhood, since the father's own masculinity was on the line. In an unstable social and economic climate in which self-reliance was at a premium, this was a matter of acute anxiety to many fathers. The Hertfordshire brewer, William Lucas, in 1847 felt 'an inexpressible anxiety' about how his seven sons would turn out (but made no mention of his two daughters). Men tended to take seriously the responsibility of reproducing masculinity in the next generation. The traditional view had been that sons who spent too much time in the company of their mothers and other female inmates of the home would grow up effeminate. The new distribution of parental responsibilities in the middle-class home made it all too likely that this would happen, especially if the father was often away on business. It is this doubt about the masculine potential of boys at home which explains much of the Victorian emphasis on 'manliness', conventionally defined as independence, energy, endurance and straightforwardness. Those qualities, it was believed, might possibly be acquired by a boy living at home, but certainly not if they were instilled by his mother. The most reliable instrument of manly upbringing was the public school. Of course the vastly expanded public-school sector of mid-Victorian England catered to other concerns as well: social climbing, professional advancement, and sometimes sound religion. But a fundamental and unvarying aspect of the appeal of these schools was that they compelled boys to 'shift for themselves', and shielded them from the feminine attractions of mother and sisters. In 1864 when nine-year-old Arthur Heaton showed signs of 'petulant' behaviour, his medical father decided the time had come to remove him from the contagion of his sisters' company and send him to preparatory school (and thence to Rugby). The next generation was to demonstrate that the public schools had suppressed the allure of domesticated femininity all too well.

The 1880s and 1890s witnessed the continuing growth of masculine domesticity, but also its first real crisis. The scene of greatest expansion was the growing ranks of the lower middle class. In *The Diary of a Nobody* by George and Weedon Grossmith (1894) the family rows and neighbourly tensions which troubled Mr Pooter so much were predicated on an undeviating attachment to domestic values, not least because his social standing depended on it. The lower middle class became firmly associated with a decorous and domestic respectability, with terraced housing in the burgeoning suburbs to match.

But the situation was very different among the professional and commercial classes which had lived in domesticity for two or three generations. More and more men of this background were taking the measure of the costs they had incurred through accepting the conventions of domesticity so readily – the diminished patriarchal authority, the boredom and the men-only pleasures forgone. Domesticity, like other features of Victorianism, became more rigid and formulaic with every decade. Beset by nice distinctions of social status and policed by etiquette manuals, domestic routine grew more comprehensive and more constraining. Since this routine was in the hands of women, the effect was to emphasise still further feminine authority and feminine ambience in the home. As the journalist T. H. S. Escott put it in 1879, 'the acceptance gained by the rite of five-o'clock tea is the symbol of the ascendancy of the softer over the sterner sex'. Two generations of domesticity had shifted the balance of power within the middle-class household and called into question much of its appeal for men.

Events in the public sphere also undermined men's attachment to the home. The well-publicised proceedings of the new Divorce Court after 1857 placed an uncomfortable spotlight on the excesses of domestic patriarchy which judges now interpreted to include mental as well as physical cruelty. A succession of legal changes – the Married Women's Property Act of 1882 and the Custody Act of 1886 being only the most notable – for the first time diluted the principle of untrammelled private patriarchy. A group of articulate feminists led by Mona Caird questioned the ideological foundations of marriage itself. At the same time the New Woman (or 'the revolt of the daughters') suggested a more autonomous model of womanhood – and not only on the pages of women novelists, but in the office, the street, the drawing-room and even perhaps the bedroom. By the 1890s the rigid *paterfamilias* was beginning to look like a vestige from the past, mocked in public and teased or resisted in private.

The outcome was a discernible male revolt against domesticity among the established middle class towards the end of the century. Marriage was postponed to an average age of thirty for men. Many more men now remained celibate for life – sometimes whole families, like the children of Edward Benson. This was the hey-day of the gentleman's club, where the pleasures of homosocial society were available to all – married men as well as bachelors. Club life itself was telling evidence of one of the most enduring legacies of the new public schools, which was to confer an unreality on the home and its female inmates. Domesticity was often hardly more congenial to boys who had attended day school: the prolongation of both schooling and professional training condemned them to continue living under the parental roof until their late twenties, resentful of both patriarchal power and domestic routine.

Rejection of domesticity – or at very least a sensitivity to its more irksome features – had important social implications, not always in obvious contexts. It was one of the springs of the growing middle-class attraction to the idea of Empire as a bracing, men-only environment. Writers like H. Rider Haggard and G. W. Henty allowed young men to experience undomesticated masculinity in its most agreeable fantasy form: 'there is not a petticoat in the whole history', Allan Quatermain reassures his readers at the beginning of *King Solomon's Mines* (1885). The middle-class vogue for emigration and imperial service reflected not just indoctrination by the public schools or career pressures in Britain, but a restless impatience with settled domestic existence.

To lead a rigorous life of adventure free of home ties had become a powerful fantasy by the late Victorian period, and because Britain possessed an expanding Empire the fantasy could be enacted by tens of thousands of young middle-class men. As one newly arrived concession-hunter discovered in Bulawayo in 1888, 'There is no old woman here to tell you "You are looking pale", . . . or having people fool around you with a cup of tea or soup or other things you do not want'. Twenty years later Baden-Powell propagated the same idea in the safety of the English countryside. The Boy Scouts were intended to place the day-schoolboy on a more equal masculine footing with his public school age-mate, by giving him a practical outdoor training and by filling his head with frontier lore from the remote corners of the Empire. In B-P's words, 'Manliness can only be taught by men, and not by those who are half men, half old women'; he did not need to specify the carpet-slippered clerk, snoozing by the fire while his sons grew up without pluck or backbone. By the Edwardian period the association between domesticity and middle-class mores was beginning to wear thin.

The twentieth century has seen a continuing process of ebb and flow in men's attachment to the home, the most powerful determinant being the two World Wars. But there have been striking signs of continuity. The middle-class men of the 1830s and 1840s invested more heavily in domesticity than their counterparts in any other country, and their legacy is perceptible even now in the phenomenon of the New Man whose loyalties and energies are centred on the home. Against this must be set the negligent or absent father, recently highlighted by the activities of the government's Child Support Agency.

As the Victorian period shows, there is inherent tension in the relationship between masculinity and domesticity. Once home and work had moved apart, homosocial and domestic attachments were set on collision course. The alienated breadwinner might yearn for home, but there was no shortage of settings where the pleasures of a bachelor life could be tasted by the married man. Adventure and danger exerted their appeal, even as domesticated masculinity became the social norm. Then, as now, domesticity for men raised intractable questions to do with the balance between authority and affection, between homely and homosocial pursuits, and between security and adventure. How these tensions were resolved or repressed constituted the very foundation of masculine identity in Victorian times, as it does today.

For Further Reading:

A. James Hammerton, *Cruelty and Companionship: Conflict in Nineteenth-Century Married Life* (Routledge, 1992); Leonore Davidoff and Catherine Hall, *Family Fortunes: Men and Women of the English Middle Class, 1780–1850* (Hutchinson, 1987); Michael Roper and John Tosh (eds), *Manful Assertions: Masculinities in Britain since 1800* (Routledge, 1991); John Tosh, 'Authority and Nurture in Middle-Class Fatherhood: the Case of Early and Mid-Victorian England', *Gender and History*, 8, no. 1 1996; John Gillis, 'Ritualization of Middle-Class Family Life in Nineteenth Century Britain', *International Journal of Politics, Culture and Society* 2 (1989).

7

Titus Salt
Enlightened Entrepreneur

Ian Campbell Bradley

*Opposite: Saltaire in the mid-1870s, after the expansion of the mill.
(Mansell Collection)*

THE PARABLE OF THE TALENTS was never far away from the minds of many of the Victorian tycoons and magnates who made their fortune from industrial processes. Storing up treasure in heaven by constructing a new Jerusalem in the West Riding of Yorkshire was the particular achievement of the industrialist Sir Titus Salt (1803–76). Ian Bradley looks at Salt, his rise from humble origins to millionaire status by mastery of new fabrics and fabric processes, his creation of the model village of Saltaire and the philosophy by which he and many other Victorian businessmen lived – philanthropy with an eye to profit.

———————

Sir Titus Salt was in many ways the archetypal Victorian industrialist. He rose from comparatively humble origins by dint of hard work and commercial acumen to become one of the richest and most powerful of the West Riding textile barons, directly employing more than 3,500 hands. An ardent Congregationalist, a strict teetotaller and a campaigner for temperance reform, he embodied the stern but enlightened values of the Nonconformist Conscience. He was involved in many of the great radical and reforming movements of his day and took a prominent part in Liberal politics. As an employer he was a true paternalist, taking his workers out of the polluted environment of Bradford, providing them with good housing and amenities in the model village of Saltaire and expecting them in return to be sober, God-fearing and hard working.

Titus Salt was born in 1803 in the West Yorkshire village of Morley, the eldest of seven children. At the age of seventeen he was apprenticed to a woolstapler in Wakefield to learn the rudiments of the woollen textile trade in which West Yorkshire was already beginning to lead the world. He learned how to buy good fleeces at auction, how to sort out the wool according to the length, fineness and softness of its fibre, and how to wash and comb it in preparation for spinning into yarn. Characteristically, he remained an apprentice for two years until he had thoroughly mastered each of these processes and it was not until he was twenty-two that he joined his father's firm of Daniel Salt & Son as wool buyer. His main job was to attend sheep clippings in the Yorkshire dales, Norfolk and Lincolnshire and auctions of imported fleeces at the London and Liverpool docks.

Despite his constant travelling, Titus Salt rapidly established himself as a lively and energetic force in the religious and civic life of Bradford. He was actively involved in the affairs of the Horton Lane Congregational Chapel where he held the offices of librarian, teacher and superintendent of the Sunday School. He was also sworn in as a special constable and helped to quell violent demonstrations on the part of striking mill workers.

On his buying trips around the country, Salt was constantly on the lookout for new materials. He bought a large quantity of Donskoi wool from south-east Russia which had been rejected by other manufacturers. Unable to find anyone prepared to spin it, he tried himself and found that it made a very good worsted yarn. This experiment led to the opening of a spinning mill in Bradford. In 1833 Daniel Salt retired and Titus took over the business, concentrating as much on spinning and weaving as on preparing the wool. He continued his search for new materials, at one stage even trying to see if he could spin yarn from the fibres of the seaweed which grew in copious quantities on the beach at Scarborough.

In 1834, while on a buying visit to Liverpool docks, he noticed a pile of 300 or so dirty-looking bales lying in the corner of a warehouse. They turned out to be fleeces of the alpaca, an animal closely related to the llama and native to Peru. Out of interest Salt pulled out a handful of the evil-smelling wool and examined it. He was impressed by the straightness and length of the fibres, took a sample back to Bradford in his handkerchief and experimented with spinning it. He found that it produced a high-quality glossy yarn. To the astonishment and delight of the brokers, who had long given up all hope of selling them, he offered to buy the alpaca fleeces at eightpence a pound.

Salt's chance discovery on the quayside started a new industry which was to make Bradford and the surrounding district one of the most prosperous regions of Britain over the next half-century. Cloth woven from the alpaca had the gloss and rustling 'frou-frou' effect of silk but at much less cost and with greater durability. In 1837 Salt introduced Alpaca Orleans, a fabric made of cotton and alpaca, which became a favourite dress material with Victorian ladies for the next fifty years. It was particularly suitable for crinolines and was also in heavy demand for mourning wear. The success of the fabric was assured when Queen Victoria sent Salt the fleeces of the two alpacas she kept in Windsor Park to be made up into cloth.

By 1839 the price of alpaca wool had risen to thirty pence a pound and two million pounds of it was being imported every year, much of it destined for Salt's mills. He was also making much use of mohair, another long-staple combing wool, which came from the fleece of the angora goat found in Turkey and which also produced a fine lustrous cloth when combined with cotton. It was through his exploitation of the properties of these two unusual wools that Salt was to establish his position as king of the burgeoning West Yorkshire worsted industry and accumulated a personal fortune.

In 1844 he moved his wife and eleven children out of the increasingly polluted and noisy environment of Bradford to a large house at Lightcliffe about ten miles outside the city. But, although he was now rich and secure enough to do so, he did not take up the lifestyle of a country gentlemen. He was at his mill by six o'clock every morning, before the machines started turning and often before the first worker arrived. It was later said of him that he made £1,000 a day before his rivals were out of bed. He was a fanatic for punctuality, both in his mills, where lateness was punished, and at home, where he demanded prompt attendance at meals and family prayers. He had iron self-discipline and expected the same from others, but he was also remarkably generous. On the way to work he often stopped his carriage to give £5 to an employee whom he knew to have been ill or in difficulties.

Salt's generosity showed itself in the year that he spent as mayor of Bradford. He took on the office in November 1848 at a time of acute distress and high unemployment in Bradford where the quality textile market had been depressed as a result of revolutions on the Continent. The town was also suffering a cholera outbreak which claimed more than 400 lives. As mayor, Salt inaugurated a proper system of drainage and sanitation, opened soup kitchens and even devised a scheme for emigration to the New World. And despite the fact the sales from his own mills had fallen by £10,000 a month because of the slump in trade, he took on 100 unemployed woolcombers and laid by their work against better times returning.

During his mayoralty Salt took a particular interest in the moral condition of the populace of Bradford and was determined to encourage the development of alternative places of recreation and entertainment to the ubiquitous public house. He was instrumental in having St George's Hall built in the centre of the town and was also actively involved in the planning and building of music halls and mechanics' institutes where people could enjoy and improve themselves free from the temptations of alcohol. He was one of the first employers in the area to grant a half holiday on Saturdays, believing that it might end the rush from the factory gates into the pub which took place every Saturday evening and often resulted in workers drinking away much of their weekly wages.

In his concern with punctuality, sobriety and self-improvement Salt was very much a man of his time. But in one important respect he was very much ahead of it. He realised the importance of environmental factors in determining people's behaviour. He did not believe that anything excused the drunkenness, the violence and the indolence of many of the poorer classes in Bradford but he realised that they would not be eradicated unless housing, sanitation and working conditions in the town were radically improved.

Mid-nineteenth-century Bradford was the fastest growing town in the western world. Its population increased from 43,527 in 1831 to 103,778 in 1851 as people poured in from the countryside to work in the rapidly expanding woollen textile industry. Bradford became the dirtiest and most insanitary place in the country with a higher proportion of malformed, undernourished and crippled children than anywhere else in England and an average life expectancy at birth of just eighteen years. Conditions were worst for the woolcombers, traditionally the lowest paid workers in the textile industry. It was not uncommon for twenty of them to live together in a cellar just four yards square, sleeping in rotas with four or more to bed. Hardly surprisingly, 70 per cent of woolcombers' children died before they reached the age of fifteen.

Salt was determined to clean up this appallingly unhealthy environment. He started by trying to tackle the atmospheric pollution. Bradford had more than 200 mill chimneys emitting sulphurous fumes. Salt himself fitted special smoke burners to the chimney stacks on his own mills to reduce pollution. As mayor he tried hard to get the council to pass a by-law making such devices compulsory in all factories and mills throughout the town, but his fellow industrialists objected that this would put up their costs. Next, he sought to provide open spaces in the town where people could get away from the crowded streets and breathe some relatively fresh air. Once again he gave a personal lead by giving to the town in 1850 a 61-acre park which he named after Sir Robert Peel whose repeal of the Corn Laws four years earlier had boosted the principles of free trade which Salt, like all Victorian in-

dustrialists, held so dear. Other similar schemes followed, but by
now Salt had something altogether bigger and more fundamental
in mind – the creation of a model industrial community in the
countryside.

Titus Salt took up what was to be the great philanthropic
project of his life at a time when he might have been expected to
be contemplating retirement or at least an easing up in his activities. He involvement in the planning of Saltaire began when
he was approaching fifty and continued until his death at the age
of seventy-three. He himself later admitted that he had been briefly tempted to invest his wealth in landed property and enjoy the
last twenty years of his life free from the stresses of business, but
he had rejected this option for two reasons:

In the first place, I thought that by the concentration of my works in one
locality I might provide occupation for my sons. Moreover, as a landed
proprietor I felt I should be out of my element. Outside of my business
I am nothing – in it, I have considerable influence. By the opening of
Saltaire, I also hope to do good to my fellow men.

Salt's motives for wanting to move to what would nowadays be
called a green-field site were a mixture of sound business sense
and philanthropy. By 1850 he had five mills in Bradford employing more than 2,000 people. A single factory would make
considerable economic sense and would enable him to take advantage of new machinery which performed the wool combing
that had traditionally been done by outworkers scattered around
the town. He also badly needed a better water supply than was
available in Bradford. On top of this there were the undoubted
benefits that his workers would gain from being moved out of the
overcrowded city slums.

The site which he chose was three miles north-west of Bradford
on the south bank of the River Aire. It had the advantage of
superb communications, being adjacent to the Leeds – Liverpool
canal, the Midland Railway line and the turnpike road from Leeds
to Keighley. It was also close to the moors and to some spectacular wild scenery. In 1850, Salt commissioned two local
architects to design a model industrial community.

The mill was the first building to be erected at Saltaire. It was
also the world's first totally integrated woollen textile factory in
which all the processes from sorting the raw, greasy fleeces to
dispatching the dyed and finished cloth were brought together
under one roof. Built in an Italianate style, it was supposedly

modelled on Osborne House, Queen Victoria's residence on the Isle of Wight. It stood six storeys high, covered an area of 6¾ acres and was equal in length to St Paul's Cathedral. Salt was determined that his mill should be the biggest and best in Europe. The spinning hall on the top floor was, at 550 by 72 feet, easily the largest single room in the western world. Adjoining the main building was a glass-covered weaving shed where 1,200 power looms turned out more than 18 miles of cloth a day. Salt had originally contemplated buying part of the Crystal Palace, used for the 1851 Great Exhibition, for a weaving shed but he found that it was not substantial enough to withstand the vibrations of the 3,000-horsepower engines used to drive the machinery.

Salt's mill was unprecedented, not just in its size but also in its design. Large flues and plate-glass windows made the whole building light and airy. Noise was minimised by placing much of the shafting which drove the machinery under the floor, and special conduits on the roofs supplied rainwater to a 500,000-gallon reservoir. The 25-foot-high mill chimney was designed to look like the campanile of an Italian church and was fitted with a special smoke-burning device to cut down the pollution from the 50 tons of coal which were burned every day in the ten boilers.

Initially nearly all the 3,500 people who worked in the mill, or the 'Palace of Industry' as it came to be known, travelled in from Bradford every day by train, but Salt told the assembled guests at the opening that it was just the first stage in a massive building programme which would result in the creation of an entire new village:

I will do all I can to avoid evils so great resulting from polluted air and water and hope to draw around me a well fed, contented and happy band of operatives. I have given instructions to my architects that nothing is to be spared to render the dwellings a pattern to the country.

Sir Titus Salt was not the first employer to establish a model community for his workforce. Robert Owen, the Utopian socialist, John Grubb Richardson, the Quaker flax spinner, and Edward Akroyd (like Salt a West Yorkshire worsted manufacturer) had all activated similar schemes in the first half of the nineteenth century. A general awakening of interest in working-class housing was stimulated partly by Lord Shaftesbury's Society for Improving the Condition of the Labouring Classes and partly by Prince Albert's model cottages which were exhibited in the 1851 Great Exhibition. Salt was undoubtedly influenced by these earlier ventures but his model village stands out both in its scale and its scope.

The dwellings in Saltaire were built over a twenty-year period. In all about 850 houses were put up, accommodating 4,500 people. The twenty-two streets were laid out according to a strict geometric plan and covered a total area of 49 acres. The main thoroughfare, which ran down to the mill, was named Victoria Road after the Queen and there was also an Albert Terrace to commemorate her husband. Salt named the other principal streets after his wife and children and the architects who designed the village. The houses varied in size and grandeur according to the status of their occupants. Managers got semi-detached houses while ordinary workmen got cottages with a living room, scullery and three bedrooms. All the dwellings were well built, with gas and water laid on and back yards with privy, coalstore and ashpit – a considerable improvement on the cramped and squalid conditions of the back-to-back terraces of Bradford.

Titus Salt was very clear about both what he wanted and what he did not want in his model village. He was emphatic that there was to be no public house, no pawn shop and no police station. A notice at the entrance to the village warned 'Abandon beer all ye who enter here'. Significantly, the first public building to be erected was a magnificent Congregational church in Italianate style with seating for 600. It was sited directly opposite the main entrance to the mill. Salt did not insist that his workers went to church (though it was said that they stood more chance of getting one of the better houses in Saltaire if they did so) and he certainly did not insist that, like him, they went to the Congregational church. He provided land for a Methodist chapel and was on good terms with the local Anglican church.

He took care to provide for the physical as well as the spiritual cleanliness of his workers. The next public building to be erected after the church was an impressive complex of public baths and wash-houses equipped with the latest in washing machines, wringers, drying frames and hot-air closets. Then came forty-five almshouses provided rent-free and with a pension of ten shillings a week to retired people 'of good moral character', schools, a hospital, a library and finally in 1870 a club and institute, the purpose of which was clearly set out in a circular sent to all the inhabitants:

It is intended to supply the advantages of a public house without its evils; it will be a place to which you can resort for conversation, business, recreation and refreshment, as well as for education – elementary, technical and scientific. In the belief that 'It is gude to be merrie and wise' provision is made for innocent and intelligent recreation.

Salt was unstinting in his efforts to provide his workers with the means for innocent recreation. In 1871 he gave them a large park, laid out with cricket pitches and giving access to the beauty spot of Shipley Glen and the moors beyond. He even had the course of the River Aire altered to improve the view and allow boating and he provided a handsome boathouse. Numerous societies were started up in the village under his patronage, the most popular being the Horticultural, Pig, Dog, Poultry and Pigeon Societies. He also laid on works outings with an improving flavour – in 1857, for example, he took the mill workers to the Art Treasures Exhibition in Manchester.

Life in Saltaire had a disciplined, wholesome quality. Work in the mill started at 6 am and finished at 6 pm with an interval from 8.00 to 8.30 am for breakfast and 12.30 to 1.30 pm for dinner. Six times a day the streets were filled with the workers hurrying to or from their homes, their clogs clattering on the cobbles. Public drunkenness and violence were virtually unknown even after an off-licence was allowed in the village in 1867. Salt banned smoking, gambling and swearing in the park and frowned on villagers hanging out washing in the streets. There may have been a slight sense among his employees that Big Brother was watching them all the time. The house occupied by the mill's security officer stood on a street corner and had a glass-windowed tower on top of the roof so, it was said, that he could observe the activities of the villagers. But in general Saltaire seems to have been a particularly happy and energetic community. When the young Charles Dickens went there in 1857 he reported that 'all looked prosperous and happy' and another journalist who visited in 1871 noted 'a better looking body of factory "hands" I have not seen'.

Salt did not confine his philanthropic attentions to the village which bore his name. He contributed generously to many national projects and retained a strong interest in the civic affairs of Bradford, being elected MP for the city in 1859. Although an ardent Liberal and a strong supporter of the principles of free trade and religious equality, he did not enjoy the rough and tumble of political life at Westminster and resigned his seat in the Commons after only two years.

Meanwhile, the business was also demanding his attention. In 1868 he became the first textile manufacturer to produce worsted influence over his workforce, he was in some ways a very humble figure. He hardly ever used the special gallery which was built for him above the door of Saltaire Congregational church, preferring on his visits there to sit with the rest of the congregation in the body of the church. His own tastes were simple – his one personal indulgence was to buy a gold watch when his savings reached £1,000. His favourite pastime in later years was tending his bananas in the greenhouse at Lightcliffe.

In common with many other Nonconformist industrialists of his age, he did, perhaps, display a certain philistinism and lack of cultural interests, as when he replied to a question as to what books he read, 'Alpaca – if you had four or five thousand people to provide for every day you would not have much time left for reading'. But he was passionately committed to the extension of education at all levels, believing it to be the route to self-improvement and advancement. He was stern, and to our modern eyes even harsh in his attitudes to his workforce. He employed child labour and opposed legislation raising from eight to ten the age at which children could be employed in factories as 'half-timers'. He had little time for trade unions and none at all for direct industrial action by workers.

Yet in many ways Salt was a remarkably enlightened employer. His views on the importance of giving his workers a clean and pleasant environment and facilities for education and recreation were far in advance of those of most entrepreneurs of his time, as was his strong advocacy of profit sharing. Unfortunately, he was not able to carry his fellow partners on this last point, but a compromise was reached whereby employees were placed on piece work and so given a direct interest in the produce of their labour without any pecuniary risk. Salt was an unashamed paternalist with all the faults which that style of management implies in twentieth-century eyes, but he was not a tyrant. He believed firmly in the essential harmony of interest between capital and labour and felt that the betterment of the lot of the working classes lay within their own hands, to be encouraged by political reforms, education and the cultivation of self-help.

Salt's massive mill which once drew visitors from around the world as a showpiece of British industry now has a new role as the home of electronics workshops, a gallery devoted to the works of the Bradford-born artist, David Hockney, a café and specialist shops. Its recent re-opening by Jonathan Silver to provide 1,500 jobs after almost a decade of lying silent and empty following the ending of textile manufacture provides a contemporary example of West Yorkshire entrepreneurship of which Salt himself would surely be proud. In other respects, however, modern Saltaire has departed from the Victorian values of its creator. The model houses put up for workers are now occupied by middle-class commuters. The Institute set up for the promotion of temperance and self-improvement now has a licensed bar and hosts weekly discos and bingo evenings. Even the village grocer sells alcohol. It is perhaps just as well that the statue of Sir Titus Salt erected in the park has its back to the village and its gaze fixed on the hills to the north.

For Further Reading:

Jack Reynolds, *The Great Paternalist: Titus Salt and the Growth of Nineteenth Century Bradford* (Maurice Temple Smith, 1983); and *Saltaire: An Introduction to the Village of Sir Titus Salt* (Bradford Art Galleries and Museums, 1976); Ian Bradley, *The Optimists: Themes and Personalities in Victorian Liberalism* (Faber & Faber, 1980); and *Enlightened Entrepreneurs* (Weidenfeld & Nicolson, 1987).

8

Samuel Smiles
The Gospel of Self-Help

Asa Briggs

Overleaf: The road to improvement: 'The Night School' by Edgar Bundy. (Ferens Art Gallery, Hull City Museum & Art Galleries/Bridgeman Art Library)

FEW BOOKS have been held to be more symbolic of the Victorian era than *Self-Help* published in 1859. The concept, together with thrift, perserverance and responsibility, was bundled into a programme for individual living approved at the time, criticised as selfish smugness since and enjoying a renaissance on the political platforms of the western world in the 1980s. But as with so many other 'eminent Victorians' its author, Samuel Smiles (1812–1904), did not easily square off with the caricature that such a combination implies. Asa Briggs argues here that while a prophet of honest toil, Smiles in propounding his views did not feel he was saying anything stunningly original, and that in some of his social views he was an advocate of positive and radical state intervention.

Self-help was one of the favourite mid-Victorian virtues. Relying on yourself was preferred morally – and economically – to depending on others. It was an expression of character even when it did not ensure – even, indeed, when it did not offer – a means of success. It also had social implications of a general kind. The progressive development of society ultimately depended, it was argued, not on collective action or on parliamentary legislation but on the prevalence of practices of self-help.

All these points were made succinctly and eloquently, but none of them originally or exclusively, by Samuel Smiles whose *Self-Help* appeared in one of the golden years of mid-Victorian Britain, 1859, the year that also saw the publication of John Stuart Mill's *Essay on Liberty* and Charles Darwin's *The Origin of Species*. Mill examined the attractions of individuality as well as the restraints on individualism: Darwin explored struggles as well as evolution, or rather explained evolution in terms of struggle. Neither thinker escaped attack. Smiles by contrast was not looking for argument and counter-argument. He believed that he was expounding not something that was new or controversial but something that was old and profoundly true, a gospel, not a thesis; and that behind that gospel was a still more basic gospel, the gospel of work.

Smiles did not claim that all his contemporaries practised self-help. He rather extolled the virtues of self-help as part of an 'old fashioned' but 'wholesome' lesson in morality. It was more 'natural', he admitted, to be 'prodigal' than to be thrifty, more easy to be dependent than independent. What he was saying had been said by the wisest of men before him: it reflected 'experience,

example and foresight'. 'Heaven helps them who help themselves.'

As far as individuals were concerned, Smiles was anxious to
insist on the value of perseverance, a favourite word of one of his
heroes, George Stephenson. 'Nothing that is of real worth', he
insisted, 'can be achieved without courageous working. Man owes
his growth chiefly to that active striving of the will, that encounter
with difficulty, which he calls effort; and it is astonishing to find
how often results apparently impracticable are then made possible.' As far as society was concerned, 'national progress was the
sum of individual industry, energy and uprightness' as 'national
decay' was of 'individual idleness, selfishness and vice. What we
are accustomed to decry as great social evils will, for the most
part, be found to be but the outgrowth of man's perverted life'.
'The spirit of self-help is the root of all genuine growth in the
individual; and exhibited in the lives of many, it constitutes the
true source of national vigour and strength. Help from without is
often enfeebling in its effects, but help from within invariably in-
vigorates. Whatever is done for men and classes to a certain extent
takes away the stimulus and necessity of doing for themselves;
and where men are subjected to over-guidance and over-govern-
ment, the inevitable tendency is to render them comparatively
helpless.'

Smiles adopted the phrase *Self-Help*, which proved to be very
difficult to translate into other languages, from a lecture by the
American reformer and prophet, R. W. Emerson, delivered in
1841; and while Smiles' own book first appeared in 1859, its contents had first been delivered by Smiles in lectures to Leeds
working men fourteen years before – one year, indeed, before the
passing of the repeal of the Corn Laws. While the book belonged
unmistakably to mid-Victorian Britain, the message, therefore,
was an early-Victorian transatlantic message, delivered in years
not of relative social harmony in Britain but of social conflict. The
point is of crucial importance in any discussion of Victorian values
in the 1980s. Smiles emerged not from a conservative but from a
radical background, the background of Chartism, and the Anti-
Corn Law League. He was not encouraging Leeds working men
to be quiescent or deferential but to be active and informed.
Richard Cobden was one of his heroes. Another was the radical
Joseph Hume, and both figured prominently in *Self-Help*. Smiles
knew them both personally, and in a letter to Cobden in 1841
he had described the extension of the suffrage as 'the key to all

great changes, whose object is to elevate the condition of the masses.'

Smiles' direct political involvement was limited, however, after the 1840s, and he settled down during the next decade to the more complacent view, which he expressed in 1852, that 'as men grow older and wiser they find a little of good in everything . . . they begin to find out that truth and patriotism are not confined to any particular cliques or parties or fractions'. Indeed, he moved well to the right of Cobden, and by the late-Victorian years, when new political causes, radical or socialist of which he disapproved were being canvassed, what he had had to say had come to sound 'conservative', as it has done to late-twentieth-century defenders of 'Victorian values'.

Yet there is a difference in the response. Whereas late-Victorian rebels attacked Smiles for his cheerful economics, claiming – unfairly – that he was interested only in individual advancement reflected in material success, late-twentieth-century defenders have praised him primarily for his hard economic realism. In particular, Sir Keith Joseph, himself writing from a Leeds vantage point, in the introduction to a new and abridged edition of *Self-Help* (1986), has set out to rehabilitate Smilesian trust in the *entrepreneur* and 'the virtues that make him what he is'. While describing *Self-Help* as 'deeply expressive of the spirit of its own times', he does not note that these were changing times and that modes of economic organisation and responses to 'entrepreneurship' were very different by 1904, the year when Smiles died, from what they had been when *Self-Help* was published.

Smiles was born not in Leeds but in Haddington, a few miles east of Edinburgh, seven years before the birth of Queen Victoria, and he took a medical degree from Edinburgh University. His first book was called *Physical Education: or the Nurture and Management of Children*, and was published in 1838, the year he moved to Leeds. There is an evident Scottish strain in his writing before and after, although curiously it is less apparent in *Physical Education* than in some of his other work. It was, after all, Robert Bruce who had had attributed to him the motto 'if at first you don't succeed, try, try, try again', and Calvin who had provided Scotsmen with a religion which made the most of austerity and vocation.

In more modern times Thomas Carlyle, born seventeen years before Smiles, had described life as 'a scene of toil, of effort, of appointed work', and had extolled 'the man who works' in the warmest language: 'welcome, thou art ours; our care shall be of thee'. The mill-owner economist, W. R. Greg, writing one year after the publication of *Self-Help*, praised Carlyle above all others for 'preaching upon the duty and dignity of work, with an eloquence which has often made the idle shake off their idleness and the frivolous feel ashamed of their frivolity. He has proclaimed, in tones that have stirred many hearts, that in toil, however humble, if honest and hearty, lies our true worth and felicity here below'.

Smiles himself took as one of his examples of perseverance in *Self-Help* Carlyle's prodigious effort to rewrite the first volume of his *French Revolution* after a maid had used the manuscript to light the kitchen and parlour fires: 'he had no draft, and was compelled to rake up from his memory facts, ideas and expressions, which had long been dismissed'. No one could have appreciated this experience more than Smiles who was a prodigious writer who followed up *Self-Help* with many volumes, including three related works *Character*, (1871), *Thrift* (1875) and *Duty* (1880). He also produced a history of his publisher, John Murray and 'his friends' in 1891.

Self-Help was full of anecdotes. Essentially it was a case-book drawing its material, including some of its most apposite quotations, from personal biographies. 'Our great forefathers still live among us in the records of our lives', he claimed, again very much as Carlyle had always claimed. 'They still sit by us at table, and hold us by the hand'. There was more than a touch of Victorian hero worship here. Yet Smiles always broadened the range to include the humble as well as the great, extending the range as far as he possibly could in his *Life and Labour* (1887). Biographies offered demonstrations of 'what men can be, and what they can do' whatever their station. 'A book containing the life of a true man is full of precious seed. It is still a living voice.' And much as he made his own living out of books, Smiles maintained that living examples were far more potent as influences than examples on paper. His book *Thrift* took as its motto a phrase from Carlyle 'Not what I have, but what I do is my kingdom'. He might have chosen instead Emerson's motto, 'The importance of man as man . . . is the highest truth'.

Smiles himself was a lively phrase-maker, interlacing his anecdotes, which by themselves were memorable and well set out, with short phrases that linger in the mind – 'he who never made a mistake never made a discovery'; 'the tortoise in the right road will beat a racer in the wrong'; 'the nation comes from the nursery'. Such phrases bind together the whole text of *Self-Help* which is far more readable – as it is pertinent – today than the verse of Martin Tupper's *Proverbial Philosophy* (1838), the popularity of which (on both sides of the Atlantic) reached its peak during the 1850s. It is far more readable too than most of the many other Victorian books designed to inspire young men like the anonymous *Success in Life* (1852), the original idea of which had been suggested by 'an American publication', perhaps John Todd's *Hints Addressed to the Young Men of the United States* (1845), which included one chapter on 'industry and economy' and another on 'self-government and the heart'. Smiles himself acknowledged a debt to G. L. Craik's *Pursuit of Knowledge under Difficulties* (1831), published by Charles Knight who specialised in diffusing knowledge. Indeed, he had been so inspired by it, Smiles wrote, that he learnt some of its key passages by heart.

The transatlantic element in the self-help literature demands a study of differences as well as of influences. There were to be many American 'success' books aiming, as Smiles aimed, at large audiences, some of the first of which were influenced, as Smiles was, by the cult of phrenology. The later line of descent can be traced through books, which move from phrenology to popular psychology, like J. C. Ransom's *The Successful Man in his Manifold Relations with Life* (1887), A. E. Lyons' *The Self-Starter* (1924), Dale Carnegie's *How to Win Friends and Influence People* (1936), C. E. Poppleston's *Every Man a Winner* (1936) and Norman Vincent Peale's *The Power of Positive Thinking* (1955). Yet many of these authors are slick where Smiles was sturdy, and consoling where he was inspiring. Few would have had much sympathy either with Smiles' attack on 'smatter knowledge'. Such 'short-cuts', he explained, as learning French or Latin in 'twelve lessons' or 'without a master', were 'good for nothing'. The would-be learner was more to blame than the teacher, for he resembled 'the lady of fashion who engaged a master to teach her on condition that he did not plague her with verbs and particles'.

One American with whom Smiles has sometimes been compared is Horatio Alger (1832–99) after whom a twentieth-century American business award was named. In his own lifetime Alger's sales were spectacular, though his books took the form of stories rather than biographies or homilies. *Ragged Dick* was one title, *Upward and Onward* another. The *genre* has been well described as 'rags to riches stories', although the twentieth-century award was endowed more generally to honour a person who had 'climbed the ladder of success through toil and diligence and responsible applications of his talents to whatever tasks were his'.

There are as many myths about 'Holy Horatio' as Alger himself propounded. In fact, he allowed a far bigger place to luck (sponsors appearing by magic at the right time and place) than Smiles ever could have done, and he grossly simplified the nineteenth-century social context, particularly the city context, in which poor people found or failed to find their chances. As the late-nineteenth-century American institutional economist, Richard T. Ely, put it neatly, 'if you tell a single concrete workman on the Baltimore and Ohio Railroad that he may get to be president of the company, it is not demonstrable that you have told him what is not true, although it is within bounds to say that he is far more likely to be killed by a stroke of lightning.'

Smiles was less concerned with social 'mobility' than with mental and physical 'effort', but he, too, could be accused of living in a land of myth when he exclaimed that 'energy accomplishes more than genius'. It was a favourite mid-Victorian statement, however, which implied a contrast between what was happening then and what had happened before, and between what was happening in Britain and what was happening elsewhere. By stating it so simply Smiles actually did influence *entrepreneurs*, few of whom depended on great intellects or on deep and systematic study. William Lever, for example, fittingly born in 1851, was given a copy of *Self-Help* by his father on his sixteenth birthday, and treasured it so much that he in turn gave copies to young men he employed in his works at Port Sunlight. On the front page of one such copy the words are inscribed, 'It is impossible for me to say how much I owe to the fact that in my early youth I obtained a copy of Smiles' *Self-Help*'.

Andrew Carnegie (1835–1919) would have made no such comment. Yet his own biography not only proclaimed many Smilesian virtues, but might well have provided the basis for an Alger true story. Carnegie was born in a tiny weaver's cottage at Dunfermline, and he had his first real break in life when he became a messenger boy in a Pittsburgh telegraph office at a salary of $2.50 a week. In 1901, when he had sold his steel business for $480 million, he became the richest man in the world. 'It's a God's mercy I was born a Scotsman,' he declared in a remark that might have appealed to Smiles, 'for I do not see how I could ever have been contented to be anything else.'

The testimonials Smiles himself received from readers of his books often came from people very differently placed from Lever or Carnegie. Thus, a working man in Exeter told him that his books had 'instructed and helped him greatly' and that he wished 'every working man would read them through and through and ponder them well'; a surgeon in Blackheath declared that *Self-Help* had given 'fresh energy and hopefulness to his career'; and an emigrant to New Zealand exclaimed that self-help had 'been the cause of an entire alteration in my life, and I thank God that I read it. I am now devoted to study and hard work, and I mean to rise, both as regards my moral and intellectual life. I only wish I could see the man who wrote the book and thank him from my heart.'

There was at least one late-Victorian socialist, a man who was himself capable of inspiring 'the millions', who was deeply impressed by Smiles. Robert Blatchford, pioneer of *Merrie England*, wrote an essay on *Self-Help* after Smiles' popularity had passed its peak in which he condemned fellow-socialists who spoke mockingly of Smiles as 'an arch-Philistine' and of his books as 'the apotheosis of respectability, gigmanity and selfish grab'. Blatchford himself considered Smiles 'a most charming and honest writer', and thought *Self-Help* 'one of the most delightful and invigorating books it has been my happy fortune to meet with.' He paid tribute to Smiles' indifference to worldly titles, honour and wealth, and declared that the perusal of *Self-Help* had often forced him 'to industry, for very shame'.

The prolific rationalist writer Grant Allen, a leading spokesman of the late-Victorian revolt, took a very similar view. In a little book published in 1884 called *Biographies of Working Men* he asserted his debt to Smiles and made explicit what many of Smiles' critics then and since failed to see in Smiles' work. 'It is the object of this volume', Grant Allen began, 'to set forth the lives of working men, who through industry, perseverance and high principle, have raised themselves by their own exertions from humble beginnings. Raised themselves! Yes, but to what? Not merely, let us hope, to wealth and position, nor merely to worldly respect and high office, but to some conspicuous field of real usefulness to their fellow men.' Smiles made the same point in *Self-Help*. He would not have shared Allen's view, however, which brings out clearly the difference between the mood of the 1850s and the 1880s, that 'so long as our present social arrangements exist . . . the vast mass of men will necessarily remain workers to the last, [and] no attempt to raise individual working men above their own class into the professional or mercantile classes can ever greatly benefit the working classes as a whole'.

Nonetheless, on certain social matters, Smiles had often expressed radical views. Like many people trained as doctors he was deeply concerned with public health. As Mary Mack has pointed out, Jeremy Bentham had used medicine as a source of *analogy* for the understanding of morals and legislation, and Smiles, who as a young man met Edwin Chadwick and Dr Southwood Smith, Bentham's disciples, never believed that the environment should be left uncontrolled if it threatened the private health not only of the deprived but of people and power and influence. Smiles supported measures, too, to deal with the adulteration of food. Drawing a distinction between economic and social *laissez-faire* – and he was not alone in this – he was fully aware of the presence in mid-Victorian society not only of Adam Smith's beneficent invisible hand but of a 'terrible Nobody'. Indeed, Charles Dickens could not have written more forcefully than Smiles did:

When typhus or cholera breaks out, they tell us that Nobody is to blame. That terrible Nobody! How much he has to answer for. More mischief is done by Nobody than by all the world besides. Nobody adulterates our food. Nobody poisons us with bad drink . . . Nobody leaves towns undrained. Nobody fills jails, penitentiaries, and convict stations. Nobody makes poachers, thieves, and drunkards. Nobody has a theory too – a dreadful theory. It is embodied in two words: laissez-faire – let alone. When people are poisoned with plaster of Paris mixed with flour, 'let alone' is the remedy . . . Let those who can, find out when they are cheated: *caveat emptor*. When people live in foul dwellings, let them alone, let wretchedness do its work; do not interfere with death.

Like many other believers in economic *laissez-faire* Smiles was prepared to use the machinery of the law to provide a framework for dealing with abuses:

Laws may do too much . . . but the abuse of a thing is no proper argument against its use in cases where its employment is urgently called for.

Throughout the whole of his life Smiles was far too active a Victorian to believe that *vis inertiae* was the same thing as *laissez-faire*. Nor was he ever tempted, as many Americans were, into the entanglements of social Darwinism. There is no reference to Herbert Spencer in his *Autobiography*, which appeared in 1905, one year after his death, and only one reference to Darwin. One of the lectures he had heard at Edinburgh, he observed *en passant*, had already expounded very similar views 'or at all events had heralded his approach'.

There was another subject which fascinated Smiles and which he believed required very positive state intervention – national education. He had forcefully urged the need for a national system in Leeds in 1850, and he paid tribute in his *Autobiography* to W. E. Forster, MP for neighbouring Bradford, who 'by a rare union of tact, wisdom and common sense, introduced and carried his measure [the 1870 Education Act] for the long-wished education of the English people. It embodied nearly all that the National Public School Association had so fruitlessly demanded years before.'

In pressing for nationally provided primary education in Leeds in 1850 and later, Smiles had been drawn into controversy with Edward Baines, editor of the *Leeds Mercury* and one of the most vociferous advocates, then and in 1870, of education managed by voluntary agencies and not by the state. In the course of a continuing controversy Smiles had no doubts about his own position. There were no analogies between education and free trade in commodities, he pointed out:

The classes who the most require education are precisely those who do not seek it. It is amongst the utterly uneducated that the least demand exists. In the case of bread it is very different. The consumer wants it, knows he wants it, and will give every present consideration for it.

A further false analogy, he thought, was that between education and the freedom of the press:

Nobody proposes to establish newspapers for everybody supported by the government, and the want of such a Press is not felt. But let it be shown that it is of as much importance to the interest of society that everybody should have a newspaper as that everybody should be educated, and then the analogy may be admitted . . . but not till then.

It was through his philosophy of education that Smiles blurred any divisions that others might have made between 'self-help' for the individual and 'mutual self-help' for the group. He always attached even more importance to adult – or continuing – education than to school education, necessary though the latter was. The process which started at school had to be followed through: 'the highest culture is not obtained from teacher when at school or college, so much as by our ever diligent self-education when we have become men'. Such education could be fostered in groups like the group of young working men he had addressed in Leeds. There were possibilities of other forms of 'mutual self-help' also, for example friendly societies. Indeed, in *Thrift* Smiles made as much as he could of the mutual insurance principle. He could never have been accused of neglecting 'welfare', provided that it did not lead to dependence.

The Smiles message was not merely a transatlantic one. It made its way round the world, sometimes to the most unlikely places. It was translated into Dutch and French, Danish and German, Arabic and Turkish, 'several of the native languages of India' (in the words of a happy publisher) and Japanese. Victorian values, it was implied, were universal values, and there was confidence in their power to change societies. The Japanese, in particular, treasured it, and many of them continue to treasure it. 'The English work forms an octavo of moderate size,' *The Times* wrote; 'in Japanese it is expanded into a book of fifteen hundred pages.' This was no handicap to its sale, for it seemed as useful as looms and steam engines. In Latin America, the Mayor of Buenos Aires is said to have compared Smiles with Rousseau and to have added 'Alexander the Great slept with his Homer, Demosthenes and Thucydides, and every notable man of the times should have at hand the social gospel'.

The universalism was restricted, however, although it went with the universalism of steam power and railways, in particular. Smiles had become secretary of a railway company in 1845 and he wrote *The Life of George Stephenson* two years before *Self-Help*. Nonetheless, he ended *Self-Help* with a chapter which introduced a word which was at least as difficult to translate from English into other languages as 'self-help' itself – the word 'gentleman'. Hippolyte Taine, convinced that the three syllables 'gentleman' summed up the whole history of English society, felt that the syllables expressed all the distinctive features of the English upper class – a large private income, a considerable household of servants, habits of ease and luxury and good manners, but it also implied qualities of heart and character. Smiles, however, felt that:

For Englishmen a real 'gentleman' is a truly noble man, a man worthy to command, a disinterested man of integrity, capable of exposing, even sacrificing himself for those he leads; not only a man of honour, but a conscientious man, in whom generous instincts have been confirmed by right thinking and who, acting rightly by nature, acts even more rightly from good principles.

Taine's reference to Mrs Craik's novel *John Halifax, Gentleman* (1856) is a practical illustration of the extension of the old ideal of the gentleman in a new nineteenth-century society. He might have referred instead to the last pages of *Self-Help*, where Smiles chose a 'grand old name' to express the kind of character he most wanted to see in action. Smiles drew out the 'grand old name' of the gentleman from its upper-class context. It had no connection with riches and rank, he argued, but with moral worth.

The equipoise of society rested on such ideological balance as well as on the balance of interests. From the 1870s onwards, however, both kinds of balance broke down. Britain was never again the same.

For Further Reading:

Samuel Smiles, *Self-Help* (first edition 1853, Penguin Books with an introduction by Keith Joseph, 1986); Asa Briggs, *Victorian People* (Penguin Books, 1985); Grant Allen, *Biographies of Working men* (1884); J. Burnett (ed.), *Useful Toil: Autobiographies of Working people from the 1820s–1920s* (Penguin Books, 1974); T. Travers, *Samuel Smiles and the Pursuit of Success in Victorian Britain* (Canadian Historical Association, 1971); M. D. Stephens and G. W. Roderick, *Samuel Smiles and Nineteenth-Century Self-Help in Education* (Nottingham Studies, 1983). A comprehensive index to the illustrations in *The Builder* 1843–83, compiled by Ruth Richardson and Robert Thorne, was published in 1994.

9

Building Bridges
George Godwin and Architectural Journalism

Robert Thorne

Opposite: Houses built on rock – Captain Henry Scott testing a new cement with workmen on an arch, 1861. Godwin was always keenly interested in new materials and techniques. (Trustees of the Science Museum, London)

PERHAPS THE MOST DRAMATIC and visibly continuing legacy of the Victorian period is its architecture – now venerated and often embalmed by conservationists throughout the western world, after decades of denigration and demolition. What Robert Thorne describes here as the 'buoyant though turbulent architectural developments' of Victorian Britain encompassed not just the aesthetic rejection of eighteenth-century neo-classicism in favour of Gothic revival and the eclectic adornment of the new industrial cities, but a serious and thoughtful debate among architects, conscious of a newly acknowledged professional status and responsibility and anxious to make their contribution as problem-solvers in the community and social reformers. Thorne's profile of the life and work of the architect George Godwin (1815–1888), editor of *The Builder* for thirty-nine years, illustrates this process and Godwin's own belief that 'art offers itself as a social bridge of no ordinary size and strength'.

If there were any direct relationship between the quality of a nation's architecture and the number of its architectural magazines, English architecture would be in a flourishing state. The coverage of architecture in national newspapers and on radio and television, though it has recently increased and improved, is still mean and unoriginal, but within the specialist press the subject is generously provided for, at least in comparison with other countries. Of four weekly architectural magazines published in Europe, three are produced in London. One of them, now called *Building* but known for most of its life as *The Builder*, can claim a pedigree going back to the origins of professional journalism in the early Victorian period. After a slightly shaky start in 1842–3 it got into its stride in 1844 and has been published weekly ever since.

The editor responsible for making *The Builder* 'one of the finest properties in the categories of the weekly press' (as it was described in 1872) was George Godwin, who presided over it from 1844 until his retirement thirty-nine years later. The formula of its success lay in the breadth and moral fervour of his interests, encompassing such a wide range of concerns that the magazine was known far outside the confines of the architectural world.

Towards the end of his life Godwin described his career as 'one of earnest and continuous endeavour to spread information, to sustain the dignity of the profession, and to contribute to the welfare of all classes'; a threefold ambition which, taken as a whole, represented a dynamic role for the journalist in the service of architecture and society. Godwin achieved a substantial following not just by reporting the news his readers wanted to hear but by nurturing a vision of social reform and of the role that the building interests, from architects to bricklayers, engineers to navvies, might play in it.

The foundation of *The Builder* in 1842 looks at first glance as if it was a journalistic ploy to exploit the buoyant, though turbulent, architectural developments of the time. The Institute of British Architects had been founded in 1834 (the Royal prefix came later), apparently signifying that the profession had come of age and was ready to accept the collective discipline and responsibilities expected of it. The founder members intended that it should combine the conviviality of a club with the dignity of a learned society and the vigour of a representative organisation, and that its probity should be marked by the exclusion of builders from its ranks. Those that were committed to the Institute in its early years, and equally those who were not, were delighting in many new spheres of architectural practice that were opening up; for whereas their predecessors had been confined largely to domestic and church work, with the occasional government, civic or theatre project, they now could find routes to fame through other specialisations. The design of institutions such as workhouses and asylums could almost sustain an architectural practice, with a few other commissions to fill the gaps, or the new realm of railway architecture could be developed in the same way. In the City of London insurance companies and banks were showing their first interest in having their own recognisably distinct headquarters, and speculative developers were following not far behind in exploiting the needs of those unable to afford anything quite so grand. Add to these and other specialisations the continuing resilience of church work, to which a demand for Catholic churches had recently been added, and it appeared that architects had never been so fortunate.

However such developments, apparently indicative of professional progress on all fronts, concealed a number of weaknesses in the position of architects. The foremost of these involved their relationship with building contractors and the building trades. Eighteenth-century building practice, using a system known as 'measure and value', made the architect responsible, having designed a building, for choosing the craftsmen to erect it, supervising them on site, and on completion measuring their work and paying them accordingly. During the Napoleonic Wars an alternative system developed whereby a single, general contractor, to whom the craftsmen were subordinate, managed all the works on site, with a price agreed beforehand according to a contract 'in the gross'. The spread of general contracting distanced the architect from the building trades and deprived him of direct control over them. The new system, whatever its virtues, redefined the building process in a way that put the architect in a vulnerable position. Against that background the foundation of the RIBA, and the banning of builders from its membership, can be looked at in another way as an attempt to stabilise the status of the architect; instead of relying on an intimate involvement in every aspect of construction to assert the virtues of independence.

A second, related problem which affected architects in the 1830s concerned the attitude of central government. The friendships and opportunities which, some twenty years earlier, had enabled John Nash to embark on the creation of a processional route from Regents Park to St James's Park reached their final episode in the creation of Trafalgar Square and the making of the West Strand improvement as a feeder to it. By the time these schemes were finished Nash had fallen from favour, not least because of his incautious conduct in crossing the boundaries between architecture and development, and when the subject of further improvements was taken up expectations were set much lower. Streets such as New Oxford Street and Endell Street, which were under construction as the first issues of *The Builder* began to appear, originated in far more hard-headed plans than those associated with Nash and Prince Regent. In place of an imaginative urban aesthetic the requirements of utility – the flow of traffic and the ventilation of the slums – had first consideration: individual plots were let on building leases with little control over their development. Whatever his fellow architects may have felt about Nash's abilities, the schemes sponsored by the government after his downfall were architecturally a disappointing setback, a loss to the profession of the kind of metropolitan showcase it felt it deserved.

The architectural world into which *The Builder* was launched was therefore less confident in some respects than it pretended to be, and the magazine almost died an early death as a victim of the problems of commitment that it had to confront. But in many ways its appearance was well-timed. Innovations in printing, a fall in the price of paper, and the introduction of the electrotype

as a means of reproducing engravings, combined to make illustrated journalism an inviting possibility: both *Punch* and *The
Illustrated London News* started life at about the same time as *The
Builder*. The growing railway network offered the chance of good
provincial distribution. As for rivals, in the architectural realm
there was only one serious competitor. In the previous decade
two architectural magazines had been started, John Claudius
Loudon's *Architectural Magazine* in 1834, and the *Civil Engineer and
Architect's Journal* in 1837. Loudon endeavoured to pitch his appeal
as widely as Godwin's *Builder* later did, offering general articles
for his lay readers combined with practical notes for specialists,
but however successful his mixture may have been, the effort of
editing the magazine, on top of all his other activities, forced him
to close it after only five years. Godwin hinted that he had
rejected the chance to take it over. *The Civil Engineer and Architect's
Journal* showed greater powers of endurance (it lasted thirty
years), but as a monthly publication it left ample scope for a weekly providing news faster and on a wider front.

Godwin had two predecessors as editors of *The Builder*, both of
whom had a style of tenure significantly different from his. The
founding editor was the architect Joseph Hansom (better known
for the cab he invented) who, inspired by Owenite ideology, had
helped found the Operative Builders' Union in Birmingham. This
was intended to be more than just an information exchange and
negotiating body, for Hansom wanted to challenge the system of
general contracting by short-circuiting it. His ambition was that
building workers should organise co-operatively under elected
master builders to take on projects, a method first put into practice in the erection of the Union's own Guildhall and in a modified way in the direct labour contract under which work on
Birmingham Town Hall was started. Both of these projects ran
into difficulties, but not such as to divert Hansom from his cause.
For him *The Builder* was a branch of the same co-operative
enterprise, a way of securing the independence of building
workers by enabling them to share their knowledge. If such
workers had responded to his call by subscribing to the new
magazine he and they could have remained free of reliance on
'the leviathan power of capital', but they failed to meet their part
of the bargain. 'Architects, master builders, and the higher class
of trades' lent their support, while to his disappointment those he
most wanted to help stood aloof.

After twenty-one issues Hansom sold the magazine to his

printers, who appointed Alfred Bartholomew as editor. In some respects he shared Hansom's vision of a building community united in a common cause, but illness prevented him from developing his views. After about a year he had to retire, to be followed by George Godwin, who was then only thirty-one but already well prepared for the post.

The heartland of Godwin's world was South Kensington; not the cluster of museums and institutions along Exhibition Road, none of which existed when he was young, but the villas and terraces which pressed westwards towards Fulham across land once occupied by nurseries and market gardens. He was born there, lived there all his life, and used his home there (first in Alexander Square, later in Cromwell Place) as his office and editorial headquarters. Beyond his house as much as within it he was in a world of his own making, for along with his father and his two brothers he was responsible for many of the building developments of Kensington in its boom years. His father used the two titles 'surveyor' and 'architect' at different times and like him Godwin varied his commitment to the projects he took on: sometimes acting as independent designer, in the pattern of the RIBA ideal, sometimes as surveyor keeping a watchful eye on the work of others, sometimes as developer, and where necessary in whatever combination of these roles offered the most appropriate solution. His first project on his own was the Brompton National Schools (1841–2), like a Tudor manor house in style, followed by an out of town commission to restore St Mary Radcliffe in Bristol. By the end of the 1840s, when his commitments as an editor would have been enough to fill the normal day of most men, he had been enlisted by the Gunter family to plan their estate north of Fulham Road. The Boltons, an oval of Italianate villas embracing a sensible Gothic church, met the suburban mood of the time perfectly. Later, on the same estate, Godwin and his brother Henry reverted to conventional terraces, but treated Redcliffe Square in a much more massive and assertive way than they earlier would have dared.

At the time Godwin took over the editorial chair most of these projects were still to come, but as a writer his name was already familiar in architectural circles. In 1836 he won the RIBA's first silver medal with an essay on concrete, a performance uniting a history of the material with up-to-the-minute advice on its composition and use. He was already known to the Institute for a talk he had given on freemasonry, largely antiquarian but tinged with a sense that the brotherhood of the medieval building community held some lessons worth heeding. On the topographical front he had published *The Churches of London* in 1838 with the help of John Britton, who had befriended him on the evening he received the RIBA medal.

The ingredients of Godwin's early career – his architectural training and knowledge of construction plus his forays into history and archaeology – made him the ideal candidate for a magazine which sought to present architecture in its widest context. If it is true that he almost ran the paper single-handedly during his first years as editor, it would have been less appealing if he had been of a narrower frame of mind. As it was, the banner across *The Builder* title page in the late 1840s was a fair representation not just of its readership but also of Godwin's interests. It read: 'An Illustrated Weekly Magazine, for the Architect, Engineer, Operative and Artist'. As time passed this was refined and extended: two new categories, Archaeologist and Sanitary Reformer, were added, Artist was changed to Art-Lover, and Operative was replaced by the more imposing term Constructor. All of these alterations, except perhaps the last, stretched its aspirations to new limits, just as Godwin's feverish curiosity constantly led him into new territories.

The easiest way to appreciate Godwin's editorial style is to select any issue from his period and examine its contents from beginning to end. Taking the number for 6 November 1852, the opening editorial, unsigned but most probably by Godwin, urges the need for working-class benevolent societies to free themselves from the 'positive wickedness' of their wasteful dependence on public house landlords. Godwin, more than Hansom or Bartholomew, acknowledged the role of capital, and therefore of the general contractor, in the building world: although not afraid to insist on the moral obligations which wealth entailed, he accepted that operatives (the term that he unfortunately dropped from his title page) would have to accommodate themselves to a seldom benevolent system. Mutual self-support was one defence, education another, and on the second theme the editorial ends: 'send your sons to the elementary drawing schools, and encourage in them a taste for reading'.

After the editorial, other contributions make their entry: verbatim reports of lectures, summaries of essays, and a piece by the prolific inventor W. Bridges Adams on a 'tension chain-net floor' he had devised for buildings requiring large unobstructed spaces.

There is news of a talk by Henry Roberts, the model housing specialist, at a sanitary congress in Brussels where he presented the costs of philanthropic housing schemes. Then there follow reports from America, including an account of the death of the architect Andrew Jackson Downing in a steam-boat accident; short pieces of provincial building news; two London theatre reviews (the Haymarket production of *Richelieu in Love* 'chiefly remarkable for terse and sparkling writing'); and finally a brief list of builders' tenders for works about to be commenced. The two main engravings of the week are of historic architectural details of the kind that contemporary architects hungered after – a doorway from Antwerp, with moulding profiles, and part of a parapet from Florence Cathedral.

The danger of presenting a casual glimpse of *The Builder's* contents such as this, regardless of where in Godwin's editorial reign the selection falls, is that it leaves a more vivid impression of his catholic coverage of events and opinion than of the major causes which he promoted through its pages. 'In this busy fighting world', he once said, 'a thing must be told many times before it will be heard.' In recognising that a cause, once adopted, had to be perservered with until the remedy was in sight he was a pioneer of campaigning journalism. Not, in his case, the strident journalism of bold layouts and catching headlines – the techniques of the New Journalism which he barely lived to see – but personal investigation followed by sustained publicity of the social evils be unearthed.

In the midst of the public health scares of the 1840s Godwin had no difficulty in choosing the prime target for his attention. Ventures into slumdom, picturesque and sensational or grimly statistical, were already plentiful, and at the end of the decade Henry Mayhew started his inquiries into the structural causes of poverty. Godwin brought the architectural contribution to an already diverse campaign. As he later recalled, 'the profession of architects had its representative in the very earliest stages of this vitally important movement'. What this role meant was less that he brought to light anything previously unknown than that he viewed familiar scenes in a particular way. Like others his explorations took him to the St Giles Rookery, then being crushed against itself by the making of New Oxford Street; to Agar Town in St Pancras, where he found houses 'planted down in very much the same manner as the wooden huts and tents at gold diggings'; and to the Old Nichol in Bethnal Green, which left him 'saddened and ill'. On trips to provincial cities, where he was less sure of his ground, he commandeered the help of local guides (in Birmingham the Chief of Police) to conduct him to districts of similar notoriety. His response to what he found lacked the personal intimacy of Mayhew's contacts, but on no grounds could it be classed as a voyeur's impression. To architectural eyes it was the fabric of the slums which sprang first to view – their construction and arrangement, condition and use – and to those matters Godwin gave particular attention. By doing so he helped edge the health movement towards a recognition of housing as a distinctive problem which called for its own set of solutions.

Godwin's reports on slum overcrowding and its results had the freshness and immediacy of a radio broadcast. Straight from a visit to the courts off Drury Lane or the brickfield encampments of Notting Hill he committed his findings to paper for next week's issue. Subsequently he collected his most powerful pieces together in three books: *London Shadows — A Glance at the Homes of Thousands* (1854), *Town Swamps and Social Bridges* (1859), and *Another Blow for Life* (1864). The two-pronged title of the middle and best-known of the three encapsulates the aim of his campaign: to portray the conditions in which the urban poor were trapped, and to suggest how they might most readily be alleviated. If at first glance his investigations seemed to make unusual material for an architectural magazine their relevance became apparent once he started to outline his remedies, for his programme of reform implied important consequences for those of the profession that cared to heed them.

Since Godwin, more than the first two editors of *The Builder*, was willing to accept the conventional values of his time, his reform proposals contained fewer radical assumptions than theirs. His principal reform was knowledge itself for, like Victorian campaigners on other fronts, he was convinced that the abolition of ignorance would produce its own remedies.

To expose the slums in writing would bring light and ventilation to other kinds. If landlords could not be bludgeoned through seeing their names in print to put their houses in order, then there were the weapons of inspection and regulation. Godwin argued that Shaftesbury's Model Lodging Houses Act of 1851 ('the best law ever passed by an English parliament', as Dickens called it) should be extended to cover all houses divided into lodgings, with a system of licensing to prevent overcrowding. And to ensure that such houses were not defectively constructed in the first place the

Building Acts required to be similarly strengthened. As a London district surveyor (yet another of the tasks which he crowded into the working week) Godwin was especially alert to builders' short-cuts and deficiencies, and *The Builder* was full of weekly tales of non-existent foundations, mortar laced with earth and un-seasoned timbers. The need to impose basic standards, and to speed the diffusion of new techniques, seemed to him to amply justify yet more vigorous regulations.

Beyond such a system of controls lay the institutional aspects of reform, in which Godwin was just as fervent a believer; always provided that such institutions offered genuine means of improve-ment. Badly-ventilated hospitals were for him, as for Florence Nightingale, a disgrace to medicine. 'There are some', he insisted, 'where patients, after an operation, have less chance of life than they would if they were taken into the fields and covered with a tent.' His advocacy of the pavilion lay-out for hospitals, with the wards strung out separately in a line or semi-circle, was one of his most thoughtfully-conducted campaigns. Public baths and wash-houses came a close second in his list of priorities, for broadly similar reasons. He delighted to chart the spreading provision for public bathing, which had reached twenty-six towns outside London by 1854, and even more to report that most estab-lishments were paying a reasonable return: 'the cost of cleanliness can now no longer be pleaded as an excuse for dirt'. In the sphere of housing, his original starting-point, he watched with caution the endeavours of charitable trusts and companies to make provision for those that commercial builders had long forsaken; wary, not because he doubted their good intentions but because the blocks they were forced to build on the sites they acquired were far from his image of how families should be housed: 'If we made them a little less like factories and barracks it would go far to give an air of home to them'. The kind of solution he preferred, cottage homes in the railway suburbs, only began to be realised in his final years.

But Godwin's main 'social bridges' were ones founded on in-dividual rather than collective action, and to that extent were in accord with the Victorian values which have recently been newly promoted. Despite the fact that he, as much as any of the reformers of his time, recognised the hopeless constraints of hous-ing and environment that bound the lives of the urban poor, and the failure of his message that 'property has its duties as well as its rights', he still believed in individual perseverance and effort as the chief engines of progress. Had it not been for the publication of Samuel Smiles' *Self-Help* the previous year his own little testament of the same kind, *Memorials of Workers: The Past to Encourage the Present* (1860), might have achieved the same kind of fame. Godwin's peep-show of useful lives had a familiar cast – Arkwright and Brindley, Watt and Stephenson – with heroes of the building world such as Thomas Cubitt thrown in; all of them, like those that Smiles paraded, intended to show that the struggling and disadvantaged could reach great heights: 'Without *will*, natural power will go but a little way: with will, small powers may be made to effect wonders'. And for those who were still held back whatever their efforts there was, he pleaded as an afterthought, the satisfaction to be had in a life of pleasure and advantage to others.

Whether self-taught or otherwise, the 'social bridge' in all of his exemplary lives was education, and it is in that sphere that one final contribution of his own career deserves to be mentioned. From the time of his first essay on housing, written in 1843, he regarded the promotion of good taste in painting and decoration as being second only to pure air and water as a way of securing moral virtue and improvement: as he put it, 'a tidy, well-arranged dwelling . . . induces neatness and industry, and elevates the character of all its occupants'. Well before he took up his editorial duties he turned this aspect of his thinking into action by accepting the post of co-secretary to the Art Union of London, an organisation which harnessed the attractions of gambling to the service of high art. Subscribers to the Art Union (over 13,000 in number by 1844) participated in an annual lottery in which the prizes were fixed sums to be spent at selected London galleries, or works of art (especially bronze statuettes) which had been specially commissioned: there were also occasional distributions of engravings to every member. The fact that the selection of prize paintings was made, not by Godwin or his committee but by the winners themselves, outraged those who felt that ill-educated choices were the result, but that missed the point. The ulterior motive of the Union, as constantly had to be pointed out, was to improve taste from below, not to impose it from above.

In the course of hearing evidence from Godwin about the Art Union, a parliamentary committee was dumb-founded that he could find time to be its secretary on top of an already full and varied life, to which came the reply: 'I constantly devote much of the night to matters of this description, simply from a desire to do good'. Confronted by such moral certainty, applied across so many fronts, it is tempting today to take his life in manageable slices rather than as a whole. *The Builder*, his chief monument, easily reinforces that tendency because its pages can be mined for countless subjects without regard to its total attitude and spirit; and indeed on first examination it is hard to appreciate the connections which bind together so many diverse topics. To say that they simply represent the fragments of a busy life is not enough, for Godwin undoubtedly did have a central ambition from which his other interest sprang: his commitment to architects. Throughout many pages of *The Builder* that is obvious, but in his reform campaigns it may be less so. Yet these, even when not architectural in a narrow sense, had implications for his profession lying just beneath the surface. They suggested a role for architects after his own mould, as problem-solvers and reformers. In our own times such claims to authority have become commonplace, though threatened and disputed more each year. In the early Victorian period, when still unusual, they seemed to offer a promising solution to the profession's dilemmas.

Godwin died in 1888 at his home in Kensington. In a testimony to his memory at the RIBA Robert Kerr, a long-standing colleague, remarked: 'We all know that he took a very deep interest in the affairs of the institute, and for fifty years he pulled the strings (I may say) in favour of it as no-one else could do'. And, he might have added, he pulled the strings for much else as well, in a most influential way.

For Further Reading

The Builder, 1842 onwards; George Godwin, *Town Swamps and Social Bridges* (1859, reprinted Leicester University Press, 1972); Anthony King, 'Architectural Journalism and the Profession: The Early Years of George Godwin', *Architectural History*, Vol 19 (1976), pp. 32–53; Anthony Wohl, *The Eternal Slum* (Edward Arnold, 1977); *The Survey of London*, Vol XLI (Athlone Press, 1983). A comprehensive index to the illustrations in *The Builder*, 1842–83, compiled by Ruth Richardson, is to be published in the near future.

10

Gladstonian Finance

H. C. G. Matthew

"I speak but in the figures."

Henry V.

RETRENCHMENT.

IN AN ERA of powerful characters, William Ewart Gladstone (1809–98) continues to tower above all but a few others – a tribute not just to his longevity but to his extraordinary energy as four times Prime Minister of Great Britain (to a queen who thoroughly disliked him), creator and sustainer of a united Liberal Party (until its fateful split over Gladstone's bold attempt, at the age of seventy-seven, to introduce Home Rule for Ireland), and embodiment of the liberal conscience.

But Gladstone cannot be easily stereotyped and indeed paradox colours a biographical analysis. He was a devoted High Church Anglican leading a party of Nonconformity, a man so far from the definition of a modern politician that his early intellectual passions were theology and philosophy and a man whose private life and temptations were, as editions of his private diaries over the last twenty years have successively revealed, taut and far removed from the magisterial public person. Here the co-editor of his diaries, Colin Matthew, writes about another source of tension in the great man's life – his commitment to fiscal conservatism set against the increasing demands on the public purse of the Nonconformist conscience at work in society.

A nachronism is an awkward business for the historian. The search for 'relevance' when teaching encourages the discovery of continuity, but close study of a period usually leads to a stress on its distinctiveness. Nineteenth-century finance used not to be thought of much interest: in the philosophy of a welfare state it was merely a detail of a period left behind. Faced today with ministers who, on the one hand, claim to support minimal state intervention but, on the other, claim with respect to any particular area of state spending to have increased expenditure (i.e. overall government spending should decrease, but no sector should be acknowledged to be suffering), historians have begun to turn their attention to both the mechanics and the ethos of the Victorian 'minimal state' and its finances.

William Ewart Gladstone's background was commercial, and it might be thought that finance would have been a natural interest. His father, John Gladstone, made a fortune speculating in commodities, particularly in the expanding Liverpool corn trade in the late eighteenth century; he became the political organiser and friend of Huskisson and Canning, the two Liverpool Members of Parliament, both Tories. But the young William never had any direct experience in the family firm, and his education at Eton and

Oxford was in the classics and in philosophy. As a young Tory MP in the 1830s his interests were chiefly theological and philosophical, and his reading and writing in those years show no particular interest in commerce or finance, though family interest required him to play an active part in bargaining with the Whig government about the terms of compensation for West Indian slave owners at the time of emancipation. Perhaps to ween him away from theology, Sir Robert Peel made him Vice-President of the Board of Trade in 1841 (at the age of thirty-one) and he was its President from 1843–5, when he resigned over the Maynooth affair (the government's proposal to give St Patrick's College, Maynooth, a Roman Catholic seminary in Ireland, a permanent endowment).

Gladstone rapidly showed an aptitude for figures and the details of tariff negotiations, and he played an important part in the making of the budgets of 1842 and 1845. Even so, his appointment as Chancellor of the Exchequer by the Earl of Aberdeen in 1852 was by no means inevitable, for having briefly been Peel's Colonial Secretary in 1846, Gladstone had become chiefly known in the late 1840s as a speaker on colonial matters. His speech attacking Disraeli's budget proposals in 1852, which contributed to the fall of the minority Tory government, and the influence of Prince Albert, seem to have led to his Chancellorship. He was Chancellor from 1852–5, and again, under Palmerston and Russell, from 1859–66. When Prime Minister, he twice appointed himself Chancellor of the Exchequer as well (in 1873–4 and in 1880–2).

Gladstone relished the Chancellorship. He enjoyed the details of figures, and he had the capacity to communicate his enthusiasm. His budget speeches raised what, under predecessors such as Henry Goulburn and Charles Wood, had been rather humdrum occasions to one of the chief moments of the political year. The importance of Gladstone's annual budget day is still symbolised by twentieth-century Chancellors carrying their budget speech from Downing Street to the House of Commons in what is believed to have been the despatch case he used for the 1853 budget. His budget speeches were huge – four hours was not uncommon – but they fascinated the Commons. They were delivered from notes only, Gladstone unfolding the record of national financial progress and the details of the financial proposals partly as if he were narrating an Homeric epic, and partly as if he was the detective at the end of a novel, unravelling a complete plot and bringing the esoteric details into clear and dramatic relationships.

The creation of the budget was the job of the Chancellor. Glastone worked out the sums himself – once literally on the back of an envelope – and rarely took advice. Indeed he usually decided on the shape of his budget proposals while at Hawarden, his brother-in-law's house in North Wales. The 1860 Cobden Treaty with France, which together with that year's budget greatly extended free trade, was sketched in the Hawarden garden. Of course, convention and the sense of what was politically possible were constraining factors, but the Chancellor bore responsibility for his proposals alone. If things went well, the reward was great; if badly, the Chancellor stood exposed, as Wood found in 1851 and Robert Lowe in 1872. Gladstone was good at spotting and anticipating difficulties, and one of his advantages to his Prime Minister and his party was that he had a safe pair of hands when it came to financial details. The Whigs in the 1830s and 1840s had acquired a reputation for financial fumbling. In the 1860s, the Liberals with Gladstone could claim to be the party of financial reliability.

Despite Gladstone's personal prominence and authority, 'Gladstonian Finance' was not a personal invention. It built on Peel, and it related to and reflected the predominant aspirations of a generation. It was in the first two periods of Gladstone's four Chancellorships that his most distinctive work was done, and it had four main consequences.

It clearly established the political and financial importance and distinctiveness of the Chancellorship (a development adumbrated by Disraeli in 1852), together with the Treasury, as the central, co-ordinating office of executive politics, second only (and not always that) to the Prime Minister. The Treasury as it developed in the 1850s and 1860s was essentially, though not in every case, a negative influence. Stressing the virtues of probity in public affairs, it and its legislative ally the Public Accounts Committee (begun by Gladstone in 1861), chased waste and corruption, and were the final stage in the long process, begun in the late eighteenth century, which made public service in Britain exceptionally free from bribes. 'Oiling the wheels' ceased to be the way to get things done in British government. This was partly because British government at the centre, outside the area of defence, had few ambitions to construct or to innovate – a point which will be shortly returned to.

A great emphasis was placed on balanced budgets and the annual national account presented in the spring budget. The dramatic performance of these budgets helped to emphasise the central place of finance in the government's annual legislative programme, as well as promoting the personal political position of the Chancellor. A chief purpose of a single annual account was to force spending departments into public accountability by directly relating their expenditure to the raising of revenue.

Revenue was to be raised (or lowered) by a balance between direct and indirect taxation. Direct taxes – the income and property tax revived by Peel in 1842, succession duties and the like – contributed about 30 per cent of central government revenue in the late 1840s and about 40 per cent by the early 1880s. The regressive indirect taxes, levied on a very small number of highly remunerative articles – chiefly food and drink – correspondingly decreased from about 70 per cent in the late 1840s to about 60 per cent in the early 1880s. The income tax – the chief contributor to the direct tax side of the equation – was only paid by those with incomes of £100 and over (i.e. it excluded the labouring classes almost completely, and some lower-middle-class people as well). Gladstone believed the £100 line was 'the dividing line . . . between the educated and the labouring part of the community', and Dudley Baxter, the Tory statistician, described it as 'the equatorial line of British incomes'.

Thus the propertied classes, which until 1867 constituted almost the whole of the electorate, taxed themselves through the income tax, bearing through the century an increasing proportion of the taxation raised by central government. This fact is all the more distinctive when it is remembered that the shouldering of this burden was refused by the equivalent classes in many of the larger European and North American states. France could only get an income tax approved in the extreme circumstances of 1914, Germany an Imperial income tax not even then, the United States only after a long struggle when the attempt to introduce an income tax was ruled unconstitutional in 1894. When a budget surplus allowed a reduction in taxation, the generally agreed rule of thumb was that each of what Gladstone called the 'twin sisters' of direct and indirect taxation should receive remission. Similarly, when extra revenue was required, the rich and the poor were both expected to contribute.

There was a complete absence of protective tariffs, the reforms begun in the 1820s being carried to an absolute conclusion in the

1860s. No British manufacturer or farmer received any protection from foreign competition; the economy was a completely open market. Taxes on imports were on goods like tea which were not produced in Britain. This openness was rigidly maintained; even the registration of foreign meat importers was frowned on for its protectionist implications. This free trade or *laissez-faire* reflected much more than merely a preference for cheap imports and an enlarging of the scale of the world market. It represented a political ethos: the government should be above economics, neither the manager of the economy nor the prisoner of economic pressure groups. Protection was, Gladstone said, a 'poison' sheltering nothing 'but the most selfish instincts of class against the just demands of the public welfare'. It armed producers with 'power and influence largely gotten at the expense of the community, to do battle, with a perverted prowess, against nature, liberty and justice'.

Parliament should balance its accounts as a neutral onlooker, beholden neither to employer nor worker, merely ensuring in the world market-place the cheapest bargain for the British consumer. The consumer was seen as a consumer only, not as one who consumes in order to produce. Or rather, productive factors were assumed to receive their stimulus elsewhere. Certainly, government took on responsibility for the standard of living. When Daniel Jones, a miner from Newcastle-under-Lyme, wrote to tell him of his unemployment and to complain of low wages, Gladstone made the classic mid-Victorian reply:

The only means which have been placed in my power of 'raising the wages of colliers' has been by endeavouring to beat down all those restrictions upon trade which tend to reduce the price to be obtained for the product of their labour, & to lower as much as may be the taxes on the commodities which they may require for use or for consumption. Beyond this I look to the forethought not yet so widely diffused in this country as in Scotland, & in some foreign lands; & I need not remind you that in order to facilitate its exercise the Government have been empowered by Legislation to become through the Department of the Post Office the receivers & guardians of savings.

These precepts of central government finance rested on a variety of assumptions. They presupposed, and indeed the whole strategy emerged from, the energy and drive of early-Victorian entrepreneurial activity. The precepts of Gladstonian finance did not try to create this activity and its accompanying investment, but rather sprang from it. They recognised the central feature of early British capitalism and responded to it; they did not set out to create what was not there. Gladstonian finance also presupposed the success of voluntarism in the provision of welfare services. It is quite wrong to suppose that, because the central government did not set out to supply welfare services, they did not exist. Education, for example, was assumed to be a state function, managed largely by the established churches; when it became clear that the churches could no longer cope in England and in Scotland, Gladstone's first government supplemented their efforts by a national system of elementary schools in the Acts of 1870 and 1872, soon made, with all-party agreement, both compulsory and free. Religious charities of all sorts, sizes and denominations were assumed to cater for other welfare needs often locally defined. A strong role was presupposed for local government acting on its own initiative, to 'municipalise' if it wished. The low profile of central government was in considerable measure premised on a high profile for local government in a wide variety of areas. Indeed the classic Victorian scenario was for central government to identify a problem (or to have a problem brought to its attention) and to solve it by setting up a locally accountable, controlled and financed institution, sometimes helped by a 'grant-in-aid' from the centre.

The financial consensus of the mid-nineteenth century also assumed that the economy would balance at a point close to full employment of available resources of capital and labour, that, as J. S. Mill wrote, 'a general over-supply' is shown to be 'an impossibility'. The process of adjustment by individuals which the prevention of this phenomenon required was painful but unavoidable. Contemporaries were aware that the process of bringing into balance was often prolonged. Gladstone when Chancellor seemed to nod – as Engels was quick to note – towards Marx's view of the 'reserve army of the unemployed' when he said that the economy worked with a chronic 'enormous mass of paupers . . . what is human life, but, in the majority of cases, a struggle for existence? and if the means of carrying on that struggle are [in 1864] somewhat better than they were, yet the standard of wants varies with the standard of means, and sometimes more rapidly'. He was also aware that 'great vicissitudes mark the industrial condition of society; and we pass rapidly in a series of cycles from periods of great prosperity to periods of sharp distress'. He throught this, of course, at a time when the trade cycle had not yet been identified by political economists either as a concept or as a set of statistics.

All these presuppositions were in the minds of those – an overwhelming preponderance of the electorate – who supported the chief thrusts of Peel–Gladstone finance, which thus expressed the assumptions of society more than if formed them.

In certain respects, this was in its own terms an extremely successful system. Its incorporation of the Treasury at the centre of the machine had an enduring effect felt far beyond the Victorian years. The concentration on codification of the accounts and on low expenditure produced an even relationship between central government expenditure and GNP as Table 1 shows.

This result is all the more remarkable considering that Victorians had only a vague concept of 'national product'. Table 1 shows that even the Edwardian crisis of expenditure was really a readjustment to take account of a greater GNP.

The willingness of the propertied classes to tax themselves and to help pay for the defence of the Empire they had created (about a third of government expenditure went on defence throughout the period after the 1840s) was an important contribution to political stability and to the legitimating of the political system. There was a marked contrast with Germany, where the introduction of an income tax was one of the Social Democratic Party's chief objectives.

But this was a financial system responding to the needs of a capitalist society at an early stage of its development. It was a system which occurred at a particular moment of British history

Table 1 Proportion of central government gross expenditure to gross national product

	Expenditure(£m)	GNP(£m)	%
1853	55.3	642 (1855)	8.6
1860	70.0	702	10.0
1865	67.1	846	7.9
1970	67.2	953	7.0
1875	73.0	1136	6.4
1880	81.5	1101	7.4
1885	88.5	1120	7.9
1895	100.9	1459	6.9
1905	149.5	1814	8.2
1913	220.2	2322	8.7

Source: Mitchell and Deane, *Abstract of British Historical Statistics* (1971) and Feinstein, *National Income, Expenditure and Output of the United Kingdom 1885–1965* (1972)

because it represented a particular phase of historical development. By the end of the century many of the assumptions which underpinned it were felt to be wrong or irrelevant. Late-Victorian values, as the older Gladstone frequently lamented, were very different from those of the early years of the Queen's reign.

The failure of 'voluntarism' to meet changing needs and expectations of welfare was widely admitted across the political spectrum, just as much on the 'right' as on the 'left' (terms which became fashionable in the 1880s). The capacity of local government and of *ad hoc* elected boards for the Poor Law and for education to provide a national service with equal standards across the country was successfully called into doubt.

Understanding of the trade cycle began to make possible a much more sophisticated attitude to and treatment of 'unemployment' (again, a term which came into use in the 1880s), and the assumption that those without employment were so because of laziness or personal inadequacy was accepted to be disproved: most of the unemployed were so as a result of forces beyond their control. Analysis of the 'enormous mass of paupers' became sophisticated and particular. Poverty came to be seen as an identifiable, curable and unnecessary condition. The notion that those on weekly wages either could or would pay for their own welfare through voluntary saving was disproved by a succession of Royal Commissions and individually sponsored inquiries.

Expectations of the tax system changed as the propertied classes became less electorally significant and the economy became rich enough to allow the tax system to attempt active redistribution, building on the moderate redistribution already existing in the low-level income tax. Consequently, different expectations emerged about the scope and function of central government revenue-raising and expenditure.

Nothing could be more anachronistic, more dangerous in the long term to political stability, more ignorant of the development of British society, more foolish in its economic and social consequences, than the assumption that the nostrums of Gladstonian finance can be simply or successfully imposed today.

For Further Reading:

H. C. G. Matthew, *Gladstone 1809–1874* (Oxford University Press, 1986) and 'Disraeli, Gladstone and the Politics of mid-Victorian

Budgets', *Historical Journal*, 1979; M. Wright, *Treasury Control of the Civil Service 1854–1874* (Oxford University Press, 1969); J. A. Schumpeter, *History of Economic Analysis* (Oxford University Press, 1954) 'Gladstonian Finance' in Part 3, ch. 2; D. H. MacGregor, *Public Aspects of Finance* (Oxford University Press, 1939); F. W. Hirst, *Gladstone as Financier and Economist* (Benn, 1931); R. McKibbin, 'Why was there no Marxism in Great Britain?', *English Historical Review*, 1984; B. Baysinger and R. Tollison, 'Chasing Leviathan: the case of Glastonian finance', *History of Political Economy* (1980).

A WARD

THE DISPENSARY

11

Ministering Angels
Victorian Ladies and Nursing Reform

Anne Summers

Opposite: Scenes of life at St Saviour's Hospital, Osnaburgh Street, London, in the 1860s – stressing the close association with religion and female community that nursing often evoked. (Mansell Collection)

PERIODS OF HISTORY stamped with the personalities of their female rulers are not necessarily the most fruitful in advancing the interests and self-awareness of fellow members of the sex. Yet it is undeniable that Victoria's reign sees the emergence of a striking number of individual women making contributions of significance in public life that sharply colour our overall impression of the nineteenth century and its values – the Brontë sisters, Mrs Gaskell, Josephine Butler, Isabella Burdett Coutts, Mrs Beaton, Elizabeth Browning – a medley of influence in social, literary and philanthropic activity.

In recent years historians have begun to look beyond the inspiring individual biographies to examine the value-systems and self-consciousness that both trapped and liberated Victorian women, and to consider how changing economic and societal patterns affected their expression. Here Anne Summers brings this technique to bear on perhaps the most treasured female icon of Victorian civic service – Florence Nightingale (1820–1910) – arguing that in her outlook and that of her fellow nursing reformers and acolytes, many of the conflicts and paradoxes of feminine 'commitment' in the nineteenth century can be clearly seen.

Nursing reform is usually described as a straightforward nineteenth-century success story whose heroine, Florence Nightingale, can be seen as an ideal type of the Victorian reformer. She was a moderniser, a seculariser, literally sweeping away cobwebs of ignorance and irresponsibility from public institutions; a promoter of professional training for women; an apostle of statistical surveys; a tireless worker for government commissions and legislative enactment. Her work survives in the structures of barracks, hospitals and nurse training schools. But the 'nursing legacy', as one recent study has termed it, in fact consists of a far more complex and contradictory set of values than are implied in this Whig litany.

At the outbreak of the Crimean War in 1854, Florence Nightingale was only one of a large cohort of Victorian women interested in the reform of nursing; and her heroic confrontations with sickness, filth and inertia at Scutari, followed by tireless work for army medical reform and the establishment of her own training school for nurses, inspired rivals as well as acolytes. Two of her earliest disciples were Jane Shaw Stewart, who was the first Superintendent-General of the post-Crimean female army nursing service, and Agnes Jones, the pioneer of 'new nursing' at the Liverpool Workhouse Infirmary. Their careers are far less celebrated than hers, but they are well worth examining for the light they throw on the many different ideas at work in nursing's 'Age of Reform'. They reveal, not the dedication to rationalisation, modernisation and sanitation championed by their preceptress, but the fervour of missionary Christianity, the ideal of reconcilia- tion between social classes, and the glorification of the separate, and largely domestic, sphere of female action.

In 1847 an anonymous article in *The Athenaeum* lamented the supplanting of such terms as 'women' and even 'wife' by the now-ubiquitous 'lady', and claimed that:

This affectation was at its height some fifteen or twenty years ago . . . . women and the females are all gone – and the feminine terminations are following them very fast. To supply their places we have *ladies*, – always *ladies*. There are no authoresses – only lady-authors; and there are lady- friends, lady-cousins, lady-readers, &c.

With the outbreak of the Crimean War seven years later, the writer would have been able to add 'lady-nurse' and 'lady volunteer' to the list.

If we wish to understand why a certain class of Victorian women invested the term 'lady' with such significance, we need to look at some of the unspectacular, but nonetheless momentous changes in private life which accompanied the industrial revolu- tion. Industrialisation and urbanisation did not just change methods of production, distribution and exchange, but unsettled and threw into question social relationships at every level: be- tween men and women, adults and children, clergy and parish, as well as between employers and employed. With the growth of prosperity, many middle-class women, whose mothers and grandmothers would have lived 'over the shop', served behind the counter, and worked as active partners in a family commercial enterprise, were removed to leafy suburban villas. Here their lives were confined to the private sphere, and their work to the upbringing of children and the management of domestic staff.

These women had become 'ladies', or 'gentlewomen'. Their leisured and unwaged status, and the increased elaboration of their households, figured as emblems of the worldly success of their male kin. They were trained to no trade outside marriage or the home. Florence Nightingale's autobiographical sketch, 'Cassandra', depicted the stultifying superficiality of such an ex- istence; other writers lamented the sorry plight of those genteel women without marketable skills who failed to marry, and whose

male relatives proved unable to support them. However, the positive aspects of the 'separation of spheres' between male and
female, public and private, were celebrated with equal vigour.
The diffusion of evangelical ideas both within and outside the established Church at the turn of the century had popularised the
practice and teaching of religion within the home, and had thus
provided a greater pastoral role for the women who were
removed from the bustle of the world. They could exploit their
isolation as the means of recalling their menfolk from worldly to
heavenly preoccupations.

This domestic, religious and maternal role had, moreover, a
more than familial dimension. The lady had a moral responsibility
which extended beyond her kin to her servants. She had the right
to mould the conduct of her social inferiors both for their own
good and for the convenience of her household. Actively seeking
to discharge the responsibilities which seemed incumbent upon
wealth and leisure, she could and did enter into a similar relationship with the poorer families of her neighbourhood. Many
clergymen and social reformers saw a pattern of relations between
the classes emerging from the practice of visiting the homes of
the poor, and from the lady's successful management of, and co-
residence with, her domestic employees. As the Reverend Brewer
wrote in 1855:

If then it were possible, . . . for the ladies of England to extend that influence over all classes of the poor which, for the great good of this
country, they are extending over one large portion of the classes below
them, . . . you would find no invincible prejudices in the way of moral
and sanitary improvement; you would not find large masses of the poor
standing heedlessly and offensively on their rights and independence . . .

It seemed to be 'woman's mission' (but for 'woman' read 'lady')
to offer society the benefits of the domestic model: to bridge
the gulf between the 'two nations' of rich and poor, to perform kindnesses which would transform mutinous sentiments into grateful ones, and to refashion the lower orders
in the image of their betters. But these expectations contained many contradictory elements. How could ladies preserve in the alien public sphere the qualities developed in private? And if the gulf between classes was healed would not
the social distinctiveness and, indeed, the authority of the lady be
softened? Somehow social divisions had to be bridged without
being dissolved. Jane Shaw Stewart, for one, had no qualms on

this point, confidently asserting in 1857 that 'what God made us we die. The real dignity of a lady is a very high and unassailable thing, which silently encompasses her from her birth to her grave'.

How best to harness the religious and charitable impulses of the lady became a subject for quite intense debate with the growth of the movement to revive sisterhoods within the Protestant churches. The High Church movement saw in the female orders of the Roman Catholic Church the best demonstration of the value of collective organisation for charitable work. The Sisters of Charity of the Order of St Vincent de Paul, founded in France in the seventeenth century, were cited by the poet Southey and other Anglican writers as an ideal type of the active order; evangelical or dissenting Protestants were more impressed by the revival of the deaconess movement in Germany, most particularly by the Deaconess Institution founded at Kaiserswerth on the Rhine by Pastor Theodore Fliedner. It was after her visit to Kaiserswerth in 1840 that Elizabeth Fry founded her own Sisters of Charity in London, later re-titled The Institution for Nursing Sisters. This was a Protestant but non-denominational establishment. High Anglican initiatives followed, with the Sisterhood of the Holy Cross set up under the influence of the Reverend Pusey in 1845, and the Sisterhood of Mercy of Devonport and Plymouth by his friend Priscilla Lydia Sellon in 1848. These orders undertook nursing in addition to other charitable work; the first nursing sisterhood proper of the Church of England was the Training Institution for Nurses, St John's House, established in 1848.

Why should so much of this energy and organisation have been directed to nursing? It can hardly be said that bad nursing was the greatest social evil of its day. Dickens' Sarah Gamp was a savage caricature: there were literally thousands of kindly, decent women for whom going out to nurse in the homes of their parents provided an honest livelihood at the time *Martin Chuzzlewit* went to press. The many hospitals established by charitable subscription were far from being squalid pits of despair: where nurses were found to be callous, incompetent or dissolute, they were dismissed; many spent a lifetime in post, acquiring much expertise and gaining the affection and respect of their employers. Workhouse infirmaries were indeed another, and darker story: but it was not to these that the first nursing reformers directed their attention. Their concerns were not so much medical or sanitary, or simply humanitarian, as religious. When the poet Robert Southey wrote in 1829 that he wished Elizabeth Fry to do for hospitals what she had already done for prisons, what he had in mind was a Christianising mission in an otherwise orderly institution.

At a time when cure was always uncertain, a sick body was a soul close to salvation, or its opposite. If those about the sick were not devoutly inclined, a great pastoral opportunity was going to waste. The expansion of urban centres had removed large numbers of the poor from the effective reach of parish organisation in the first half of the century. The so-called voluntary hospitals had a pronounced missionary advantage in providing an orderly and captive audience of in-patients for Christian teaching. These were indeed Anglican foundations, where chaplains were appointed, and discharged patients were required to attend church and render thanks for their recovery; but by mid-century they had become the site of medical teaching and the theatre in which surgeons could display their talents: their original ethos was largely overwhelmed by more secular functions. Nursing, unlike the occasional visit of the chaplain or the medical man, involved constant attendance at the bedside of the sick person; nurses, therefore, were the key figures in a movement to reclaim both the persons of the poor, and the practice of medicine, from creeping secularisation. To find women who would ensure that the technical aspects of nursing work were scrupulously carried out, who would prevent any descent into coarseness or indecency – on the part of either nurses or medical students – and who would, furthermore, leave no death-bed opportunity neglected, was no easy task. As Florence Nightingale's friend Mary Stanley wrote on the eve of the Crimean War, 'it is a class of women which remains to be created'.

The constitution of St John's House was designed to meet this challenge by dividing its membership, as Elizabeth Fry's institution did not, between paid nurses and unpaid sisters. The ladies who took the title of sister lived with the nurses and supervised their training, work and conduct at all times. They were not necessarily more skilled in caring for the sick than the women they employed; but it was assumed that, because they were socially superior, they were spiritually equipped to give the all-important character training required of the 'new nursing'. The system displayed, indeed, the same confusion between social and spiritual superiority which was evident in much sermonising about the hierarchy of the well-to-do household. When, in 1856, St John's House took over the nursing of King's College Hospital, London, further assumptions from the domestic realm were brought into play: St John's undertook all the nursing and cleaning arrangements for a fixed yearly fee, hiring, firing and supervising the nurses without the intervention of the medical officers. Like the mistress of a household, the sisters did not expect any mere males to appoint the servants or to interfere with their management; St John's House was – with an overtly religious justification – transposing domestic norms to the institutional sphere, and maintaining a private order intact within a public one.

King's College Hospital was a church foundation as well as a teaching hospital attached to the University of London, and its very large concession to the sisterhood ethos is at least partly explained by this. We might expect quite different conditions to be attached to Florence Nightingale's successful penetration of the Army Medical Department after the Crimean War. In 1861 she obtained the establishment of the first official (albeit very small) female army nursing service, and in 1863 the name of her trusted lieutenant, Jane Shaw Stewart, appeared in the Army List. These would appear to be achievements of quite another order to the St John's House contract with King's College Hospital; and where women were entering a government institution, and a previously all-male sphere, there would surely be no room for a female religious mission, much less the replication of the domestic arrangements of gentility. In fact, Jane Shaw Stewart, although Florence Nightingale's chosen instrument, continued to work far more within the conceptual framework of sisterhoods and 'separate spheres' than within one in which secularism, professionalism, and 'equality of opportunity' had any currency.

Jane was the daughter of Sir Michael Shaw Stewart, sixth baronet of Ardgowan, Renfrewshire. She first met Florence Nightingale 'on a certain, to me, memorable, Oct. 18/54'; a devout Anglican, and a wealthy woman, she may have considered some form of philanthropic career before this date, but henceforth she made hospital work her vocation. They next met at Balaklava, where common difficulties with the War Office and the Army Medical Department created an intense bond of sympathy between them; after the war, Jane collaborated with Florence in devising regulations for a new army nursing service, and carried out research for her on nursing arrangements and hospital layout in Paris.

Superficially alike, the two women could not have approached their life's work in a more different manner. For Jane, nursing reform was not a matter of training programmes and sanitary schemes, but a 'coarse, repulsive, servile, noble' self-sacrifice, the action and influence of one individual over others, the Christian leaven in the indifferent lump. She was horrified by Florence's enthusiasm for the government commissions and legislation which followed the debacles of the Crimean War, and could not understand her willingness to go into print, or her anger at being defeated on planning decisions as towards size and ventilation. She begged Florence to secure herself and her career within the framework of the Anglican church, and to accept that the only way to reform nursing was to: 'spend one's life . . . in silent, quiet, as well as laborious and trying work, in governing, training and organizing the women who nurse in hospitals . . .' Florence, she wrote, was in danger of abandoning 'the glorious talent of action, of female action and direction, which you have received' in favour of male principles of work, and the dubious distinction of becoming 'a mere female writer'.

Although Florence did not follow Jane's prescriptions, and continued to focus her efforts on the public sphere and the men who dominated it, she succeeded in preserving her personal privacy. Ironically, Jane, who desperately craved it, could not. Florence worked behind the scenes all her life to influence legislation on such matters as army health and workhouse infirmary reform, and after 1860 supervised the establishment and working of the Nightingale Training School at a considerable personal distance from St Thomas' Hospital, which housed it. Jane was sent to the front line as the first superintendent of the new army nursing service. Even if matters had gone well – and matters went disastrously – she would have found it a martyrdom. Far from seeing her appointment as a pioneering achievement for her sex, she saw it as being 'called to serve God in the painful way of official duty'. It may have been some consolation to know that she was the servant of a female sovereign, but the idea of publicity in any form appalled her.

While she did not wish to join a sisterhood, Jane had close links with St John's House, and the regulations which she and Florence devised together for the new army nursing service bore distinct similarities to the contract St John's had negotiated with King's College Hospital. An all-female chain of command was created, responsible neither to the military governor of an army hospital nor to its medical officers, but directly to the Secretary of State for War. Much to Florence's irritation, Jane was informally allowed to stipulate that all the nurses should be Anglicans. The Superintendent resided and 'messed' with her subordinates, and supervised much of their leisure, as well as most of their working hours. Almost from the start, this transportation of the values of the religious sisterhood and the genteel household to an all-male military institution proved unworkable, and the scheme ultimately broke down at virtually every level.

As Jane herself had predicted, the medical officers were equally resentful of her official privileges and of her social distinction: in her seven years in office she did not draw a penny of her salary. They did all they could to marginalise her position, and intrigued with disaffected nurses to denounce her to the War Office. The attitude of the nurses was a sad commentary on Jane's maxim that 'the improver must live among those she endeavours to improve and to train, one of, tho' superior to them'. The conjuring trick of bridging social divisions without dissolving them had proved beyond her powers. Her insistence on commensality had distinct disadvantages: her feeling that 'it is not good that a Nurse who has just behaved, for instance, with deceit or with gross insubordination, should sit down to dinner with the Superintendent' led, in some cases, to nurses' being disciplined by being made to eat alone for a month. More serious offences – the exchange of love letters with a patient, the discovery of empty gin bottles – resulted in instant dismissal without right of appeal. The high dismissal rate contrasted with the greater tolerance extended to the peccadilloes of the male ward orderlies. Jane had finally to undergo the ordeal of a full War Office inquiry and a pillorying in the medical press before handing in her resignation in 1868.

If 1868 was a bitter and humiliating year for Jane Shaw Stewart, it was a tragic one for another of Florence Nightingale's pupils, Agnes Elizabeth Jones. Agnes became superintendent nurse in the male wards of Liverpool Workhouse Infirmary in 1865, and left her post for the grave three years later. The immediate cause of her death was typhus, but physical and mental strain undoubtedly contributed to her collapse in no small degree. She had come very slowly to a nursing vocation and, like Jane, had done so as an expression of Christian commitment. The daughter of a devout Irish Protestant family, whose childhood ambition was to become a missionary, she found her model of the practical religious life in Kaiserswerth, which she visited in 1853 and 1861.

Florence Nightingale's belief that God's will was made manifest in the laws of hygiene and the pattern of disease and recovery had even less significance for the evangelical Agnes that it did for the High Church Jane. Agnes believed that the primary end of earthly life was personal salvation through Jesus Christ, and that her own mission was conversion through preaching and example. When in 1861 she was approached by the businessman and philanthropist William Rathbone, in connection with establishing a nurses' home and training institution in Liverpool, she asked: 'is the Christian training of the nurses to be the primary, and hospital skill the secondary object?' and was not satisfied with the answer, or with the prospect of Unitarian assistance with the project. While in her training year at St Thomas' Hospital she organised a Bible class, some of whose members accompanied her to Liverpool when she took up her workhouse post. Whilst there, she continued to hold Bible classes and prayer meetings in addition to carrying out her official duties.

Great hopes were entertained of the Liverpool workhouse experiment, which was financed by Rathbone. After the first year, when comparison was made between the 'new nursing' in the male wards and the pauper nursing in the rest of the Infirmary, it emerged that the percentages of deaths and discharges were actually unfavourable to the new system. But there was universal praise for the greater cleanliness of wards and patients, the improved behaviour of the latter, the reliable obedience to medical instructions, and 'the gentle and kind attention paid to the sick and the dying'. The disappointing clinical results did not weaken support for the experiment; and it is unlikely that they gave Agnes herself much cause for concern. Where Florence Nightingale and her professional descendants might feel a sense of loss and failure, Agnes was capable of writing 'I had a bright death-bed today to cheer me', and an even more startling entry in her diary for 1867 runs: 'a great many children die, and I can scarcely be sorry when I think of what might be; but it is often sad to see them dying. They look so pretty in their little coffins, and we lay them out very nicely.'

Agnes nursed in a far more squalid and distressing setting than Jane Shaw Stewart, but there are close parallels to be seen in their approaches to nursing superintendence. Both were preoccupied with the question of the spiritual influence which women of a higher social class might exercise on women lower down the scale. Agnes initially doubted that she had a talent for leadership, but felt it her duty, as a lady and a Christian, to develop it. She perceived the necessity of living among lower-class women as one of the most formidable trials and penalties of her decision to take up nursing, and in a striking self-exhortation, she noted in her diary a remark of Rathbone's: 'are you more above those with whom you will have to mix than our Saviour was in every thought and in sensitive refinement?'

Despite her family's protests, Agnes insisted on taking her meals with her nurses: 'the moral influence of her presence in such a mixed community, she considered not the least important part of her day's work.' To most of her friends and relatives, she maintained that she was happy and fulfilled in her work, and, clearly, would never have abandoned it. But, like Jane, she was exercising an *imperium in imperio*; her official relations with the Poor Law Guardians and medical officers, and with the workhouse master and matron, were not clearly defined, and she was professionally, socially, and emotionally isolated. 'As I know painfully', she wrote to a friend in 1865, 'no one can tell what a woman exposes herself to who acts independently. I never would advise any one to do as I have done.'

Florence Nightingale did not ever allude publicly to the resignation of Jane Shaw Stewart; she did, however, use the occasion of Agnes Jones' death to urge other women of her class to come forward to take her place. In an article entitled 'Una and the Lion' she wrote: 'All England is ringing with the cry for "Women's Work" and "Women's Mission". Why are there so few to *do* the work?' Her appeal veered uneasily in tone between professionalism and religiosity. She advanced the claims of systematic training against amateurish good will (with a heavy plug for her own school at St Thomas'), and insisted that nursing should be a properly remunerated occupation: but she did not deny that 'there have been martyrdoms', and asserted that 'it is God's work more than ours'.

It was not, indeed, realistic, to imagine that women of education and energy would embark on a physically strenuous, and even dangerous, career, which removed them from their family and friends, if they were not already possessed of a powerful religious motivation; and such women were more likely to seek the spiritual support and permanent fellowship of a sisterhood than the loneliness of a purely secular formation. Paradoxically, Florence could hope to attract to full-time nursing – as opposed to part-time philanthropy, or armchair campaigns for social reform

– only those women whose values were fundamentally different from her own. The first decades of reform and 'modernisation' in nursing depended less on the advance of medical science and public health than on a strongly developed sense of spiritual vocation and *noblesse oblige*, which often harked back to the supposed social values of an earlier and more harmonious era.

A close examination of the careers and personal lives of a number of male reformers of the Victorian period might reveal similar paradoxes. But few of them had to condemn themselves, their sons or their protégés to lives of isolation, unwarmed by any glow of legitimate personal ambition. The public sphere was not an alien and often hostile environment for them, as it was for many of their female counterparts. The personal cost to 'the lady' of leaving the private sphere in order to join the shock troops of social change and reconciliation was a heavy one. And 'woman's mission' was largely expected to be its own reward; duties, rather than rights, were proclaimed as the motor principle of women's actions outside the home. It is possible to admire self-abnegation without acquiring a taste for it; perhaps it is not too surprising that large numbers of Victorian women for whom Florence Nightingale was a heroine did not perceive it to be in their own interest to become pioneers. The ethic of female service and self-sacrifice permeated initiatives from which many have benefited, but which cannot properly be heralded as emancipatory. Not only nursing, but teaching, social work and even the feminist movement itself possess a large and dubious inheritance from the value system of the sisterhoods and ladies bountiful of the nineteenth century.

For Further Reading:

M. E. Baly, *Florence Nightingale and the Nursing Legacy* (Croom Helm, 1986); L. Davidoff and C. Hall, *Family Fortunes: men and women of the English middle class, 1780–1850* (Hutchinson, 1987); P. Hollis, *Ladies Elect: Women in English Local Government, 1865–1914* (Oxford, Clarendon Press, 1987); *Memorials of Agnes Elizabeth Jones by her Sister* (Strahan and Co., 1871); F. K. Prochaska, *Women and Philanthropy in 19th century England* (Oxford, Clarendon Press, 1980); M. Vicinus, *Independent Women: Work and Community for Single Women, 1850–1920* (Virago, 1985).

12

Josephine Butler
Feminism's Neglected Pioneer

Trevor Fisher

Overleaf: Bust of Josephine Butler by Alexander Munro. (Mary Evans Picture Library)

NEW MODELS OF MASCULINITY could emerge within the Victorian status quo as well as in challenges to it; new models of femininity, by contrast, most frequently emerged from a particular campaign that challenged received attitudes. Some women, such as Florence Nightingale, made their mark by intervening and taking charge in an area where their resolution and input offered an implicit critique of the indecisiveness of a male establishment. Others honed their skills and defined themselves by direct challenges to male assumptions and exploitation.

Josephine Butler (1828–1906) is a particularly good example of a mid-Victorian woman who took on the male establishment in the explosive area of sexual exploitation, with her campaigns against semi-licensed prostitution in army and navy towns in the 1870s and later against the toleration of child prostitution and 'white slavery' into Continental Europe. She did so, however, from an existing personal standpoint of social and political respectability.

Her crusades often incorporated lurid frontal assaults that could be tactically inept but which were very effective in bringing discussion of the issues in question to the fore. As such, as Trevor Fisher unravels them here, she contributed an essential activist component to the consciousness-raising that was being pursued in more quietist style on a literary front by writers such as Elizabeth Gaskell, George Eliot and the Brontë sisters.

In the history of British feminism, Josephine Butler occupies a marginal position. She has been overshadowed as a feminist pioneer by the dramas surrounding Florence Nightingale, the Pankhursts and the militant suffragettes. Yet in her campaign against the Contagious Diseases Acts, Josephine Butler fundamentally changed the terms of women's political lives. She not only challenged the Victorian taboo that sexual matters were unmentionable, but by taking a dominant role in a major pressure group permanently destroyed the notion that women could not take a leading part in politics.

Josephine Butler was the path-breaking pioneer of women's right to political independence. In the half-century before the formation of her Ladies' National Association in 1869, women had actively supported anti-slavery, the Anti-Corn Law League and temperance and suffrage movements, but no woman had become a national political activist. Josephine Butler did just this, and in leading her campaign to success after a decade and a half established that women were not inferior to men in terms of political ability.

But Josephine Butler did not set out to create precedents. A daughter of a Liberal upper-class family who was second cousin to the former prime minister Lord Grey, she had married into a very respectable family. Her husband, George Butler, was son of a former headmaster of Harrow who became vice-principal of Cheltenham College and principal of Liverpool College. There was little in her background which suggested a rebellion against the all-male political élites of mid-Victorian England. But an exceptional challenge propelled her into the public arena. That challenge was the passage, in 1864, 1866 and 1869, of three Acts of Parliament which established state-regulated prostitution in garrison and naval towns across Britain and Ireland.

The Contagious Diseases Acts regulated prostitution in order to control venereal disease. They gave police and magistrates the power to order any woman suspected of being diseased to be medically inspected, by force if necessary. If found to be infected, the authorities had power to have her confined to a hospital for treatment for a period of up to three months. If she refused to be inspected, or discharged herself from hospital without permission, she could be imprisoned for up to two months. No similar provisions applied to the men of the town. The Acts thus embodied the double standard of sexual morality in a particularly striking way.

The government saw the Acts as a step towards maintaining military efficiency in the teeth of a worrying venereal epidemic. Public health reformers welcomed them as a step towards state-regulated prostitution on the continental model. Puritans and feminists opposed them as a threat both to women's rights and public morality, but in the early 1860s their concerns were limited to a marginal group of health reformers around Florence Nightingale. The initiative lay with politicians deeply concerned by the abysmal performance of the British military during the Crimean War. This cruelly exposed the crippling inadequacies of the British forces. Acts of individual heroism such as the Charge of the Light Brigade and the work of Florence Nightingale's nurses could not conceal overwhelming incompetence in the military leadership.

However, it was not politic for the British establishment to admit the deep inadequacies of the officer class and a scapegoat had to be found. The most convenient culprit was the poor physique of the fighting men, in particular their susceptibility to venereal disease. Infection rates had been rising since the 1820s, and venereal disease offered a convenient excuse for officialdom.

The military establishment formed a *de facto* alliance with the public health lobby led by *The Lancet* to secure a supply of disease-free prostitutes to service the rank and file.

When Earl de Grey was appointed as Secretary for War in 1863, he swung his considerable political weight in favour of state-regulated prostitution. Support developed in Whitehall, aided by a campaign of letters and leaders in the press. Florence Nightingale counter-briefed Harriet Martineau, who produced a series of critical articles in the liberal *Daily News*, but to no avail. The first Bill was brought forward in 1864, setting up a limited system as an experiment for three years in eleven towns.

The authorities believed the system to be successful. An official committee set up in 1866 to investigate the working of the Act (the Skey Committee) recommended that it should be made permanent, and Parliament complied the same year. The wind was in the sails of the public health lobby, which started a campaign to have the system applied to the civilian population of large towns. The government did pass a new Act in 1869 extending the scope of the system, but still confined it to military and naval bases. The period of detention was extended to nine months maximum.

Anti-vice campaigners were appalled. Their anger took concrete form at the annual meeting of the Social Science Congress in October. This meeting discussed the Acts, and on October 4th passed a resolution condemning them. The following day activists decided to form a National Anti-Contagious Diseases Acts Association. This was intended to encompass both sexes, but the women decided to form their own grouping – the Ladies' National Association (LNA). Josephine Butler was not involved in the debates. However, her close friend, Elizabeth Wolstenholme, was present and saw Josephine as the ideal leader for the LNA. Consequently, she wired Butler with the call to 'haste to the rescue' and take up the campaign.

Butler was slow to respond. She was well aware that respectable opinion would censure a woman who campaigned on an issue linked to prostitution, and she was above all a respectable, middle-class woman. Her background in the Liberal landowning classes and her marriage into the Butler family provided a comfortable life as a respectable, God-fearing wife and mother.

She had much to lose from accepting the invitation which Elizabeth Wolstenholme offered in 1869, and hesitated for three months before accepting. She had, however, experienced a religious conversion in adolescence which gave her a powerful moral impetus.

This had been reinforced by personal tragedy. In 1864 her youngest child, Eva, had been tragically killed falling downstairs when rushing to greet her parents. This tragedy haunted Josephine Butler for the rest of her life. The family transferred to Liverpool where she became deeply involved in work reclaiming prostitutes. She later recalled she 'became possessed with an irresistible urge to go forth and find some pain keener than my own, to meet with people more unhappy than myself'.

Josephine was equally strongly moved by deeply held Liberal principles. The Butlers had backed the North during the American Civil War, suffering social ostracism as a consequence, and Josephine Butler gained valuable political experience in campaigning against slavery. She later made conscious links between negro slavery and the treatment of women under the Contagious Diseases Acts. Yet there was an enormous gulf between campaigning for the rights of negro slaves in far-off America, and campaigning for the rights of working-class prostitutes at home. Josephine knew she would threaten her comfortable life, and her husband's career, by entering the campaign against the Acts. But neither she nor her husband could see the call as anything but divinely inspired. Josephine Butler agreed to become the secretary of the LNA.

The campaign was launched on New Year's Day 1870, when the *Daily News* published a protest against the Acts signed by 140 women, including Florence Nightingale, Josephine Butler, penal reformer Mary Carpenter and suffragist Lydia Becker. This was a foundation document of the feminist movement in Britain.

The publication of the New Year protest caused a nine-day sensation. Josephine later recalled an MP telling her, 'we know how to manage any other opposition in the House or in the country, but this is very awkward for us – this revolt of women. What are we to do with such an opposition as this?' The first tactic was to censure the women for daring to speak; the second was to erect a wall of silence. Neither tactic worked. Within a few months all major provincial cities had repeal societies, and many had ladies' committees as well. Josephine threw herself fervently into the fray, and in the first year travelled 3,700 miles and addressed ninety-nine meetings. In the course of this, she discovered that she had very unusual talents at inspiring audiences. Trades unionists and other working men responded positively to her, being particularly conscious of the dangers prostitution and police action posed to their families.

For women, her appeal was even stronger. Beautiful and charismatic, Josephine inspired women who were doubtful about embracing so 'unrespectable' a cause. Judith Walkowitz records Mary Priestman of Bristol recalling her first sight of Josephine. She and a friend had gone to hear Butler speak at a meeting in 1870 to 'find for ourselves whether she was really one whom we could follow in the dark path we had entered on'. The hall was filled with silent ladies waiting for the speaker. The door opened and Butler entered:

... slight and very graceful – almost young (she was forty-three) and very beautiful. As she moved to the table she raised her eyes with such a look of inexpressible sadness, as if the weight of the world's sin and sorrows rested on her innocent head. A woman Christ to save us from our despair was the involuntary thought that entered my head and has never left it.

Men were also touched by her spell. The Regius Professor of Divinity at Oxford commented that 'Men could never be the same after they had seen and known Josephine Butler. A new sense of what passionate pity could mean was brought home to them'. Her appeal was not merely spiritual. There is no doubt that she possessed an unconscious but powerful sexuality. John Addington Symonds went to hear her, and later recorded that 'his sexual equipment swelled'.

While Josephine's appeal was vital in sustaining the LNA, her passionate commitment and deep moralism was a double-edged sword. The repealers rightly condemned Gladstone's government for passing the 1869 Act, but wholly failed to see that the only chance of repeal lay in converting the Liberal Party. They were blind to the need to court the Liberals in a situation in which the Conservatives were wholly unsympathetic. Repealers foolishly committed themselves to a policy of frontal attack against Gladstone's ministry which deeply alienated them from the party, notably at the Colchester by-election of 1870.

In the spring of 1870, when a by-election occurred in the garrison town of Colchester, the Gladstone ministry attempted to secure a seat for Sir Henry Storks, ex-governor of Malta and a strong supporter of the Contagious Diseases Acts. Repealers were equally determined to stop him. The only way to do this was to run a third candidate, split the Liberal vote, and thus return the Conservative. That the Conservative opposed repeal was irrelevant; the object was to move Gladstone toward repeal. Thus the

LNA stood Dr Baxter Langley as candidate, with Josephine Butler and James Stuart, Fellow of Trinity College, Cambridge, going to Colchester to run the campaign.

Liberal supporters were incensed. When Dr Langley and James Stuart held a meeting in the local theatre, a mob drove them from the platform. Langley's clothes were torn, he was covered in dirt and flour and his face was bloodied. Stuart was hit with a chair. The mob then realised that Josephine Butler was their main opponent. She risked violence whenever she appeared on the streets. Hysteria reached fever pitch when she took a room at a hotel. In the middle of the night the proprietor roused her to warn her that a crowd was attacking the hotel, smashing the windows and threatening to torch the building. She had to leave immediately, and after running down unknown streets in the dark was given shelter by an anonymous housewife.

After this, the events at Colchester became national news. The role played by Josephine Butler and her women supporters was an overnight sensation. When the result was announced, a Liberal majority of 183 in 1868 had been turned into a Conservative majority of 527. This pyrrhic victory encouraged the repealers. They repeated the tactic at the Pontefract by-election of August 1872, succeeding in reducing the Liberal majority from 233 to 80. During the campaign Josephine Butler and a friend were pursued into a hayloft by roughs who tried to smoke them out. The repealers became more determined, Butler arguing that the aim should be to 'make these fellows afraid of us' – 'these fellows' being Liberal MPs.

Sympathetic Liberals were appalled. They realised that weakening Gladstone's government paid no dividends at all. Concern grew as the 1874 election drew near and the possibility loomed of a wholly unsympathetic Conservative government. Josephine Butler was wilfully blind to the dangers. When the 1874 General Election produced just such a Conservative victory, Josephine was both shocked and dismayed.

A bitter post-mortem followed. Pro-repeal MPs vociferously attacked the policy of undermining the Liberals and putting in the Conservatives. With the Tories in government for up to seven years, the repealers had to accept the force of the argument. It hit Josephine Butler particularly badly. As she came to understand the folly of the course she had advocated, she suffered the most serious of her periodic bursts of nervous illness. The shock of her nervous breakdown in 1875 spread through the LNA, testifying to the importance of her role within it. An LNA activist, Margaret Tanner, commented that 'the mere thought of her being ill paralyses some of our workers, who almost exist by her inspiration'.

The repeal movement now had to face the unpleasant reality that they were a minority movement on the fringe of the Liberal Party. Fortunately, repealers still attracted figures of substance. The new parliamentary leader of the LNA, Sir James Stansfeld, had been President of the Local Government Board in Gladstone's first ministry. Stansfeld insisted on action designed to win a parliamentary majority, which in practice meant the return of the Liberals.

This assertion of the parliamentary wing of the campaign over extra-parliamentary action left little room for Josephine Butler's energies and talents. Failure at home, however, forced the repealers to look more closely at developments abroad. In December 1874 Josephine left for a tour of the Continent. She made many contacts, and in March 1875 the British, Continental and General Federation for the Abolition of Government Regulation of Prostitution was formed in London. Josephine Butler was its honorary secretary. Garibaldi accepted nomination to its Council, and Cardinal Manning later joined the British section. The anti-regulation movement was strong enough to hold an international conference of 500 delegates in 1877, and began to probe the international vice trade.

Late in 1879, puritan anti-vice campaigners discovered that British women were being held against their will in the state brothels of Belgium. When she heard of this, Josephine Butler was inflamed. On May 1st, 1880, she published an emotional attack on the most sensational aspect of the trade, child prostitution, alleging that 'In certain of the infamous houses in Brussels there are immured little children, English girls of from ten to fourteen years of age, kidnapped ... by every artifice ... known only to the wealthy men who are able to pay large sums of money for the sacrifice of these innocents'. Unwittingly, she had planted the seeds of W. T. Stead's 'Maiden Tribute' campaign of 1885.

The allegation of child prostitution was overshadowed by the immediate issue of the illegal detention of women in Belgian brothels. The chiefs of the Brussels morals police were dismissed in the autumn of 1880 after a prosecution depending largely on evidence supplied by Josephine. Yet the court revelations seemed to be ignored in Britain and in May 1881 Josephine drew up a petition calling for 'Such changes ... in the English laws as should make it impossible for any young girl or child in our country to be deprived of her liberty by fraud or force', and presented it in person to Earl Granville, the foreign secretary. Granville was a Liberal, and took Butler seriously. He readily moved for a Select Committee of the House of Lords to investigate white slavery.

Their Lordships' investigation in 1881 and 1882 confirmed that a serious problem of procuration by fraud existed, while discovering little evidence of child abduction. They called for measures to prohibit solicitation for foreign brothels, the age of consent to be raised to sixteen, and comprehensive measures to tighten the law against brothel keepers. These recommendations were all that the purity lobby could wish for; but the road ahead was rocky. Gladstone's second ministry nevertheless introduced a Criminal Law Amendment Bill into the Lords on May 31st, 1883, as suggested by the Select Committee.

By mid-1883, Josephine Butler was, therefore, fighting on two fronts. Stansfeld had secured a Commons Select Committee into the operation of the Contagious Diseases laws, which reported in August 1882. It provided the basis for a sharply focused offensive in the winter of 1882–83. The repealers did not ask for total repeal, but for the abolition of compulsory examination of women under the Acts. Stansfeld accurately saw that this was the aspect of the Acts which most worried Liberals. As the crucial vote on April 20th approached, the National Liberal Federation was persuaded to vote in favour of repeal. W. T. Stead, editing the *Pall Mall Gazette*, argued against the Acts in its columns, and the cabinet agreed to leave the issue as a question of conscience. With Josephine Butler leading a deputation of women in prayer outside, 182 voted for Stansfeld's resolution, and 110 against. Most MPs had abstained, but the repealers exulted at a crucial breakthrough.

Nonetheless, the Contagious Diseases Acts remained on the statute books, and their supporters threatened to reintroduce the compulsory elements should Gladstone's government fall. Worse, the Criminal Law Amendment Bill ran into serious opposition. The initial bill had to be withdrawn from the Lords and reintroduced in 1884 in a weaker form. This Bill passed the Lords, but failed in the Commons. A third and even weaker Bill was passed by the Lords in 1885, but struggled in the Commons. When the bill reached its second reading at Whitsun, 1885, a bare forty members turned up to debate it. An inconclusive debate was adjourned. With Gladstone's ministry tottering, Josephine Butler faced the grim prospect of seeing a Conservative election victory and the failure of her crusade.

This is the essential background to her involvement in W. T. Stead's notorious 'Maiden Tribute' press campaign of the summer of 1885. Stead had readily agreed to use his *Pall Mall Gazette* to aid the passage of the Criminal Law Amendment Bill. Yet it was far from clear what Stead could do. Gladstone's second ministry collapsed on June 9th, replaced by a stop-gap Conservative administration pending a General Election. When Parliament was dissolved, unfinished business would fall with it. Stead knew, therefore, that he had to raise the Bill to the top of the political agenda in a matter of weeks.

Stead, Josephine Butler and their associates calculated that only a massive sensation could force urgent action over white slavery. They therefore set out to produce such a sensation. The most explosive facet of white slavery was the allegation, which Josephine Butler had made in May 1880, that under-age girls were being kidnapped and sent to Continental brothels to be debauched by rich degenerates. Stead set up a 'Secret Commission' to discover evidence of this. Yet despite enlisting the aid of General Booth and the Salvation Army, Stead failed to do so. At the eleventh hour, Josephine Butler succeeded.

That summer Josephine had met an ex-London prostitute named Rebecca Jarrett. Jarrett claimed to be a former madam – well used to procuring young girls. Butler and Stead prevailed on her to take up her former trade and procure a girl to provide the crucial evidence for Stead's articles. Reluctantly, Jarrett went back to her old haunts and came back with a thirteen year old, Eliza Armstrong. Stead had her certified as a virgin, then spirited her out of the country, to a Salvation Army hostel in France. Convinced he had proven Josephine Butler's allegations, Stead wrote the four articles headed 'The Maiden Tribute of Modern Babylon'.

These were published in the week beginning Monday, 6th July, 1885. Stead likened London to Babylon sacrificing virgins to the Minotaur, by allowing young women to be exploited to satisfy the lusts of the rich. The language was emotional, but Stead had plenty of evidence to prove sexual corruption. Unfortunately, the centrepiece of his case, the 'abduction' of Eliza Armstrong, was not well founded. But in the second week of July, the impact was all that Stead and Butler wished. In the week before the articles appeared, the government showed no interest in the Criminal Law Amendment Bill at all. Yet on Thursday, 9th July, the Home

Secretary, Richard Cross, moved the resumption of the second reading with unseemly haste.

Cross was under intense pressure and rapidly proceeded to put the Criminal Law Amendment Bill on the statute books. The bill was strengthened, passed the Commons on August 7th, the Lords on August 10th and received the royal assent on August 14th. In less than two months the Bill had been rescued from almost certain oblivion to become the law of the land. It was Josephine Butler's greatest triumph.

Yet it rapidly turned sour. Jarrett had assured Stead and Butler that Eliza Armstrong was the daughter of drunken parents who cared nothing for her welfare. This was not so. The parents became worried at not hearing from her, and after several weeks applied to the local magistrates to discover her whereabouts. By the end of August, the police were investigating Stead's activities, and within weeks he and his Secret Commission were in the dock charged with abduction. Stead, Jarrett and others were convicted and sent to prison.

Josephine Butler was appalled. Although not placed in the dock herself, she felt morally responsible for the débâcle. She had genuinely believed that child prostitution was widespread in the capital, and believed that Jarrett would be able to tap easily into the trade. She was bitterly disillusioned by Stead's behaviour on conviction. He proved himself vainglorious, regarding his spell in prison as heroic martyrdom. Worse, he totally ignored his fellow defendants, most blatantly Rebecca Jarrett. Josephine rushed into print with a pamphlet defending Rebecca Jarrett.

It had very little impact. Stead was the martyr-hero of the purity lobby, now boosted by the passage of the Criminal Law Amendment Act. Seven days after the passage of the Act, the puritans had set up the National Vigilance Association (NVA), a militant antivice organisation. Butler was shocked by the repressive attitudes displayed by the NVA, though she was initially a council member. The new Association had none of the concern for individual rights which had driven Josephine Butler to oppose the Contagious Diseases Acts. It was far from suspicious about state and police power, welcoming these as essential weapons in its crusade. Nor did it share Josephine Butler's views that prostitutes were sisters to be rescued, seeing them as enemies to be reformed or crushed. This attitude was implicit in Stead's contempt for Rebecca Jarrett, and as Josephine Butler came to realise that Stead's harsh puritan views dominated the NVA, her spirits dropped.

They were not revived despite the final triumph of the campaign against the Contagious Diseases Acts in 1886. In the turmoil of Gladstone's third ministry, the Grand Old Man discovered he needed James Stansfeld in the cabinet. Stansfeld's price was the absolute repeal of the Acts. Accordingly, Gladstone found time for a brief Repeal Bill which was passed, on March 26th, shortly before the Home Rule crisis destroyed the government.

For Josephine Butler, triumph was bitter-sweet. Though she welcomed repeal, she knew that it had been achieved only by creating militant puritan forces which were hostile to her humanitarian concerns. She welcomed the defences against sexual exploitation which the 1885 Act provided for women. She could only deplore the harsh, repressive puritanism that had been created in the course of its passage. Now well into late middle age, she was too tired and disillusioned to do more than issue private condemnations against the oppressiveness she had unwittingly helped to create.

The events of 1885 permanently distorted her image. She has suffered from her association with Stead and his harsh, repressive morality. History has preferred to celebrate the mid-Victorians who preceded her, Martineau and Nightingale, or the suffragette militants who came later. Josephine Butler has become a marginal figure.

She deserves better than this. She was the pioneering campaigner for women's rights and for a common standard of morality for men and women. She gave herself without sparing to secure protection for the most defenceless women against gross sexual exploitation. And in her work for the reclamation of prostitutes, she exhibited a genuine regard for the most despised section of British society which is wholly admirable. Most moral puritans in 1886 followed Stead in ignoring Rebecca Jarrett as beneath contempt. Josephine Butler did not.

Above all, Josephine broke down the barrier against women's participation in politics. When the LNA published its manifesto on New Year's Day 1870, male politicians were shocked that women should take a political stand. Josephine Butler ensured that the surprise was short-lived. By her work on the hustings and in the lobbies, she broke for ever the taboo on women participating in politics. The generation of women activists represented by Harriet Martineau and Florence Nightingale had not dared to go so far. The suffragettes, a generation later, took their right to a political life for granted. Yet despite breaking the path for later generations, Josephine Butler gains barely a footnote in the history of British feminism. It is time she came out of the shadows.

For Further Reading:

Josephine Butler, *Personal Reminiscences of a Great Crusade* (Horace Marshall, 1896); Brian Harrison, 'Josephine Butler' in *Eminently Victorian* (ed.) J. F. C. Harrison et al (BBC Books, 1974); Paul McHugh, *Prostitution and Victorian Social Reform* (Croom Helm, 1980); Glen Petrie, *A Singular Iniquity – The Campaigns of Josephine Butler* (Macmillan, 1971); Benjamin Scott, *A State Iniquity – Its Rise, Extension and Overthrow* (New York, 1968); Judith Walkouitz, *Prostitution and Victorian Society* (Cambridge University Press, 1980).

13

Joseph Chamberlain and the Municipal Ideal

Derek Fraser

Overleaf: The sweeping radical reforms in Birmingham inevitably attracted the perennial charge of overburdening the ratepayers – a point of view illustrated in this 1882 cartoon, which has Chamberlain 'putting on the screw', a pun on the origins of his personal wealth and position. (Reference Library, Local Studies Department, Birmingham Public Library)

PUTTING ON THE SCREW.

(The Improvement Scheme.)

"It is now estimated that another £100,000 is wanted,"
—Is the present revised estimate a final one, or may we
expect that some time hence another £100,000 will be
found necessary.—*The Birmingham Daily Post.*

JOSEPH CHAMBERLAIN (1836–1914) never enjoyed the fruits of office as a Prime Minister of Victorian Britain, but he affected the destiny of the nation far more drastically than many of his contemporaries at 10 Downing Street. At home, Chamberlain's political initiatives had a traumatic impact on both major political parties and invite comparison with the careers both of Oswald Mosley and latterly David Owen. In 1886 his opposition to Home Rule for Ireland split Gladstone's Liberals, keeping them out of power for all but two of the next twenty years, and took Chamberlain and his Liberal Unionists to the Conservative benches. Once there Chamberlain's zeal for abandoning free trade in face of Imperial preference saddled his new party with a policy that led the Conservatives to electoral disaster in 1906.

Abroad, as Colonial Secretary in the 1890s, Chamberlain's aggressive imperialism and vision of the destiny of Anglo-German expansion set the tone for the jingoism of the Boer War and the tension of pre-1914 diplomacy.

All this can sometimes obscure Chamberlain's radical origins and continuing power base: the city of Birmingham where as Mayor and leader of the Liberals' caucus in the 1870s he championed 'gas and water socialism' – the systematic extension of local government's powers and initiatives. Derek Fraser examines the paradox of this collectivist ethos developing alongside self-help and individualism, and focused in the person of a man who became a kind of Ken Livingstone of mid-Victorian Britain.

———————

It is one of the paradoxes of the history of Victorian England that a society wedded to the principles of self-help, nevertheless created an administrative state with broad social and economic functions. An important part of the historiographical debate on this paradox concerns the apparent conflict between *laissez-faire* and state intervention in such fields as the relief of poverty and the control over conditions of work. In such questions the ideological implications were often faced head-on. In other areas, particularly those involving the local work of town councils, there was a process of collectivism by stealth.

Responding to essentially local pressures and nearly always relying on private local acts rather than national legislation, Victorian urban corporations gradually assumed responsibility for the general welfare of the citizens. Rarely did this process penetrate the national political consciousness or throw up a national leader. However, in Joseph Chamberlain of Birmingham, the practical response to urban problems, the theoretical and strategic justifications for dealing with them, and the necessary political will and power came together in a celebrated case. For both contemporaries and historians Chamberlain came to personify 'the municipal ideal'.

Chamberlain had been born in London to a staunch Unitarian family in 1836 and had moved to Birmingham at the age of eighteen. He worked in the screw business and displayed considerable entrepreneurial talents in securing for the firm of Nettlefold and Chamberlain a near monopoly position, with strong national and international connections. A natural liberal, perhaps even flirting with republicanism, Chamberlain imbibed the individualism and voluntarism characteristic of the Victorian middle class. As one of his first biographers put it, he 'leaned to individual liberty and believed it the duty of the state to interfere neither with the private right of the citizen nor the public rights of unrestricted competition'. What he learned of social conditions in his adopted town and what he achieved as a municipal leader were to compromise considerably so individualist a view. His success in business justified some kind of political prominence and he was elected a councillor in 1869.

Birmingham Town Council offered great potential to an aspiring local politician because of its stunted development. In the thirty years since its foundation it had failed to fulfil the hopes of its original sponsors, having suffered a series of debilitating humiliations. The 1838 incorporation of Birmingham had been inspired by Thomas Attwood's vision of town councils as 'real and legal political unions . . . which would give the people a better means of making their power felt'. That radical surge soon flowed into Chartism and the Birmingham Council became indelibly tarnished by this association. Peel pronounced in Parliament that the Council could not be trusted to enforce law and order, apparently confirmed by the 1839 Bull Ring riots, and Birmingham suffered the obloquy of having a Home Office police force imposed upon the town. Even when this was withdrawn and the disputed legal authority of the newly incorporated towns was confirmed, the Council's freedom of action was constricted by the sovereignty of competing parochial and township authorities. These included not only the prestigious ·Birmingham Street Commission, which since the eighteenth century had been a sort of surrogate corporation, but also puny township institutions which were able to hold municipal power at bay.

It was not until 1851 that all local powers were vested in the Corporation, and thereafter the Council was in the grip of parsimonious petty bourgeois representatives whose main aim was to keep down the rates, not surprisingly a popular if short-sighted policy. The status of councillors was low and the local élite looked to philanthropic rather than municipal outlets for their displays of public service. In the late 1860s this began to change dramatically and Chamberlain was but one of several wealthy industrialists, business and professional men who significantly altered the social composition of the Council, augmented its organisational ability, and enlarged its vision. Chamberlain was to be the main beneficiary of this political thrust in which three developments converged.

First, there occurred in mid-Victorian Birmingham a remarkable flowering of socio-religious thought which laid a duty of civic service upon the towns economic leaders. For a quarter of a century Birmingham Nonconformists were lectured by the powerful orator and unorthodox pastor George Dawson. He urged believers to express their religious conviction in terms of civic duty and he increasingly identified the municipal corporation as the modern expression of God's will. Evolving a philosophy of municipal collectivism, he saw the corporation as the parallel to the state: 'a great town exists to discharge towards the people of that town the duties that a great nation exists to discharge to the people of that nation'. Dawson was ably assisted by the Congregationalist minister, Robert Dale, who insisted that spiritual conviction should not be deflected by the distasteful aspects of political activity. Christians could, indeed must, become active political beings for they 'may serve Christ on the polling booth or on the platform, in Parliament, in the Town Council or on the Board of Guardians'.

Noting his middle-class followers' reluctance to assume municipal responsibilities, Dale pleaded for them to 'see to it that the towns and parishes in which they live are well drained, well lighted and well paved'. Dale and Dawson were the most prominent advocates of this new 'civic gospel' but other dissenting denominations also spawned similar teaching. Even among Anglican circles, the prolific local writer W. L. Sargant was to be found extolling the virtues of municipal self-government as exemplified in active town councils which exploited the growing public spirit of the urban middle class.

In Birmingham, secondly, that class had been politicised largely by concern over education. By the mid-1860s Liberals, like Chamberlain and his political colleagues Jesse Collings and George Dixon, had become convinced that the voluntary educational system could not meet educational needs despite the undoubted liberality of philanthropic supporters and notwithstanding growing state subventions. Some kind of public system was needed, made the more urgent by the local statistical evidence which revealed how small a proportion of children received continuous education. The political grouping which was eventually to bear fruit in Chamberlain's Birmingham of the 1870s had its first expression in the flurry of agitation on education from which emerged the National Education League in 1869 and the Central Nonconformist Committee in 1870, both of which were such a trial for Gladstone and his beleaguered education minister, W. E. Forster.

Moreover, it was Chamberlain perhaps more than others who made the crucial link between educational and municipal reform. 'How can we educate the children of the town', he asked, when they live in homes 'where anything like decency and honesty and morality is impossible'. He argued that it was farcical 'when the instruction of the school is contradicted by the experience of the home'. He drew the significant conclusion that it was folly 'to talk about the moral and intellectual elevation of the masses when the conditions of life are such as to render elevation impossible'. To remove such contradictions required municipal power and the means of acquiring and sustaining political control was the third element in forging Chamberlain's Birmingham.

Between 1867 and 1873 Birmingham Liberalism forged a new political device which was eventually to transform the organisation of British politics and which marked the emergence of a genuinely modern political system. Organisations and associations had already become a distinctive feature of Victorian urban politics and Birmingham built on this to apply, in a more systematic manner, the well-founded strategem that elections could be won by the efficient organisation of the vote.

The immediate stimulus was the 1867 Reform Act which massively increased the electorate and introduced the teasing challenge of the 'minority clause' (giving Birmingham a third parliamentary seat but restricting voters to the existing two votes). Until 1885 Birmingham, like all other large towns, was a single constituency and it was William Harris, the leader of the town's Liberals, who devised the system of ward organisation to deal with this unwieldy electorate. In the celebrated 'Vote As You Are Told' election of 1868 Birmingham returned all three Liberal candidates by a disciplined system of ward adoptions which restrained the natural inclination of everyone to vote for their hero, John Bright, and thus waste Liberal votes. There were some reservations about such a dictatorial system and one prominent northern politician asked Gladstone, 'How can any liberal advocate a procedure based upon the despotic obedience of thousands to a central head?'. Yet the caucus system had delivered the electoral goods and was soon to be both emulated in other towns and introduced into national politics via the National Liberal Federation.

Nor was the caucus restricted to parliamentary elections alone, for in 1870 Liberals faced the new challenge of electing a school board on a unique system of cumulative voting (where voters could allocate all their votes to one candidate or split them in any manner). Though Chamberlain was successful, the voting system deprived the Liberal non-sectarians of a majority and so a coalition of religionists controlled the first school board. This did not deter Chamberlain who rather cynically used the Council to block undesirable educational developments by starving the school boards of funds. When the Church and Conservative Party made a spirited effort to break this deadlock in the 1872 municipal elections, the Liberals evolved an even more rigorous organisation with standing ward committees, district delegate bodies and a powerful executive council directing all forms of political activity from the top of a clear pyramid of political authority. In 1873 this novel political machine, with its somewhat distasteful echoes of Tammany Hall, delivered a parallel triumph to Chamberlain. He became simultaneously chairman of the school board and Mayor, now designated by George Dixon, MP as 'the prime mover of everything good in Birmingham', and fulfilling John Morley's description (and the cartoonists' depiction) of Chamberlain as 'King of Birmingham'. Chamberlain was elected Mayor three years in succession and only ended his period of office when he entered Parliament in 1876.

His municipal regime witnessed a sustained assault upon Birmingham's social condition, transforming the authority from a laggardly sideshow into the cynosure of what came to be called 'the best governed city in the world'. At the heart of Chamberlain's civic renaissance lay the twinned municipalisation of gas and water. In neither case was Birmingham pioneering.

Half a century earlier the management of a publicly controlled gas supply was at the centre of Manchester politics and by the time Chamberlain made the purchase of the two gas companies his first municipal initiative he estimated that there were about fifty British towns which had a municipal gas supply. Similarly, the public ownership of water had polarised the politics of Leeds and Liverpool in the 1830s and 1840s, wreaking havoc with normal party divisions. Both towns along with some sixty others had assumed control of their water supply before Birmingham. What was novel about the two bills which received the royal assent on the same day in August 1875 was that this municipalisation was part of a coherent strategy which integrated the two into a practical and theoretical civic policy. Where other towns had approached these issues in a piecemeal and pragmatic fashion Birmingham's municipalisation policy was a lucidly thought out attack upon urban problems with clear objectives.

The gas question was approached from two angles. First it was asserted that monopoly services should go to the public rather than remain in private hands. To this theoretical proposition was added a powerful attraction: the profits from gas could subsidise municipal expenditure. This was peculiarly appropriate in Birmingham where public resistance to high rates was common and the town lacked any corporate property as a source of revenue. To carry off this ambitious purchase Chamberlain had to display a dazzling array of talents. He was masterly on the financial aspects and proved a canny negotiator for the two gas companies. He successfully carried town meetings, not least by offering to buy the companies himself and garner a large profit. He steered the bill through the pitfalls of the hearings in Parliament for private legislation and he allayed the fears of township institutions and neighbouring authorities. It was a great personal triumph and his anticipated £15,000 profit actually turned out to be £34,000 in the first year, a vital subvention to municipal funds at a time of increased civic expenditure.

The municipalisation of water was not seen in such stark financial terms, though the two questions were closely related in Chamberlain's plans. The monopoly argument applied equally to gas as to water. Indeed Chamberlain believed that both were public necessities: 'I do not think that our modern civilisation can any more afford to do without gas than it can afford to do without water'. Whereas gas was viewed as a source of municipal profit, water was seen as a means of improving public health. Belatedly

Birmingham had woken to the question of sanitation, as rapid urban growth had undermined the town's natural topographical advantages and Chamberlain placed the municipalisation of water firmly in the context of reducing the town's worrying and increasing death rate. In a sense the main arguments had already been fully rehearsed in the abortive attempt of Thomas Avery, the scales manufacturer, to secure civic control of the water supply in 1869.

Yet even in the short space of five years the water company's valuation had grown significantly. That same financial boom which created both the potential resources for municipal largesse and the public climate favourable to it, simultaneously augmented the assets which Chamberlain wished the town to acquire. So he had to persuade both the council and its ratepayers that whereas when municipal purchase had been first contemplated in 1851 a quarter of a million would have sufficed, now in 1875 over a million would be required, to add to the two million it had cost to buy out the gas companies. Again Chamberlain's political and financial skills carried the day, not least in fighting off a strong rearguard action by the water company against compulsory purchase. He kept firmly in the public mind that the costs were small compared to the profit to be found 'in the comfort of the town and the health of its inhabitants'.

Here, as the central plank in Chamberlain's civic programme, was the eponymous gas and water municipalisation of so-called 'gas and water socialism'. Yet to have real effect on the welfare of the citizens, to this had to be added further sanitary measures. One of the first successes of the Chamberlain group of municipal reformers was to hijack the public works committee in 1871, following the threat of legal action against the Corporation for pollution of waterways with sewage. The reformers secured the appointment of a sewage committee to oversee a new sanitary regime. This involved the removal of open privy middens and cesspools, improved sewage collection and disposal methods and the reduction in nuisances caused by the outflow of sewage into waterways.

During Chamberlain's mayoralty, his sanitary lieutenant, William Cook, organised a sanitary survey of the town using the services of the medical officer of health Birmingham had belatedly but compulsorily appointed. This survey led to the classification of houses according to condition, the worst of which would require weekly inspection. Public health inspectors were to be appointed on the basis of one per ten thousand people, instead of thirty thousand. The new inspection arrangements were resisted by William Brinsley, a grocer and representative of pre-Chamberlain shopkeeper mentality. Brinsley denounced the new regime as 'unconstitutional and un-English', and protested that through inspection the citizen would lose 'that which was has hitherto been held most dear to Englishmen – namely the sanctity of domestic life'.

The defeat of Brinsley confirmed that the new philosophy was firmly in control and a few months later Chamberlain unveiled his most ambitious project whose outcome is clearly visible a century later. He proposed a major slum clearance scheme for an area long acknowledged as insanitary. To the qualitative description of the squalor was added one vital statistic – its death rate was double that of Edgbaston, where Chamberlain and the town's élite lived. It was planned to drive a wide boulevard straight through the overcrowded and squalid alleys and lay out a central prestigious street appropriate to the town's size and commercial importance, thus neatly allying sanitary reform and civic pride. Though never quite as successful as Chamberlain hoped (the scheme actually lost money for the Council), the laying-out of Corporation Street, in the words of the town's first municipal historian:

. . . carried light, and air, and life throughout the district. Slums and rookeries, pestilential morally and physically, have disappeared as if by magic, and have given place to streets and buildings worthy of occupying the centre of a great town, while other portions of the improvement area have been so benefited and purified that an artisan population may now occupy them without injury to health or the sacrifice of self respect.

The Chamberlain years also saw new parks laid out, increased municipal and philanthropic support for art galleries, museums and libraries, and later, successful bids for Birmingham to have its own assizes, university and even bishopric. Chamberlain had promised, 'by God's help the town shall not know itself', and when he succeeded Dixon as MP in 1876 he proudly claimed that Birmingham would be 'parked, paved, assized, marketed, gas and watered and *improved* – all as a result of three years' active work'. The beneficial legacy of Chamberlain's hectic mayoralty was most pointedly seen in the fall in the death rate, dramatically so in the case of the improved areas of the town. No doubt epidemiologists would argue that mortality and morbidity were not so amenable to merely environmental factors; nevertheless it was a potent counterweight to increased municipal debt and public concern over rates when the economic climate changed in the 1880s.

Joseph Chamberlain was not the first to have a three-year term as mayor in a provincial capital. In mid-century the wealthy John Potter had served three years as mayor of Manchester. Local radicals much resented the civic pomp introduced by Potter whose term seemed to exemplify 'the tyranny of the bloated rich'. By contrast, Chamberlain's period of civic office personified the very essence of radicalism and launched a national radical career. To his progressive municipal policy was added a growing commitment to a broader radicalism spelled out in his slogan 'Free Schools, Free Church, Free Land and Free Labour'. This combination of local and national progressivism made him a kind of Ken Livingstone of his day. It certainly did not worry him that 'some timid minds' denounced his work as socialism, for this was simply 'neither more nor less than the practical admission of the duty of all classes in the community to co-operate for the common good'. In similar terms J. T. Bunce, who as editor of the *Birmingham Daily Post* strongly supported the Chamberlain programme, described the municipal ideal as 'a highly organised and well administered system of communal effort . . . ordered association for the common good'. It was its egalitarian democracy which Bunce so valued, since 'the benefits it confers are restricted to no class and are controlled by no interest, but . . . open to the whole community from richest to poorest'.

If few cities could boast a Chamberlain or so concentrated a period of civic improvement, the development of municipal services was a common feature of the mid- and late-Victorian urban scene. If we wish to identify that which was distinctively Victorian, we cannot ignore the creation of a municipal social infrastructure, as much a Victorian legacy to the twentieth century as the railways. Indeed, it took the length of Victoria's reign to transform corporations from narrow legal entities into institutions with broad social purposes. In erratic, non-ideological ways and with varying degrees of success, urban authorities gradually assumed a wide range of functions legitimised only by their ultimate responsibility for, in Chamberlain's words, 'the welfare, the health, the comfort and the lives' of Britain's town dwellers. By the end of the nineteenth century there was talk if not yet of a municipal welfare state, then of councils being responsible for the citizen 'from the cradle to the grave'. Such a phrase was used by a civic historian summarising the role of Liverpool Corporation, in terms which would have been applicable to many other towns:

> It offers to see that the child is brought safely into the world . . . It gives him playgrounds to amuse himself in and baths to swim in . . . It sees that the citizen's house is properly built and sometimes even builds it for him. It brings into his rooms an unfailing supply of pure water from the remote hills. It guards his food and tries to secure that it is not dangerously adulterated. It sweeps the streets for him and disposes of the refuse of his house. It carries him swiftly to and from his work . . . If he is sick it nurses him; if he is penniless it houses him; and when he dies, if none other will, it buries him.

For many, such municipal policies were anathema, to be resisted at all costs in defence of individual liberty and property rights alike. By the 1890s 'municipal socialism' was at the centre of a political battle for the ideological soul of the *fin de siècle*. Yet it was always easy to contain municipal intervention within an essentially pragmatic framework which did not threaten the values of *laissez-faire*. To turn on a municipal gas or water tap, to walk in a municipal park or to ride in a municipal tram hardly represented a conversion to socialism. Moreover what towns like Birmingham were doing was more aptly described as municipal capitalism rather than municipal socialism, for many of such activities were, in the words of a contemporary political scientist, 'but the application to changed conditions of the venerable principles of the individualists'. That to preserve an individualist cocoon around municipal collectivism also involved a high degree of self deception, was never better illustrated than in Sidney Webb's famous caricature of the individualist town councillor who would:

> . . . walk along the municipal pavement, lit by municipal gas and cleansed by municipal brooms with municipal water, and seeing by the municipal clock in the municipal market that he is too early to meet his children coming from the municipal school, hard by the county lunatic asylum and municipal hospital, will use the national telegraph system to tell them not to walk through the municipal park, but to come by the municipal tramway to meet him in the municipal reading-room by the municipal art gallery, museum and library where he intends to consult some of the national publications in order to prepare his next speech in the municipal town hall in favour of nationalisation of canals and the increase of Government control over the railway system. 'Socialism, Sir,' he will say, 'don't waste the time of a practical man by your fantastic absurdities. Self-help, Sir, individual self-help, that's what made our city what it is'.

Historians, like contemporaries, have to grapple with a value system in which the collectivism of the municipal ideal coexisted with the individualism of self-help. Though some today might wish it were otherwise, Victorian *mentalités* were a complex mixture of values in the past which are not easily recreated.

For Further Reading:

J. T. Bunce, *History of the Corporation of Birmingham*, I (1878), II (1885); A. Briggs, *History of Birmingham*, II (Oxford University Press, 1952) and *Victorian Cities* (Odhams, 1963); E. P. Hennock, *Fit and Proper Persons* (Edward Arnold, 1973); J. L. Garvin, *The Life of Joseph Chamberlain*, I (Macmillan, 1932); D. Judd, *Radical Joe* (Hamish Hamilton, 1977); R. Jay, *Joseph Chamberlain* (Oxford University Press, 1981); C. W. Boyd (ed.), *Mr Chamberlain's Speeches*, I (London, 1914).

14

Herbert Spencer and 'Inevitable' Progress

Robert M. Young

WHEN WE THINK OF THE VICTORIANS we think of energy, optimism and a boundless certainty that the world had improved, is improving and will improve still further. Such a view may be a caricature and seem cruelly misplaced from the cynical standpoint of the late twentieth century – but it has its basis in the dynamics of new thought and activity in the physical, biological and human sciences in the Victorian period. Apart from its impact on the theological and religious debates of the mid-Victorian church, Charles Darwin's theories of evolution based on his travels and research, codified in his 1859 best-seller *On the Origins of Species*, seemed to reflect a vision of the world as thrusting and imposing which was suited to the entrepreneurial dynamics of Victorian society in the same way that the divine clockmaker view of God derived from Newtonian physics had appealed to the culture of the Enlightenment.

It was not Darwin, however, but Herbert Spencer (1820–1903), who was the great populariser and synthesiser of such ideas through his popular journalism, and prolific output of books. The beauty of technological change, competition and survival of the fittest were Spencer's watchwords and, as Robert Young reminds us here, the darker developments of the later Victorian world are one of the reasons why this reputation and that of the 'glad, confident morning' went into eclipse.

It is hard to recapture the power of Herbert Spencer's ideas and easy to mock him. At the height of his influence more than a million volumes of his writings were in print and there were editions in all the major, and many minor, languages. He was offered – and declined – honours all over the world. One of America's leading industrialists, the Scottish emigré Andrew Carnegie, began his frequent letters to Spencer, 'Dear Master Teacher'.

Yet when I began doing historical research in the early 1960s, and was beginning my own library of primary sources, the books which were easiest to find and to obtain within my self-imposed limit of fifteen shillings, were those self-same volumes of his great work, *The Synthetic Philosophy*. The secondhand shops were full of the various editions of these and his other writings.

Spencer's best biographer, J. D. Y. Peel, explains the decline in Spencer's reputation:

Posterity is cruellest to those who sum up for their contemporaries in an all-embracing synthesis the accumulated knowledge of their age. This is what Spencer did for the Victorians.

More than that, he provided a guarantee in the laws of nature of what they most fervently needed to believe would be the result of the frantic and bewildering, disruptive and distressing, process of urbanisation and industrialisation: progress. It was clear in his first book, *Social Statics: or, The Conditions Essential to Human Happiness Specified and the First of Them Developed* (1851):

Progress, therefore, is not an accident, but a necessity. Instead of civilisation being artificial, it is part of nature; all of a piece with the development of the embryo or the unfolding of a flower. The modifications mankind have undergone, and are still undergoing, result from a law underlying the whole organic creation; and provided the human race continues, and the constitution of things remains the same, those modifications must end in completeness. As surely as the tree becomes bulky when it stands alone, and slender if one of a group; [there follow many biological analogies] . . . so surely must things be called evil and immoral disappear; so surely must man become perfect.

This book was written as an attack on Benthamite Utilitarianism at a time when there were grave doubts that the ethical and social principle of 'the greatest good for the greatest number' could be engineered. Better to guarantee it, but to do so required restraint from state regulation and interference. His first principle was that 'Every man has freedom to do all that he wills, provided that he infringes not the equal freedom of other men'. People would eventually come to do naturally what is best, even though a lengthy struggle would be necessary. Spencer therefore opposed such things as Poor Laws, state-supported education, sanitary supervision, protection of the ignorant from medical quacks, tariffs, state banking, and a government postal system.

A year after *Social Statics* he embarked on a series of essays which based progress securely on the most important scientific idea of the period: evolution. The ideological context of all this was the perennial problem of reconciling order with change. When the old pastoral order celebrated by the natural theologians began to give way, it could no longer be confidently maintained that 'All is for the best in the best of all possible worlds', and that God keeps it that way. The justification of the ways of God to man had for centuries been expressed in natural theology – the reconciliation of God's word – the Scripture – with his works – nature. But as the eighteenth century turned into the nineteenth, the natural theology of pastoralism was under threat from the need for a theology that could make order and change reconcilable.

And, of course, change is really a species of order if it is progress, that is, change for the better.

The writings of Thomas Malthus and the debate around his *Essay on the Principle of Population* (1798) addressed just this issue. Apparent chaos – hunger, war, famine – could be avoided to a considerable degree by moral restraint. Malthus saw history as a kind of learning and even invoked the principle that 'Necessity has with great truth been called the mother of invention'.

William Paley's *Natural Theology* (1802), Malthus' *Essay* and the writings of the Utilitarians competed with, and partially complemented, one another as ways of rationalising these issues. Indeed, Paley saw himself as a Utilitarian and also believed that he could accommodate Malthus' doctrine within a higher generalisation of God's ultimate benign purpose: the Good Gardener needed to prune the products of His 'superfecundity'.

But it was Spencer, writing in the decades after 1850, who finally placed change on a secure and secular metaphysical foundation. In the extent of his generalisations and the range of his use of illustrative materials he can be said to be Britain's most prolific and bold thinker – the nearest the nation has had to a domestic Hegel. Lest this conception seem far-fetched, I should add that the framework of ideas for which Spencer was the main systematiser, populariser and historical source, was also the main alternative to the dialectical mode which Hegel gave to phenomenology and Marxism. What Spencer gave was the organic analogy and functionalist thinking based on the biological concepts of structure, function, organism and adaptation as the ideas in psychology, sociology, anthropology and political theory. He was the most influencial single source for the main tradition in Anglo-Saxon thinking devoted to the naturalisation of value systems in the physical, biological and human sciences.

How did he become such a man – often called *the* man – of his age? He was born in 1820 in Derby, the eldest of nine children and the only one to survive infancy. His father was a Methodist who inclined towards Quakerism and Deism while his mother was an orthodox Wesleyan. It was not a happy marriage, and Spencer once remarked that this may have contributed to his remaining a bachelor. His education was in one sense neglected while in another sense he was allowed to range widely and to explore, though not in a formal setting. At thirteen he was sent to study with an uncle in Bristol for three years.

One source of Spencer's polymathy and optimism was that at

sixteen he went to work as a civil engineer on the railways and continued in this vocation for a decade. He travelled all over the Midlands and had a hand in many aspects of the last great achievements of the Industrial Revolution.

In the midst of this work he wrote as a journalist and supported complete suffrage. In 1848 he obtained a post as sub-editor of *The Economist*. Then, as now, this was the key financial weekly and represented the wealthy middle class. It tended to be Unitarian in religion, *laissez-faire* in economics and strong on self-help. Across the street was the office of John Chapman whose assistant was Marian Evans (later 'George Eliot'). He soon became an intimate friend (there was talk of marriage) and remained so until her death. His circle included her lover, George Henry Lewes, T. H. Huxley, John Tyndall, and many other leading intellectual and scientific figures of London. He was soon contributing to some of the radical periodicals, *The Leader*, *The Fortnightly*, *The Westminster Review*. He left the *Economist* in 1853 and devoted himself full-time to writing and survived on various legacies, subscriptions to his books and, later on, an investment of £7,000 made on his behalf by his admirers. Spencer joined the influential scientific group, the X Club (where he was called 'Xhaustive Spencer') in 1864 and the Athenaeum in 1868.

The point of all this is that we have in Spencer a man ideally placed to capture the spirit of the age. Huxley saw Spencer's aim as to show 'the mutual connection and interdependence of all forms of cognition'. Indeed, the major project he conceived in 1858, embarked on two years later and completed on 1896, comprised ten volumes, beginning with *First Principles*, moved on to a two-volume revision of his *Principles of Psychology*, to the *Principles of Sociology* and the *Principles of Ethics*, along with various new editions, popular and descriptive works and collections of essays. A volume of four of his essays on *Education* continued to be reprinted well into our own time. They criticised rote learning and classics and advocated exploration and science.

Two facts made him all the more an antenna for the ideas in the air. The first was that he never was much of a reader – more of a magpie. All he heard was grist for his mill, grinding out evermore comprehensive generalisations. Even the most loyal of his admirers pointed out that he was given to grandiosity, and Huxley said that Spencer's idea of a tragedy was a deduction slain by a fact.

The second characteristic that led to his writing *in extenso* was that like so many of his contemporaries, he suffered gravely from debilitating neurotic symptoms. He had a breakdown from over-work while writing *The Principles of Psychology* in 1855 and collapses recurred. He was left with a strange sensation in the head which he called 'the mischief', along with palpitations and insomnia. Among the consequent eccentricities was the use of earplugs which he inserted to avoid over-excitement. It was noted that these times included occasions when he began to lose out in an argument. He also had problems in sustained working and eventually reached the stage where he would row down the Serpentine or play racquets and break off to dictate to his amanuensis for twenty minutes or so until 'the mischief' returned. He lived in various boarding houses, and in one case his housekeepers – 'Two' – told all in *Home Life with Herbert Spencer*.

His last years were spent frantically trying to shore up his edifice and defend it against misinterpretations. He died in 1903 having written an extensive autobiography. He is buried at Highgate near George Eliot, George Henry Lewes and Karl Marx.

The American pragmatist philosopher, William James, was one of his admirers but said of him that never were greatness and pettiness more oddly mixed. Spencer was monotonous, petty, small-minded, hypochondriacal and self-pitying. He was also a pure intellectual and devoted his entire adult life to the writing of his great work.

The leading idea of his huge theoretical edifice is simply put: take *laissez-faire* quite literally; don't interfere. The law of evolution will bring about the progressive adjustment of internal relations to external relations unless we muck it up. The scientific principle of the uniformity of nature should be applied to human nature and society. The final formula which underpins the whole system and which he continued to modify until the last revision of his work is as follows:

Evolution is an integration of matter and concomitant dissipation of motion; during which the matter passes from a relatively indefinite, incoherent homogeneity to a relatively definite, coherent heterogeneity; and during which the contained motion undergoes a parallel transformation.

Semi-mystical slogans such as 'homogeneity to heterogeneity' and 'the physiological division of labour' lent an *ersatz* biological aura to his psychological and social doctrines.

To unpack all this and to put it starkly, Spencer claimed that there was no need for politics. Indeed, his devoted American disciple, E. L. Youmans, was once recalled by Henry George to have said the following about the state of American society in response to the question, 'What do you propose to do about it?': Youmans replied 'with something like a sigh':

Nothing! You and I can do nothing at all. It is all a matter of evolution. We can only wait for evolution. Perhaps in four or five thousand years evolution may have carried man beyond this state of affairs. But we can do nothing.

This is, of course, the *reductio ad absurdum* of naturalistic ethics. However, it is not difficult to imagine its attractiveness in the period of primitive accumulation of capital in America. His ideas (though much distorted and exaggerated) were used as the basis for the 'Social Darwinism' of the Robber Barons, and they dominated American universities between 1860 and 1890. When Spencer visited the United States in 1882 he was treated like royalty. The behaviour of John D. Rockefeller in creating the Standard Oil Trust, along with other attempts at monopoly, were often defended by invoking Spencer's theories. Such rapacious behaviour was claimed to lead to progress through struggle, and the elimination of the weak, along with the hierarchical division of labour, was rationalised. Competition, it was argued, gave us the 'American Beauty' rose.

Spencer was the veritable author of the phrase 'survival of the fittest'. He can also be said to have condoned starvation of the idle and the shouldering aside of the weak by the strong. However, his own writings on the theory of population and on 'Progress: Its Law and Cause' (1857), along with his systematic writings, were all predicated on optimism and were in no way designed to condone cruelty. Indeed, on one reading, what he defended was individual competition and not corporate or state rapaciousness. One of his main bugbears was 'collectivism'. He argued for old-fashioned 'true' liberalism and defended a negative concept of liberty as the absence of restraint. The idea was to remove impediments to 'natural' progress. This also led him to oppose collective bargaining and trade unions.

Underlying Spencer's belief that evolution was inherently progressive was the theory of inheritance of acquired characteristics. This meant, quite literally, that life, humanity and society learned from their mistakes and the inheritance of 'functionally produced modifications' was for the best. In the human realm individuals would see the reason to move from egotism to altruism and societies from militarism to industrialism. Although the inheritance of acquired characteristics is not now thought to be the mechanism of evolution it was a perfectly respectable theory in Spencer's own time.

It should also not be thought that Spencer was uniquely over the top in his optimism while more sober thinkers, for example, Darwin, saw no directionality in evolution. Here is the last sentence from the chapter on instinct in *On the Origin of Species*:

Finally, it may not be a logical deduction, but to my imagination it is far more satisfactory to look at such instincts . . . not as specially endowed or created instincts, but as small consequences of one general law, leading to the advancement of all organic beings — namely, multiply, vary, but the strongest live and the weakest die.

Indeed, Darwin's book ends:

Thus from the war of nature, from famine and death, the most exalted object which we are capable of conceding, namely the production of higher animals, directly follows. There is grandeur in this view of life, with its several powers, having been originally breathed into a few forms or into one; and that, while this planet has gone cycling on according to the fixed laws of gravity, from so simple a beginning to endless forms most beautiful and most wonderful have been, and are being, evolved.

Darwin was cautious about what he said about man. There was only one sentence: 'Light will be thrown on the origin of man and his history'. In the sixth edition, that sentence reads:

In the future I see open fields for far more important researches. Psychology will be securely based on a foundation already well laid by Mr Herbert Spencer, that of the necessary requirement of each mental power and capacity by gradation.

It can even be said that Spencer put in caveats about evolution being counterbalanced by 'dissolution', but the second note was seldom heard. Yet the times betrayed him, and towards the end of his life he lost his optimism. More and more collectivism was introduced in the name of creating space for the very individual initiatives which the policy of *laissez-faire* had been designed to enable. This led eventually to the Fabian Society and the modern Labour Party.

Spencer was horrified when 'Social Darwinism', of which he was really the main founder, was used to justify policies to which he was deeply opposed. When he first put forward his ideas in the 1850s the acme of civilisation could be glimpsed. In the early 1860s and subsequently his hopes were dashed. One need only think of the Crimean War (1854–6), the American Civil War (1861–5), the Great Depression (1876–96), and the Boer War (1899–1902). He was as opposed to these as he had been to the Jamaican atrocities of Governor Eyre during the controversy in 1865–7. The high tide of industrialism had led to industrial obsolescence and the perceived need for colonial and imperial expansion. It was a terrible irony that Social Darwinism was the rationalisation for the most shocking excesses in this era.

People often outlive the period of which their ideas were a perfect expression. Spencer was the most influential writer of this times on general philosophy and man's place in nature. When he died he was the most famous and most popular philosopher of his age and was seen by many as a 'second Newton'. His ideas were esteemed in Russia, China, Mexico and Brazil, and in Japan his influence was greater than any other foreign thinker.

His entry in *The Dictionary of National Biography* (1912) says:

Spencer's place in the history of thought must be ranked high. His influence in the latter half of the nineteenth century was immense: indeed it has so woven itself into our modern methods of thinking that its driving revolutionary energy is nearly spent, there is little likelihood of its being hereafter renewed. It was the best synthesis of the knowledge of his times.

By the 1930s the American functionalist sociologist, Talcott Parsons, was quoting an historian's ironic query, 'Who now reads Herbert Spencer? It is difficult for us to realise how great a stir he made in the world.'

Once again, however, Peel provides an answer:

At a time of unprecedented, seemingly uncontrolled and terrifying change, Spencer reassured the bewildered by interpreting the transition that man experienced and setting it within a larger arc of change covering all nature.

His influence remains in the loose clichés still used around evolution and progress. It is also reflected more precisely and pervasively in the social and psychological theories called 'functionalist'. These, as I said above, draw explicitly on biological analogies – structure, function, adaptation, organism – and continued to flower until the 1960s in the work of the most eminent anthropologists, Bronislaw Malinowski and A. R. Radcliffe Brown in Britain, the functionalist and behaviourist psychologists William

James, John Dewey and J. B. Watson, and Parsonian functionalist sociologists in America. The dominance of this way of thinking has recently been challenged by phenomenological and Marxist ideas, but there has been a powerful revival of biologism in socio-biology and behavioural genetics.

There has also been a resurgence of *laissez-faire* ideas, which are powerfully reminiscent of the starkest version of Spencer's thinking, in the social and economic philosophies of Reaganism and Thatcherism. The argument is the same: that one should de-emphasise suffering and distress in the name of the grander scheme, and social and class antagonisms should be set aside in the name of the larger family or social organism, while renewed industrialisation will produce sufficient prosperity for all. This is the new Anglo-American version of the slogan which captured the spirit of the age which Spencer codified and which still adorns the flag of Brazil – 'Order and Progress'. It has inspired scientific and evolutionary philosophers around the globe, and its current form draws on versions of the Spencerian organic analogy in computing and in theories that treat all domains as 'systems', open to computer modelling and mathematical solutions. Conflicts, it is thought, can be calculated away in a higher ordering of society, and intractable contradictions – of class, of gender, and power relations between peoples – need not arise. Spencer's vision is now thoroughly secularised but is not less a religion of progress for all that.

For Further Reading:

Robert C. Bannister, *Social Darwinism: Science and Myth in Anglo-American Social Thought* (Temple, 1979); Walter Bagehot, *Physics and Politics: or Thoughts on the Application of the Principles of 'Natural Selection' and 'Inheritance' to Political Society* (King, 1869); James G. Kennedy, *Herbert Spencer* (Twayne, 1978); J. D. Y. Peel, *Herbert Spencer: The Evolution of a Sociologist* (Heinemann, 1971); John Watson, *Comte, Mill and Spencer: An Outline of Philosophy* (Maclehose, 1895); Robert M. Young, *Mind, Brain and Adaptations in the Nineteenth Century* (Oxford, 1970) and *Darwin's Metaphor: Nature's Place in Victorian Culture* (Cambridge, 1985).

15

Stewart Headlam and the Christian Socialists

Edward Norman

*Overleaf: Scripture reading in a night refuge; from Doré's 'London', 1872.
(HT Archives)*

RELIGION NOT ONLY DOMINATED the minds of Victorian laymen much more than many historians have previously appreciated – but the implications and obligations of being a 'Christian gentleman' could be far-reaching in their social and political impact as well. Overlapping in chronology (and sometimes in personnel) with the twin religious revivals of Evangelicalism and the High Church 'Oxford Movement' was a movement of like-minded 'Christian Socialists' – critical of the economic orthodoxies of their day which had, as they saw it, a pitiless effect on the working class. This did not make them champions of state intervention or proto-Marxists – but it did establish a critical moral agenda for *laissez-faire* capitalism that in time, it could be argued, ripened into the 'anti-Victorian values' of the end of the nineteenth century.

Edward Norman examines the career of one of the most colourful of this Christian Socialist group, Stewart Headlam (1847–1924), who in a varied career as Church of England priest, friend of the outcast (including Oscar Wilde), Fabian activist and London County Councillor stirred up a 'divine discontent' that far outpaced the more temperate aims of the movement's early leaders.

Victorian Christian Socialism hardly constituted a 'movement' or even a 'school' of thinking. Its leaders were too idiosyncratic, too individualistic, and far too much given to internal dissension for that. The development of social criticism, furthermore, often indicated an expression of only one dimension of their general attitudes: others continued to reflect the unreconstructed assumptions of the old world of their social class and professional status. They were drawn from established sections of society, and were, until quite late in the nineteenth century, mostly Anglicans and academics.

What they shared was a rejection of the effects of competitive economics, as they understood them, on the lives of ordinary working people. They were critics of classical Political Economy. That did not, in itself, particularly distinguish them from the Tory Paternalist churchmen and the backwoods squires who were also, in the mid-century, declaiming against 'the dismal science' as Carlyle so memorably called it. The Christian Socialists, furthermore, tended to produce moral and educative solutions to the encompassing social ills – not political or structural ones. They were in agreement with most of their contemporaries in espousing limited doctrines about the competence of the state to interfere in social and economic relationships and were therefore enemies, in general, of collectivism.

That did not necessarily diminish the authenticity of their 'socialism', since socialist ideas in the most formative decades of Christian Socialism, the 1840s and 1850s, were extremely incoherent and not characteristically biased towards collectivist solutions either. But the greatest of the Christian Socialist thinkers, Frederick Denison Maurice – to whose ideals all others in the Christian Socialist tradition throughout the century in some sense acknowledged a debt — was emphatically opposed to political action to achieve the social reforms he so earnestly desired. Politics, he supposed, were 'sectarian'; they obscured the whole of social truth by exclusivity about a mere part of it.

Maurice was influenced by Coleridge and Idealist thought: he believed that the 'universal and spiritual Kingdom' of Christ, the real brotherhood of all men, was already in actual existence. The working men were brutalised by the terms and conditions of their labour and so were incapable of recognising either the Kingdom or their place in it. What was needed was not mere political change, which he saw as a dangerous tinkering with order, but mass education. Since, like so many in his day, he still regarded education as the due preserve of religion, this implied a renewed role for the church.

When the Christian Socialists published their famous placard *Workmen of England!* (actually drawn up by Charles Kingsley), at the time of the great Chartist demonstration in 1848, it stated this conviction rather baldly: the working men were told that they were not yet fit for political participation, and that charters and Acts of Parliament would not help them to be free. What they needed was to be educated. As a first and important step, the Christian Socialists began to set up co-operative workshops. They were, from their point of view, the ideal way forwards. Associationism was non-political; through self-help and individual responsibility for labour it was morally elevating, and it had the potential to permeate other working relationships. In 1854 Maurice proceeded to found the Working Men's College in London, as a spearhead for the adult education of the working class.

There were some beneficial, but in the end rather slight consequences of these initiatives. They acquainted a number of men from the skilled élite of the working classes with the fact that at least a few representatives of established religion were sympathetic to their needs; they stimulated the general movement for

adult education; they formed a link between the co-operative experiments and evolving trades unionism largely through the
efforts of three of the Christian Socialist leaders, Edward Neale,
Thomas Hughes, and John Ludlow. But the contribution of
Christian Socialism to the development of labour politics was
not great.

Why then were the Christian Socialists important? The answer
lies in the elevated view of humanity which Maurice and his followers promoted, and in its effects in their social criticism.
Maurice believed that Christ was in all men. This was the very
heart of his social concern. He even came to regard the term
'Christian' as confining, since it seemed to separate mankind into
categories. As a result of examining social misery through a screen
of interpretation provided not by transient modes of social thinking but by a theological statement about some human
fundamentals, the Christian Socialists were able to enunciate
opinions of enduring value. They were able, as only a few men
in any age are able to do, to stand outside the common assumptions of their times and to declare some permanent truths. In this
sense they were authentic prophets, and are not to be judged
worthwhile, as some have done, because they said things which
later generations found sympathetic or compatible with their own
social attitudes, but are to be judged as valuable for discerning
ultimate meanings and lasting moral lessons in the conditions of
their own day.

They recognised dignity and potential in those whom traditional society had tended to relegate to the permanent periphery; to
see the injustices of a system that resulted in blighted lives and
actual disease and premature death. That they also retained
strong attachments to many of the assumptions of their own class
and culture should neither surprise nor shock. So did other early
prophets of social emancipation. The Christian Socialists were
sceptical (and sometimes even hostile) to the practices of
democracy, they tended to assume the virtues of social deference
and the landed basis of society, and – perhaps the feature which
most distanced them from a realistic appraisal of social fact – they
failed to appreciate the existence of a class conflict. Yet they saw
that society was materially ready for the advance of the working
people, and correctly blamed prevailing economic ideas and practices for inhibiting the educational and moral development of the
masses.

The first Christian Socialists came together at the end of the

1840s – 'the Hungry Forties' – in order to promote the co-operative ideal, and to show the working men that although they sympathised with the social injustices that precipitated Chartism the points of the Charter were not in themselves the way of social salvation. Under the influence of Maurice they were very unpolitical. In the second generation of Christian Socialists, however, there were men who, whilst still imbued with Maurice's religious humanism, were anxious to associate more immediately with progressive developments in secular politics. Stewart Headlam was the greatest of these.

He has not had, it is true, a particularly good press. While Maurice and Kingsley, and others of the Christian Socialist Leadership, were unpopular for a time in the church, because of their social radicalism and sometimes for their supposed doctrinal heterodoxy, they were eventually rehabilitated and received some sort of recognition (Maurice got a Cambridge chair and Kingsley received two prestigious canonries and a royal chaplaincy). Headlam was always out in the cold. There were features of his personality that help to explain this. He was reckless and mischievous, and lacked the deference to authority which those in authority always expect; he was markedly insensitive to those whose opinions were unlike his own. He seemed eccentric to his contemporaries: a priest who applauded atheists and secularists for their authentic 'religious' insights, and who befriended the raffish world of artists, interior decorators, and ballet-dancers and actors. He was certainly guilty of poor judgement in his triumphalist and paradoxical exaltation of those whom the society of his day rejected – but this was not because he was wrong to love those despised by conventional society, but because of his inability to convey his feeling sympathetically to the leaders of religious opinion.

His love of those whom convention loathed was in fact Christlike, and his sense of the damage done to the interior lives of men by their wrong social priorities and their unwillingness to elevate collective needs above individual ones was expressed, if not with great originality, at least with great clarity. He saw the fragility of accepted social orthodoxies – how men were forever, and especially in his own day, mistaking the transient for the permanent in human orderings of society. Though not possessed of a mind of great genius his human sympathies were sometimes released in a series of social diagnoses whose penetrating qualities surely had something of genius about them. In evaluating Headlam, therefore, it is helpful to set his eccentricity and perversity into one dimension of his being, and to recognise his social insights as belonging to another. Few men have paid so dearly for their convictions. Headlam valued his own priesthood above all things, yet in 1878, while still a curate in Bethnal Green, he had his licence to preach revoked by the Bishop of London and was never thereafter, until his death in 1924, given any kind of post in the church. His offence had been to give a public lecture in which he encouraged young people to go to the theatre and to the ballet in order to cultivate an understanding of theatrical art. His brief marriage also ended in failure and separation: that, too, it later transpired, had told against him.

The possession of private means enabled Headlam to survive. He was the son of a prosperous Liverpool underwriter, and was sent to Eton. That was in 1860, and the experience of Eton endured throughout his life. Headlam regarded the College as a 'liberating influence', partly because he supposed it to be internally free of social class distinctions (his fag was the son of the Archbishop of Canterbury), and partly because he thought its official Anglicanism was in practice an essay in secularism. He went on to Cambridge, and to a low third-class degree in Classics. There, however, he attended Maurice's lectures and was directly inspired to seek a vocation in the church. Ordination followed in 1872, and then a curacy in Drury Lane. That was where he made the acquaintance of the theatrical world which proved so fatal to his relations with ecclesiastical authority. In 1873 he moved to a second London curacy, in Bethnal Green, where he fell under the influence of Septimus Hansard, the Christian Socialist incumbent.

At Bethnal Green, Headlam's social beliefs and political opinions were formed and they did not greatly change through the rest of his life. What he did was to combine Maurice's view of man, emancipated from the thrall of Evangelical notions of inherent depravity, with a close and authentic experience of working-class conditions. Men and their needs now became the centre of his understanding of Christianity. 'The Church exists to bear witness to men that they are brothers', he declared in 1875, 'that God is now and for ever, here and everywhere, the Father of all men.' Though Headlam practised ritual and called the Anglican eucharistic rite 'the Mass' he was not really an Anglo-Catholic. His theology was far too Broad Church for that – he accepted most of the liberal Biblical criticism of the day – and his attitude to ecclesiastical authority notably lacked the hierarchical deference of the Oxford reformers. He fully supported evolutionary teachings about the origins and nature of human life.

During the first years of his ministry he joined a number of other young and radical priests in a society which met regularly in the vestry of St Martin-in-the-Fields. The exchange of views with men like George Sarson, John Elliotson Symes, and Thomas Hancock confirmed Headlam's social progressivism and gave him the confidence of knowing that his was not an isolated voice in a largely hostile church. The discussions among these young friends assisted Headlam's assembly of a grid of social interpretation: he began to give a wider shape and system of interpretation to the first-hand knowledge of working-class society he was receiving through actual residence among the poor in Bethnal Green.

The result of this was the Guild of St Matthew, whose history and ideas were inseparable from the attitudes and beliefs of Headlam, Warden of the Guild throughout the thirty years of its existence. The element of 'Sacramental Socialism', so crucial to Headlam's political vision, was clearly evident at the very foundation of the Guild. It was begun by some girls in the Bethnal Green parish who were trying to secure regular attendances at early-morning services. That was in 1877. When Headlam was dismissed from his curacy at St Matthew's the following year the Guild became his main preoccupation, and he soon converted it into a largely political body with a national basis. Local branches were organised by sympathetic High Church clergy. Early in the 1890s the Guild attained its highest level of membership, with about 400 – a quarter of them priests. It was intended to be, and was, a propagandist body, to influence church opinion and to give its members an experience of active work for social change. George Bernard Shaw learned public speaking by attending its debates. Despite the atmosphere of mild eccentricity that hedged some of its proceedings the Guild did in fact exercise an influence out of all proportion to its size.

It had three points. First, it existed to show the secularists that Christianity was not an enemy, since both sought ethicist and humanist goals for society. Secondly, it encouraged sacramental worship. Thirdly, it was 'to promote the study of social and political questions in the light of the Incarnation'. With Headlam's adhesion to Henry George's land reform programme, in 1883, the Guild added – not uncontroversially – some agrarian priorities as well. At first mainly taken up with the Secularists, the Guild became more and more political. The change confirmed Headlam's position as the first serious Socialist, in the modern sense, in the Victorian tradition of 'Christian Socialism'. Unlike Maurice and his circle, Headlam really did intend to work for structural changes in society, and the Guild, whatever its shortcomings, was the first Christian body in England to achieve some real insight into the dynamics of Socialism.

The Guild, as ideologically conscious societies usually are, was accordingly filled with dissensions and doctrinal splits over political theory and practice. Headlam's own inability to consult adequately with others, and his tendency to regard the Guild as the automatic agent of his own opinions, did not help internal accord either. When he went on early in the 1880s to support Disestablishment, secular education, and agrarian reform, different sections were offended by turns. In 1909 Headlam himself dissolved the Guild. 'The only thing we do,' he observed sadly, 'is to talk about a definition of Socialism.' But that, in itself, had provided a forum for the education of religious opinion much greater than Headlam himself ever recognised.

Headlam's own Socialism was militantly secular. He took Maurice's doctrine about the immanence of the divine in the material world, which was primarily Maurice's Idealist way of reconciling men to their circumstance, and gave it a political meaning. Secularism, Sacramentalism, and Socialism were, for Headlam, overlapping expressions of God's historical destiny for mankind. They conveyed the essential truth, as he saw it, that the material nature of things disclosed the divine directly; of the church he concluded 'the Incarnation compels us to regard it as a great co-operative organised institution for human welfare'. The Secularists had 'absorbed some of the best Christian truths which the Churches have been ignoring.' The history of the church showed it to have been, time and time again, 'opposed to progress', and the object of the Guild of St Matthew, he told the members in 1883, was to 'restore' Jesus as he really was, a man of the people. Jesus was 'the social and political *Emancipator*, the greatest of all secular workers, the founder of the great Socialistic society for the promotion of righteousness, the preacher of a Revolution.'

Headlam also insisted that Jesus had said very little about the after-life, but a great deal about the present one – in terms of justice and righteous dealings between men that the conventionally religious always ignored. The sayings of Jesus, he persisted, 'tell of a Kingdom of Heaven to be set up upon earth, of a righteous Communistic Society.' In 1884, at a chance meeting in the Athenaeum, the Bishop of Newcastle told him: 'Why, you talk as if you believed that Christ's Kingdom were coming here on earth!' Headlam replied, 'What else should I believe? Of course I do.'

Yet Headlam's understanding of Socialism was also indebted to that strain of nineteenth-century English radicalism – found also in Tory parsons and urban literateurs – that represented an aesthetic reaction to industrialism. In his case, however, it surfaced not in rural romanticism or a hankering after an idealised version of traditional social relationships, but in the idea of a popular culture based upon art. Hence the Church and Stage Guild of 1879, which attempted to educate religious opinion out of its horror of the performing arts. Jesus, Headlam assured a scandalised ecclesiastical hierarchy, was 'with us now in the Theatre as well as in the Church'. And hence, also, Headlam's Anti-Puritan League which resulted in his public support for Oscar Wilde at the time of the trial in 1895. Headlam was drawn to Wilde through a Christian sense that, as a representative of Christ, he had a duty to befriend outcasts. Others saw things differently, and one of those who resigned from the Guild of St Matthew in horror said he was all for building up the new Jerusalem, but not for 'wading through Gomorrah first'. There can be little doubt that Headlam's work on behalf of the socially and morally despised prejudiced many against his simultaneous espousal of Socialism.

Among the Victorian Christian Socialists, Headlam was the one who most realised the need for political action to secure social change. He became a champion, furthermore, of collectivist solutions, and despite some reservations about the threats to individual liberty he advanced to an expansive role for the state in social regulation. He also supported collective bargaining and trade union rights, a redistribution of wealth by state action, and a full programme of educational and welfare provision by government. Sometimes, it is true, he left the actual means by which the state was to promote these benefits unclear. But he was emphatic, as he explained in his Fabian Tract of 1892, that it was the duty of all good men 'to seize the State and to use it for the well-being of the masses instead of the classes'. He was, above all, impatient of the empty declamations of good intention made by philanthropic and charitable bodies in his day: change had to be concrete; an actual shift of power was needed, 'some tremendous social reorganisation.'

Just as education had become the priority for Maurice, so it did for Headlam – but for quite different reasons. The earlier Christian Socialists, and some later ones, wanted to educate the masses in order to make them capable of entering into social and public institutions which were to remain more or less the same. Headlam, on the other hand, linked popular education directly with social and political transformation. The purpose of education, he said very frequently, was to stir up what he called 'divine discontent' with the existing social order. Even the liturgy of the church was to be regarded as an education in political change: the *Magnificat* was a statement of Socialism, in which the humble were exalted and the rich were sent empty away.

In 1882 Headlam was elected to the London School Board, as representative for Hackney, and entered into the work of educational administration and reform that was to take up the rest of his life. He, Annie Besant, and A. W. Jephson, were the Fabian presence on the Board, and they contended for secular education – the only way, in Headlam's judgement, that education could be truly just in a society of increasingly divided denominational allegiance. When the Board was wound up in 1903 and its work was taken over by the Education Committee of the London County Council, Headlam was for a short while without a voice; but in 1907 he was elected to the London County Council and resumed his work for another seventeen years.

On public platforms Headlam called himself a 'Christian Socialist', and it is quite clear that he intended this description, unlike his predecessors in the tradition, as a political rather than only a moral identification. He combined his Socialism with work for the Liberal Party, and was for a time chairman of the Bloomsbury ward of the Party. It was not uncommon for this kind of dual affiliation to exist: Thomas Hughes, one of the greatest of the Christian Socialists' publicists, sat in Parliament as a Liberal. In Headlam's case the assumption of a Party loyalty was not easy. His personal idiosyncrasies and the sacramental aspect of his religious understanding of Socialism did not fit easily with the party groupings that were available in his day. He gave some support to Hyndman's Democratic Federation in 1884, but he refused to become involved with the Independent Labour Party, regarding its socialism as too diluted. He had doubts, also, about the immediate admission of the working classes to political participation,

and believed, like the earlier Christian Socialists, that more education was required first. In the artistic and cultural interests of
many of the leading Fabians he found at least something that ap-
proximated to his own priorities, and he became an active
member in 1886, serving on the Fabian Executive on three occasions. In 1887 he was one of the special committee of fifteen
who drew up the 'Basis' of the Society. Yet his influence on the
Fabians was slight. His policy of not speaking, at its meetings,
from a distinctly Christian perspective, meant that his one great
insight – the Sacramental Socialism of his Incarnational theology
– was excluded from the Fabians' counsels.

Headlam was at his best when actually working among the
poor, and it was to Bethnal Green that he asked to be taken as
he lay dying. Like the Founder of Christianity, he eschewed the
company of the socially respectable and sought out the companionship of outcasts. 'Priesthood binds me to Radicalism', he
declared. It was not so much his Socialism that shocked his contemporaries as his moral originality. In his mind there were no
dazzling constructions of intellectual penetration, but a perception
of the fearful effects on human lives of the appalling conditions
in which the masses of working people were obliged to exist. His
Socialism, though so full of personal qualities, survived him in
the generation of Christian activists, trained in the Guild of St
Matthew, who were to take a leading part in the rise of social
priorities in the English Christianity of the first decades of the
twentieth century.

For Further Reading:

F. G. Bettany, *Stewart Headlam* (London, 1926); Kenneth Leech,
in *For Christ and the People, Studies of four Socialist Priests and
Prophets*, ed. M. Reckitt (SPCK, 1968); P. d'A. Jones, *The Christian
Socialist Revival 1877–1914* (Princeton University Press, 1968);
D. O. Wagner, *The Church of England and Social Reform Since 1854*
(New York, 1930).

16

William Morris
Art and Idealism

Charles Harvey and Jon Press

Overleaf: For 'practical and noble ends': the chintz printing section at Morris & Co.'s workshops at Merton Abbey, Surrey. (William Morris Gallery)

THE RELATIONSHIP BETWEEN INITIATIVES in political and social thought
and the aesthetic developments of Victorian Britain is inevitably a complex one. There was certainly little of a functionalist nature to explain
why Victorian Gothic began to sweep all before it in architecture and the
decorative arts from the 1840s onwards. But there is much that can be
traced back to the 'fair chivalry' of the 'Young England' movement and
the nostalgia for an idealised medieval world as sponsored by Pugin and
others as a backlash against the mechanistic Industrial Revolution.

One figure straddles the range of creative impulses that goes from the
years immediately after the Great Exhibition through the Arts and Crafts
movement to the cusp of fin de siècle Art Nouveau. With a genius for
popularisation paradoxically underpinned by a political outlook and philosophy that increasingly challenged the Victorian status quo, William
Morris (1834–96) is a central figure. His aesthetic achievements drew
their inspiration from an idealised egalitarianism of a communal and
guild-based Middle Ages rather than hymning the feudal order.

The multitalented Morris was also a pioneering socialist activist and
here Chris Harvey and Jon Press, key contributors to the 1996 Victoria
& Albert Museum exhibition and catalogue marking the centenary of
Morris's death, show how his catherine-wheel enthusiasms span out of a
sometimes naive but strongly-felt critique which influenced both urban
and suburban elites not just in mid-late Victorian Britain but beyond into
the 20th century.

William Morris was a man of extraordinary creative energy
who dedicated his life to the cause of art. Personal experience convinced him that art should not be the preserve of a small
minority of professionals of refined taste and sensibilities, but
should be a universal activity, natural to life, work and leisure.
He wished to live in a society which eschewed the production of
inferior, ugly wares, made without pleasure by tormented workers. In a decent society, which strove for beauty and relaxation
instead of profit and personal advantage, the only goods worth
making would be the necessities of life, and objects which were a
source of pleasure to maker and user alike. Hence his famous
dictum: 'art which is made by the people and for the people, as a
happiness to the maker and the user'.

Born in 1834 into a wealthy commercial family, William Morris
had the opportunity and the means to pursue the career of his
choice. Abandoning his initial intention to enter the Church, he
tried his hand at architecture and painting before turning to the

decorative arts. Here he found his true *métier*. Though he was also to become celebrated as a writer, a pioneer of English socialism, and a typographer and printer, it was above all through his talents as a designer, and through the highly successful business which depended upon those talents, that he was to make his mark.

The influences upon the young Morris were many and diverse. Like many of his generation, he was deeply influenced by the Romantic and religious revivals. He read widely and voraciously, and throughout his life his friends and acquaintances often remarked how he always 'seemed to know', whatever the topic under discussion. At an early age, he became personally acquainted with leading figures in the world of art and architecture, including Dante Gabriel Rossetti, Ford Madox Brown, G. E. Street and John Ruskin. But though biographers have identified an ever-growing list of influences upon the young Morris, the most important – at least as far as the subsequent development of his ideas and working practices are concerned – were Street and, above all, Ruskin.

G.E. Street is one of the most significant figures in the history of Victorian architecture. In his office in the 1850s and 1860s were to be found some of the brightest of the younger generation – men like Norman Shaw, Philip Webb, and John and Edmund Sedding, who were to rise to the top of their profession. Morris was articled to Street for nine months after leaving university. Though it quickly became apparent that he was not suited to a career as an architect, and he later clashed with Street over the latter's drastic restorations of medieval churches, Morris nevertheless drew much from Street's example. Most notable were Street's scholarly approach to architecture – he was amongst the most knowledgeable medievalists of his day – and his insistence that the architect should acquire a good all-round knowledge of the crafts which contributed to interior design and decoration. He himself was proficient in embroidery and designing church silver and metalwork.

Ruskin, however, was the main influence. During the course of the 1850s, his investigations into art and architecture gradually led him towards social criticism and political economy. The first stirrings occur in *The Seven Lamps of Architecture* (1849). In 'The Lamp of Life', Ruskin began to evolve a new understanding of the nature of men's work and what it meant for society. Like Carlyle before him, Ruskin was insistent that it was through work

that man fulfilled himself. For Ruskin, however, it had to be creative labour, which drew upon the workman's intellectual and
moral strengths as well as his physical powers. Such ideas were
further developed in *The Stones of Venice* (three volumes, 1851–
53), where they are drawn together in the famous chapter entitled 'The Nature of Gothic'. Here Ruskin set out his belief that
the architecture and art of a particular society express the values
of its entire culture.

According to Ruskin, architecture and its attendant arts should
be judged according to the amount of freedom of expression allowed to the individual workman. He contrasted favourably the
arts and crafts of the Middle Ages and the relationships they
engendered with the industrial society of the nineteenth century,
which seemed to him to place more restrictions on the workman
than any preceding age had done. Modern society – and in particular the Political Economists who supported the new liberal
industrial order – was thus indicted for having alienated and
dehumanised workers, forcing them to perform monotonous and
soul-destroying tasks. This critique of contemporary society, industrialisation and economic thought culminated in *Unto this Last:
Four Essays on the Principles of Political Economy* (1862), where
Ruskin argued that Britain's industrial society was morally de-
generate and pernicious, driving the labouring class into cultural
and material poverty.

Morris had read Ruskin's work at Oxford with fellow under-
graduates like Edward Burne-Jones, and by the late 1850s he had
become a good friend. As Morris embarked upon a career in the
decorative arts – not, after all, a 'suitable' occupation for a man
of the upper middle classes – he must have taken heart from
Ruskin's assertion that the decorative arts were serious arts, because, along with architecture, they created the visual environment in which men and women lived. Ruskin's elevation of
medieval society, his preference for hand-crafted wares, and his
insistence that the artist, designer and craftsman should be seen
as one, must also have struck a chord. Ruskin's ideas on business
ethics, which are in essence an appeal to the business leader to
behave in a socially responsible, paternalistic fashion, 'shaping
the market' and encouraging good taste rather than merely responding to the current demand for cheap, shoddy goods, likewise had an enduring impact.

Morris was not unusual in responding to these ideas, which
touched a widening cross-section of Victorian society. What

distinguished him, however, was the immense effort he made during his lifetime to give them practical expression. His vehicle was the firm of Morris, Marshall, Faulkner & Co., a partnership established in 1861 with a mission to influence public taste and lead the market. Morris's partners were Ford Madox Brown, Dante Gabriel Rossetti, Edward Burne-Jones, the architect Philip Webb, and two lesser-known figures, Charles Faulkner, an Oxford mathematics don, and Peter Paul Marshall, a surveyor and amateur painter. Though all the partners contributed designs in the early years, it was Morris who took the leading role in running the firm. In 1875 it was reconstituted under his sole ownership, by which time most of the others had effectively withdrawn from active involvement.

In the 1860s the firm concentrated upon ecclesiastical stained glass, though it also produced hand-painted tiles, table glass and furniture. Its furniture ranged from simple, rush-seated 'Sussex' chairs, which became a staple product for almost eighty years, to spectacular, one-off projects like the St George cabinet, designed by Philip Webb and decorated by Morris with scenes from the life of the saint. In 1866–67, there were important secular commissions for St James's Palace and the Green Dining Room at the South Kensington Museum, won in the face of fierce competition from more established firms like Queen Victoria's favourite, Crace & Co.

In the 1870s, Morris reoriented the firm towards the rapidly growing middle-class secular market, widening the product range and providing a complete interior design service. He breathed fresh life into a succession of arts and crafts: wallpapers, printed and woven textiles, carpet making and tapestry all gained from his efforts. Morris had to work hard to ensure that the firm's goods were produced to the highest standards. Where he could find a manufacturer who met his needs he was happy to sub-contract; but the range of products produced in the firm's own workshops grew steadily as he sought greater control over the manufacturing process. Morris & Co. became known for its use of traditional methods, machinery and processes. For example, ceaseless experimentation during the 1870s and early 1880s enabled Morris to master vegetable dyeing techniques which had fallen out of commercial use and provided him with the indigo blues and madder reds which may be seen in many of his best designs. Such techniques were often relatively expensive, but they enabled the firm to charge premium prices for its hand-woven fabrics and carpets, and its hand-painted textiles and wallpapers.

Morris's ideology strongly influenced succeeding generations of designers and artists, as in Walter Crane's wallpaper design for a panel of 'Swan, Rush and Iris'. (Courtesy of the Trustees of the V & A)

By the 1880s, the reputation of Morris & Co. was firmly established. Its shops in London and Manchester were patronised by the cultured and wealthy, and prestigious agencies had been established in the great cities of Europe and America. Its workshops at Merton Abbey, Surrey, were described in the pages of middle-class journals as the embodiment of a 'Ruskinian dream', where craftsmen produced top quality wares in idyllic, semi-rural conditions for higher than average wages.

Morris himself was by now a widely respected figure. He was frequently consulted by the South Kensington Museum (now the Victoria & Albert) on the acquisition of textiles, carpets, tapestries and embroidery, and was formally appointed as one of its Art Referees in 1884. Additionally, he served as an examiner for the South Kensington School of Design from the late 1870s, and in 1882 was called before the Royal Commission on Technical Instruction as an accomplished and well-informed witness. In the 1890s he felt able to launch into another round of creative endeavour with the founding of the Kelmscott Press – a pioneer of the private press movement which revitalised typography and printing in the late nineteenth and early twentieth centuries.

Yet at the very time that Morris & Co. was at the pinnacle of its success its owner was becoming increasingly dissatisfied with his achievements. Morris's personal development is charted in fascinating detail in his correspondence and, more publicly, in the long series of lectures which he gave between 1877 and the early 1890s. They set out the deep practical knowledge which underlay his craftsmanship, for Morris's ideas on the nature of art, labour and human happiness were based squarely on his practical experience in the decorative arts. Unlike Ruskin, he needed practical knowledge of a subject before he felt able to pronounce upon it. In each case he completely mastered the principles and techniques of design and manufacture, and whenever necessary acquired the practical skills of the hand-worker as well as those of the designer and organiser of production. Morris delighted in the work. This, more than any abstract argument, convinced him that all working people might, if society was properly ordered, find deep satisfaction in the creative process.

This, of course, was a very big 'if', and Morris's personal experiences led him to develop in these lectures a wide-ranging critique of nineteenth-century industrial society. Fundamentally it seemed to him that the nineteenth century – the 'Century of Commerce', as he called it – had seen an appalling decline in standards. 'England has of late been too much busied with the counting-house and not enough with the workshop', he argued. The manufacturers, 'who never did a stroke of hand-work in their lives', had become 'nothing better than capitalists and salesmen', concerned with profit margins rather than the maintenance of quality. Artists, designers and craftsmen had likewise been forced to respond to the dictates of the marketplace for, with the separation of entrepreneurial, design and production functions, their status had been debased and they had become the hirelings of manufacturers who knew little, and cared less, about art or industrial design. Hence the prevalence of 'sham' or 'shoddy', as Morris often called the products of nineteenth-century industry.

Morris's hostility to the Industrial Revolution was largely based on the belief that mass production was pernicious. Though not opposed to machines and new technology *per se*, he was deeply critical of the consequences of machine production in a capitalist society. Three particular causes for concern were identified. The first of these was the division of labour, since it was through this, and the de-skilling that generally accompanied it, that work became joyless. Thus Ruskin had looked back to the medieval period, when the labour of the artisan was a source of interest and pleasure, and resulted in products which were fitting and beautiful. The freedom to take full responsibility for the manufacturing process – and indeed, the freedom to make mistakes – ennobled the worker and satisfied his creative needs.

Whilst Morris's medievalism was less pervasive than that of Ruskin (and a good deal less pervasive than critics and admirers alike often assumed), he likewise placed a high value upon the virtues of the guild system of the late Middle Ages. In particular, he was attracted by the existence of a direct relationship between producer and consumer, and the local nature of craftsmanship. In his evidence to the Royal Commission on Technical Instruction, Morris stated that 'division of labour does a good deal to cheapen goods, but on the other hand I think it does a great deal to deteriorate them'. In capitalist production, 'the creation of surplus values being the one aim of the employers of labour, they cannot for a moment trouble themselves as to whether the work which creates the surplus value is pleasurable to the worker, or not'.

Secondly, goods should not be over-finished. 'Never demand an exact finish for its own sake, but only for some practical or noble end', said Ruskin in 'The Nature of Gothic'. Fitness for purpose was a guiding Ruskinian principle, which was frequently reiterated by Morris in his own writings. It was partly for this reason that Ruskin and Morris shared a dislike of the eighteenth century's quest for perfection and repeatability.

Finally, the awful conditions in which so many working people spent their lives contrived to make their work joyless and uncreative. Nineteenth-century housing, for example, was castigated by Morris as 'the basest, the ugliest, and the most inconvenient that men have ever built for themselves, and which our own haste, necessity, and stupidity, compel almost all of us to live in'. The destruction of trees and fields by the sprawl of monotonous, cheaply built suburbs around Britain's great cities was the target of his particular ire. 'How can I ask working-men passing up or down these hideous streets day to day to care about beauty?' he asked. Indeed, Morris's concern over the environment in which his fellow men had to live and work – his attacks on the pollution of Britain's rivers by industrial dyestuffs, or the fouling of her atmosphere by industrial chimneys – mark him as a notable forerunner of today's Green campaigners.

Taken together, Morris's lectures of the late 1870s and the 1880s provide a profound analysis of work and art in industrial society. Solutions to contemporary problems, however, were harder to produce – not surprisingly, considering that many of them continue to plague us today. Indeed, he was distinctly pessimistic about the situation, believing that contemporary civilisation was indifferent or even hostile to art, and recognising how hard it would be to bring about a fundamental change. In the fullness of time, he concluded that art could only flourish if capitalism itself was to disappear.

Thus, though the theme and tone of his lectures often seems to echo Ruskin, the outcome was very different. Ruskin remained convinced of the merits of a hierarchical society, in which individuals were rewarded according to their skill and experience. He argued that 'the distinction between one man and another [should] be only in experience and skill, and the authority and wealth which these must naturally and justly obtain'. What mattered in his view was the avoidance of extremes of wealth, and that money should be put to work to good purpose. Morris, however, made the transition from social criticism to revolutionary communism, earning himself a place amongst the pioneers of English socialism. In 1883, he wrote: 'both my historical studies and my practical conflict with the philistinism of modern society have forced upon me the conviction that art cannot have real life and growth under the present system of commercialism and profit mongering'.

Of all the central tenets of the Ruskinian model, the only one which Morris fully discarded was the belief that the benevolence of individuals could combine to better the world. He turned to Marxism and politics in pursuit of a social rather than an individual solution to the evils of the age. Socialism could not be achieved by the actions of individuals, no matter how able and well-meaning they might be.

Yet if Morris was disappointed with his achievement, it remains true to say that his ideas and example provided a powerful influence upon the development of the decorative arts. More than through his lectures or writings, it was through his own practice that Morris was to influence successive generations. Thus Morris's own example demonstrated that there was a market for better-quality products which did not compete solely on price, and that industry had to concern itself far more with considerations of taste and quality. Like Ruskin, Morris actively encouraged manufacturers to abandon the production of ugly dross and to lead by example in the creation of standards of good taste in manufactured goods, so 'forging the market' and educating public taste. He once exhorted businessmen that their duty lay in

... educating the public ... so that we may adorn life with the pleasure of cheerfully *buying* goods at their due price; with the pleasure of *selling* goods that we could be proud of both for fair price and fair workmanship; with the pleasure of working soundly and without haste at *making* goods that we could be proud of.

This vision of the socially responsible businessman, as one who put purpose before profit, and education before convenience, was accepted as an ideal by William Morris: he set for himself the very highest standards in design and manufacture; he preferred to set new trends rather than merely follow fashions; he never wasted an opportunity, at exhibitions or in publicity materials, to educate the public.

Another essential element of Morris's philosophy was his belief that the maker of any object should strive for originality in design. Originality in design pleases and elevates life, whereas uninspired goods reduce the quality of life. 'Never encourage imitation or copying of any kind except for the sake of preserving great works', Ruskin exhorted in 'The Nature of Gothic' – a sentiment with which Morris concurred wholeheartedly. Coupled with originality of design were high standards of manufacture. It was this that led Morris to the constant search for best quality materials and methods in dyeing, weaving, tapestry and other media which characterised his business career in the 1870s and 1880s. Morris was not unaware that this conferred competitive advantage in a fiercely contested market. The importance of a reputation for originality and quality is asserted in Morris's evidence before the Royal Commission on Technical Instruction in March 1882, when he remarked that 'beauty is a marketable quality, and . . . the better the work is all round, both as a work of art and in its technique, the more likely it is to find favour with the public'.

Coupled with Morris's emphasis on originality and beauty was his insistence on a full understanding of the medium in which the designer was working. Only in this way would the design properly complement the nature of the material and the capabilities of the production process. As always, Morris invariably followed the prescriptions he set out for others. In all his many activities – painting, pattern design, weaving, dyeing, printing – he applied a common method of working, beginning with systematic research and exploration of the topic, and then passing on to identification of best practice or suitable models; experimentation to identify through personal experience the problems involved; and modification of ideas, techniques or methods to bring his own work to fruition.

Such views and practices placed William Morris in opposition to some of the prevailing values of his age. His was a creed which idealised craftsmanship, beauty, naturalness and simplicity in design and manufacture, and eschewed the dubious benefits of cheap, mass-produced goods. But though aesthetics were of vital importance to him, he was equally hostile to Aestheticism. 'Art for art's sake' was anathema. He believed that art was for everyone; all men and women needed creative work and the everyday experience of beautiful things – well-designed, well-made objects which stood the test of 'fitness for purpose'.

Here lies a paradox, for many people associate the name of William Morris with High Victorian opulence and intricacy of design. What they do not appreciate is the extent to which Morris felt compromised by his reliance on the custom of what he called 'the swinish rich'. His real views on art and design, however, have never been lost. Any number of designers, artists, craftsmen and architects have acknowledged the importance of his ideas and example to their work. From the 1880s, a younger generation, often loosely described as the Arts and Crafts Movement, began to implement the principles enunciated in his lectures and confirmed by his example – men like Walter Crane, C. F. A. Voysey, A. H. Mackmurdo, C. R. Ashbee and William Richard Lethaby. The societies which they established, such as the Art Workers' Guild and the Arts and Crafts Exhibition Society, had clear educational goals, and thus served to disseminate Morris's ideas more widely still. Nor was Morris's influence confined to Britain. In Europe, he was acknowledged, amongst others, by Van der Velde and Walter Gropius, the founders of the Bauhaus. Though their work stood for all that was modern, it was made in Morris's spirit.

The most fitting comment on Morris's legacy to us is that the best of his work has retained its appeal down to the present day. Indeed, his designs continue to inspire such admiration that they may fairly be regarded as a major part of the cultural legacy of nineteenth-century Britain. In similar fashion, the ideas which he set out in his writings and many public appearances continue to exert a fascination on people around the world. The centenary of his death in 1996 generated a spate of radio and TV programmes, publications and exhibitions; all this will help to bring this most multifaceted of Great Victorians to our attention.

For Further Reading:

C. E. Harvey and J. Press, *William Morris: Design and Enterprise in Victorian Britain* (Manchester, 1991); C. E. Harvey and J. Press, *Art, Enterprise and Ethics: The Life and Work of William Morris* (London, 1996); F. MacCarthy, *William Morris: A Life for Our Time* (London, 1994); L. Parry, *William Morris Textiles* (London, 1983); W. S. Peterson, *Kelmscott Press: History of William Morris' Typographical Adventure* (Oxford, 1991); C. Poulson, *William Morris* (London, 1989); A. C. Sewter, *Stained Glass of William Morris and his Circle* (London, 1975); E. P. Thompson, *William Morris: Romantic to Revolutionary* (New York, 1976); P. Thompson, *The Work of William Morris* (Oxford, 1993); R. Watkinson, *William Morris as Designer* (London, 1990).

17

Mary Kingsley and West Africa

Dea Birkett

THE STRIKING IMAGE of the intrepid explorer penetrating the 'heat of darkness' in Africa and the hold it exercised on the popular imagination has tended, both then and since, to be associated with the grass-roots enthusiasm for imperial expansion that characterised the later Victorian period.

Yet the most celebrated of these exploits – the expeditions of David Livingstone which opened up central and southern Africa and prompted Stanley's famous rescue mission via the Congo – were prompted by zeal for evangelism and geographical discovery rather than empire-building, and often the men and women iconised as discoverers in the imperial pantheon had sturdy doubts about the unalloyed benefits that 'civilisation' was bringing to the people they encountered. Here Dea Birkett considers the career and outlook of one of the most striking women explorers, Mary Kingsley, and her discovery not just of West Africa but of her own distinctive and dissenting feminist identity.

Imagine what a Victorian spinster looked like, and you have imagined Mary Henrietta Kingsley. Whether tramping down Piccadilly or trekking through tropical forests, she always dressed entirely in black, with a high-necked buttoned blouse, small sealskin bonnet and wielding the indispensable black umbrella. But imagine what a Victorian spinster did, and Mary Kingsley breaks every rule. For in 1893, for a thirty-year-old spinster to take a cargo vessel to West Africa was an extraordinary step. The unorthodoxy of Mary Kingsley's response to her stifling domestic life has cast her as an isolated heroine, removed from the cultural milieu of late-nineteenth-century Cambridge in which she was raised. But the roots of her long voyage from the confines of her mother's sickroom to the Ogooué rapids lay in the dreams and aspirations shared by many middle-class Victorian women who responded in less dramatic and memorable ways.

While her contemporaries might choose the settlements of the East End of London, where as middle-class women they could escape the limits of their genteel homes and wield power over working-class women and men, Mary Kingsley looked further afield for an arena where her gender was no longer of primary importance. She found it in Africa where she was, first, white, and only secondly a woman. Travelling as a 'white man', she revelled in a new kind of freedom which 'took all the colour out of other kinds of living'. Rather than challenging the hierarchies of her time, Mary Kingsley's physical and psychological journeys were predicated upon them.

Her contribution to the image of Africa also exploited an ideology in which it was believed that Africans and Europeans, as women and men, were essentially different. The doctrine of 'separate spheres' found expression in her pleas for the recognition and preservation of African traditional custom and culture. The methods through which she propagated these views were determined by her own place, as a woman, within them. For she was excluded from the burgeoning number of circles concerned with African and colonial affairs, so turned to behind-the-scenes, hidden ways of politicking, exploiting the informal networks and social sphere to which women were relegated. Both her personal motives and political method reveal a woman firmly rooted in her time, responding to the disadvantages of being female and the privileges of being white which late-Victorian Britain and imperial expansion gave her. Although bearing the name of Kingsley, Mary had neither the education, money, nor established class status her literary uncles and cousins enjoyed. Born only four days after Dr George Kingsley married his housekeeper, Mary Bailey, in October 1862, Mary's first thirty years were consumed in tending to her sickly mother and acting as secretary to her father's amateur anthropological work.

When both parents died within weeks of each other in 1892, she felt like 'a boy with a new half crown'. Enticed by the tales of travel and adventure in her father's library, and with the intention of collecting 'fish and fetish', she sailed for West Africa – 'the white man's grave'. But alongside the spirits and jars for preserving her specimens packed in her large black waterproof bag, she took her cultural baggage. The isolation of Mary's early life had forced her on to the companionship of books, and from these she culled an image of the 'Dark Continent' and its exotic 'savage' inhabitants prevalent in both the academic and popular press. So strong were these images, that when the SS *Lagos* drew towards the West African coast in August 1893, it all seemed so familiar.

By 1896, after two journeys to West Africa, Mary Kingsley was a celebrity, a regular presence in the daily press and an enormously popular lecturer. Her quest in search of 'fish and fetish' had led her into more far-reaching discoveries, and what she saw and recorded questioned the images she had taken with her. 'One by one I took my old ideas derived from books and thoughts based on imperfect knowledge and weighed them against the real life surrounding me, and found them either worthless or wanting . . . the greatest recantation I had to make was my idea of the traders'.

Popularly derided as the 'palm oil ruffians', the European traders in West Africa were mostly single men, some with African wives, caricatured in the British press as debauched and drunken rogues who had reluctantly given up dealing in slaves when 'legitimate trade' offered greater financial inducements. For Mary Kingsley, however, they were men she was 'proud to be allowed to call friends and know were fellow-countrymen'.

It was not only her trader friends she believed were maligned. Africans, at the hands of the missionary party – eager 'not to tell you how the country they resided in was but how it was getting towards being what it ought to be' – were portrayed unfairly. Kingsley challenged:

. . . the stay at home statesmen, who think that Africans are awful savages or silly children – people who can only be dealt with on a reformatory penitentiary line. This view is not mine . . . but it is the view of the states-man and the general public and the mission public in African affairs.

Looking for consistency, practicality and humanity to be under-stood and explained, rather than vices and immorality to be manipulated and eradicated, she argued for a new approach to anthropological study by looking at African societies from the in-side out, to 'think in black'. Her passionate desire to 'penetrate the African mind-forest' made her travel as a trader, living as her African companions and depending upon them entirely for her safety and well-being. Long before anthropologists had developed the idea of fieldwork, she argued:

. . . unless you live among the natives you can never get to know them. At first you see nothing but a confused stupidity and crime; but when you get to see – well! . . . you see things worth seeing.

Although questioning many of the popular images of Africa, Mary Kingsley was steeped in the racial theories used to justify and support the expansion of British interests in West Africa. She espoused a by now out of fashion polygenesist outlook, believing that Africans and Europeans, as men and women, were essential-ly rather than evolutionarily different. 'I feel certain that a black man is no more an undeveloped white man than a rabbit is an undeveloped hare, and the mental difference between the races is very similar to that between men and women among ourselves'. The fault of the missionary endeavour, she believed, was in trying to Europeanise Africans. Missionary-educated Africans were 'the curse of the Coast', embracing 'a secondhand rubbishy white culture' rather than traditional African social customs. When writing about her travels, she focused on her contacts with the Fang people of Gabon, 'unadulterated Africans', as she called them, 'in the raw state'.

Her attitude towards women's rights shared this conservative and separatist philosophy. When approached by petitioners for women's admission to the learned societies she brushed aside their entreaties. 'These androgynes I have no time for', she complained. Women and men were different in kind rather than degree, as Africans to Europeans, and these differences should be recognised and encouraged rather than glossed over. While not denying a hierarchy within these differences constructed on racial and sexual lines, she nevertheless argued for areas of specialist knowledge, in line with the popular doctrine of 'separate spheres'. Opposed to the admission of women to societies of travellers, she argued for a separate women's meeting where things could be discussed without the presence of men. 'Women like myself know many things no man can know about the heathen' she told the Secretary of the Royal Geographical Society, 'and no doubt men do ditto'. On her return from West Africa in December 1895, her first venture into print was not, as commonly believed, in defence of European traders or 'real Africans' but in response to an article in the *Daily Telegraph* describing her as a 'New Woman'. Infuriated by this label, she wrote to the editor denying any such allegiance: 'I did not do anything without the assistance of the superior sex', denying the independence she had so desperately sought.

Mary Kingsley's philosophy of separate development of the races and sexes led her into direct opposition to the missionary party and their stress on a common humanity. Her defence of polygamy, domestic slavery, and even cannibalism as appropriate social forms in West Africa, shocked the conservative press and quickly brought her notoriety. But with this came a popular platform from which to air her views. Her first book, *Travels in West Africa*, published in January 1897, was an immediate bestseller. Based on an account of her second journey, its vast amount of new anthropological material established her as the leading West Africanist of the time. But Mary Kingsley was no longer content with confining herself to the issue of ethnology. Soon she was arguing for the recognition of anthropology as a tool of imperialist expansion; to govern the African, she argued, you must first know him. She wrote to the eminent Oxford anthropologist E. B. Taylor:

. . . I will force upon the politicians the recognition of anthropology if I have to do it with the stake and thumbscrew. Meanwhile the heathen unconsciously keeps on supporting anthropology gallantly, and official-dom says it won't have anything but its old toys – missionaries, stockbrokers, good intentions, ignorance and maxim guns. Well we shall see.

The imperial expansion Mary Kingsley envisioned was of a very different kind to that the new Colonial Secretary, Joseph Chamberlain, had in mind. In opposition to his plans for administrative intervention in West Africa and the establishment of the Crown Colony system, supported by the missionary parties, Mary Kingsley advocated informal economic imperialism, looking back to a mythical golden era when British interests in West Africa were protected by European traders and fair commerce between African and European flourished. Economic ties under British merchants rather than administrative control under 'pen-pushers and ostrich feathers' was her aim. She argued:

England is the great manufacturing country of the world, and as such requires markets, and requires markets far more than colonies. A colony drains from the mother country, yearly, thousands of the most able and energetic of her children, leaving behind them their aged incapable relations. Whereas the holding of the West African markets drains a few hundred men, only too often for ever; but the trade they carry on and develop enables thousands of men, women and children to remain safe in England in comfort and pleasure, owing to the wages and profits arising from the manufacture and export of articles used in that trade.

Only this system – eventually outlined in her 'Alternative Plan' – would, she claimed, also benefit Africans, by leaving their cultural and social organisations intact.

Mary Kingsley's means of raising support and realising her plans were limited, for her gender excluded her from the burgeoning number of forums concerned with African affairs. The admission of women to the Royal Geographical Society in 1892 had drawn such fierce opposition that the decision was hastily rescinded. Other societies of travellers were equally hostile to women's participation. Outspoken women's activities were confined to the field of missionary and philanthropic work, but even here public speaking could be frowned upon. For a woman to actively campaign against the missionary endeavour and on behalf of the 'palm oil ruffians' and 'heathen Africans' threatened her femininity in a way less controversial standpoints would not have done. Mary Kingsley's response was to emphasise her ladyhood, almost to the point of caricature, reminding her audience at public lectures that she appeared as their maiden aunt, dressed as a woman far beyond her mid-thirties. She appealed to a close friend to help her in the maintenance of this public persona. 'I implore if you hear it said in Society that I appear on platforms in African native costume, a billy cock hat, and a trade shirt, to contradict it', she wrote, 'honour bright I'd got my best frock on'.

As the corridors of official power were closed to her, she began to exploit unofficial methods and behind-the-scenes networks, soon earning the name of 'Liverpool's hired assassin' for her pro-trader politics and clandestine ways of operating. In private, she asserted pressure on individual politicians, exploited old networks and created new ones, and encouraged ventures into the political arena. Her political development was inextricably knitted to the ways and means through which she could work. It is this infor-mal, behind-the-scenes, nature of her politics that has often led to an underestimation of her influence in West African affairs.

Mary Kingsley felt bound to defend the European traders, Africans, and her own reputation against the allegations being paraded in the press. The first public debate in which she became involved was over the 'liquor traffic'. In 1895 a combination of factors – humanitarian and commercial – launched the 'liquor traffic' debate into a new phase, to which Kingsley's own efforts would soon be added. The British fear of the domination of the West African spirit trade by Hamburg firms reached a new height. The return to power of Salisbury in June, with the temperance supporter Joseph Chamberlain as his Colonial Secretary, was cited by Colonel Frederick Lugard, commissioner for the hinterland of Nigeria, as giving 'hope to those interested in the question that the time had at last come when effective steps would be taken to deal with this evil'. The language of the 'liquor traffic' debate be-came the 'demoralisation of the native' and 'the evil trade' versus 'legitimate commerce' – all reminiscent of earlier anti-slavery arguments – rather than profit and administrative control.

Sir John Kirk's enquiry following the 1895 Brass uprising had reopened the debate around the future of the Niger Delta, and different interests were vying for influence in the area – the Royal

Niger Company under the persuasive leadership of Sir George
Goldie, the Niger Coast Protectorate government, Liverpool and
Manchester trading houses, the Colonial Office, and the missionary bodies. The liquor traffic was, to a large extent, a pawn in this
contest, a highly emotional issue which could be used to draw
public support in the propaganda war.

For Mary Kingsley, the temperance party's argument had two
main fallacies. Firstly, it painted a picture of an African population
easily manipulated and less able to resist the enticements of
alcohol than Europeans. Secondly, the curtailment on the impor-
tation of trade alcohol to West Africa would inhibit the
'free-trading' practices of the Liverpool merchants, who used it as
a form of currency to obtain the palm oil and other raw materials
of their trade. The pro-liquor lobby, however, had little ability to
raise the sympathies of the general public against the appeal of
the temperance party's tales of the degradation wrought by 'trade
gin'. In Kingsley, the pro-liquor party found an advocate who
could couch their economic arguments in terms more acceptable
to the popular palate. While the leading Liverpool merchant John
Holt had earlier complained that the anti-liquor leaders were
'professional agitators and old women', within a few years he
would be extremely grateful that someone conforming to this
image had come over to the traders' side.

The debate took place as much in extra-governmental forums
as behind the walls of the Colonial Office. Lugard spoke to the
Colonial Institute, the letters pages of *The Times* were dominated
by the altercation between West African bishops and governors,
and missionary societies hosted public discussions. The thrashing
out of the issue in these unofficial forums allowed Kingsley,
excluded from the official arena, to be fully immersed in the centre
of the debate.

Mary Kingsley's first attacks on the temperance party were
made from her position as an ethnologist, to counter the image
of the African as a 'drunken child'. She was drawn into the fray
by an article appearing in the *Spectator* accusing Africans of being
'a people abnormally low, evil, cruel . . . It is in Africa that the
lowest depth of evil barbarism is reached, and that we find the
races with the least of humanity about them except the form . . .
they are all degraded'. Kingsley's reply argued for an understanding of African culture:

I do not believe the African to be brutal, degraded, or cruel. I know from
wide experience with him that he is often grateful and faithful, and by

no means the drunken idiot his so-called friends, the Protestant missionaries, are anxious, as an excuse for their failure in dealing with him, to make out.

Although a reluctant speaker, Kingsley embarked upon a vigorous and exhausting programme which took her throughout the country, from local geographical societies to 'magic lantern at YMCA'. The popular image of an intrepid lady explorer in the jungle which had initially so angered her could draw large crowds who would then receive political statements sugared in tales of African adventure.

While the propaganda war was being fought out in the pages of the press and on the public platform, in private the correspondence between Kingsley and her temperance adversaries was more wordy and considered. 'I am going for this mission party with feminine artfulness, not like a bull at a gate', she told Holt. As Lugard's damning account of the 'witty and amusing Miss Kingsley' appeared in *The Nineteenth Century*, in private his correspondence with her was a more mutual exchange of information and opinion. And while *The Times* paid her the ultimate insult and ignored the publication of her book, widely reviewed elsewhere, she met the editors for dinner. In this manner she hoped to exert private influence where public access was denied.

Kingsley was building up a network of contacts throughout the political spectrum, exploiting the social sphere controlled by women. Her first approach to her Liverpool ally Holt was made by writing to his wife, who had invited her to attend a meeting of the local Literary and Scientific Society. The wife of the Assistant Under Secretary at the Colonial Office, Reginald Antrobus, provided her with invaluable information and insight into Colonial Office wranglings by spying on her husband's papers. The leading Anglo-Irish social hostess Alice Stopford Green's ability to speak French enabled Kingsley to keep in contact with members of the French embassy in London.

Communications with West Africa were also developed, as Kingsley kept in regular contact with Africans on the coast and hosted them on their visits to London. 'I have quantities of blacks here', she wrote to Holt – including the leading lawyer Samuel Lewis and Edward Blyden, editor of the *Sierra Leone Weekly News*.

The value of this diverse network of contacts would prove itself in the 'hut tax' controversy in the Protectorate of Sierra Leone. The British merchants had always opposed a tax on African property, accurately predicting that the resulting opposition would disrupt trade. When the first outbreak of resistance to payment occurred in early 1898 their fears were proved founded, but a wavering Colonial Secretary was reluctant to remove a tax in the face of persistent support for its implementation by the Governor of Sierra Leone and allegations by humanitarian pressure groups that clamping down on slavery had caused the rebellion. Realising she had once again to fight opponents who appeared to have humanitarian concerns entirely on their side, Kingsley pleaded for an understanding of Africans – sympathy for the black man as she put it, 'not emotional but common sense sympathy and honour and appreciation'.

But the sympathy she invoked also recalled earlier arguments with the temperance lobby over their misunderstanding of the African situation. The pro-hut taxers, she believed, suffered from a similar ignorance of African society, though a different aspect – not the misrepresentation of the African as a 'drunken child', but of the nature and value of indigenous African legal systems. The hut tax, Kingsley argued, offended African law. 'One of the root principles of African law is that the thing that you pay any one a regular fee for is a thing that is not your own – it is a thing belonging to the person to who you pay the fee'. But behind these initial objections lay her deeper opposition to an interventionist policy in West Africa. The real cause of the rebellion was the 'reasonable dislike to being dispossessed alike of power and property in what they regard as their own country'. While publicly sticking to her claim that the tax was the root cause of the disturbances, in private she admitted that it was 'merely the match to a train of gunpowder'. By 'sticking severely to native law' however, other arguments would 'come by and by'.

How can the influence of someone who operated in such a behind-the-scenes and informal way be measured? Her prominent position on African affairs led the Colonial Secretary to write to her at this critical time. But he was reluctant to be seen to countenance the opinion of such a controversial figure. He sought her advice, therefore, as covertly as possible. 'He is horribly frightened of being known to communicate with the witch of Endor', Kingsley told Holt. She responded in kind, marking all her letters to him 'Private' and 'Strictly Confidential' – doubly underlined. When Sir David Chalmers was sent out to Freetown as Special Commissioner to investigate the cause of the disturbances, Chamberlain first briefed him on Kingsley's views. Governor Cardew of Sierra Leone paid her frequent visits on his return to London, and the Acting-Governor Matthew Nathan, sent out in his place, zealously courted her friendship before his departure. His reading on board ship from Liverpool to Sierra Leone was Mary Kingsley's second book, *West African Studies*. In this manner she was in touch with all those involved in policy-making around the hut tax.

As her political experience grew, her methods of politicking became more sophisticated, subtle and therefore hidden from subsequent history. Not wanting to appear as a one-woman opponent to the hut tax, she encouraged others to commit themselves to print. Using her contacts with leading pressmen such as St Loe Strachey, editor of the *Spectator* and, Kingsley thought, a 'backstairs to Chamberlain', she introduced young journalists into print, most notably E. D. Morel, correspondent for the *Pall Mall Gazette*. She encouraged Holt to write to the papers, but warned him 'don't for goodness gracious sake let the mention of me occur'. As her contacts grew, she increasingly relied on these methods. 'The truth is Mr Holt', she wrote in 1899, 'every bit of solid good work I have done has been done through a man. I get more and more fond of doing things this way. It leaves me a free hand to fight with.' To St Loe Strachey she wrote, 'In the seclusion of private life, in the gentle course of private friendship, I shall do my best in language worse than you have ever heard from me, to weld my men together and I'll fight to the last shot in my locker against the existing system'. Soon the Colonial Office christened her 'the most dangerous person on the other side'.

Her book, *West African Studies*, published in early 1899, contained a strong attack on the Crown Colony system. 'The sooner the Crown Colony system is removed from the sphere of practical politics and put under a glass case in the South Kensington Museum, labelled Extinct, the better for everyone', she wrote. She described its system of government as a waste of life and money, and a destroyer of African social organisations on which peace and prosperity depended. In its place she drew up an 'Alternative Plan'. This was innovative firstly, in giving governmental and administrative control to European trading interests in West Africa embodied in a Grand Council who appointed a Governor General of West Africa, and secondly, by officially incorporating African opinion – filtered through a council of chiefs – into the administrative network. But although the 'Alternative Plan' was presented as a new option for British control of West Africa, in fact it looked back to a former era rather than forward to a new one. The infor-

'Mavungu', the three-foot nail fetish which Mary Kingsley brought back from West Africa on her first journey in 1893, and which stood in her South Kensington flat. (Pitt Rivers Museum, Oxford).

mal economic ties which Kingsley hoped would form the basis of British imperialism were central to this plan, as was their implementation by a European trading class. The failure of this scheme would depend not only on the impracticality of re-establishing an informal empire in a time of increasing European intervention in West Africa, but also the reluctance of British trading interests to take on the added responsibilities of government. British traders also wanted a non-trading European administrative class to run West African affairs and protect their markets from European and African rivals.

While on the public platform Kingsley appeared as the professional politician, in private she felt more and more drawn to the Africa she had left behind. While maintaining a professional façade of feminine conformity, in the privacy of her Kensington home she decorated her rooms with souvenirs from her journeys – enormous wooden drums and a yard-high nail fetish – and jangled about in her African bangles. To a childhood friend she wrote of the stresses of her two personalities, the public politician and the private African:

The majority of people I shrink from, I don't like them, I don't understand them and they most distinctly don't understand me . . . I cannot be a bushman *and* a drawing-roomer. Would to Allah I was in West Africa now, with a climate that suited me and a people who understood me, and who I could understand.

She longed to return to 'skylark' in West Africa and experience a freedom 'this smug, self-satisfied, sanctimonious, lazy, *Times*-believing England' could never give.

Her identity with the African had been strong and heartfelt since her return from West Africa. Emotional revelations of this personal sympathy to close friends found more public expression in the use of terms usually reserved for non-European peoples to describe her own experience. Calling herself a 'savage' and a 'member of the tribe of women', she would even describe herself as 'an African'. 'We Africans are not fit for decent society', she told Alice Stopford Green, and to the Indianist Sir Alfred Lyall, she wrote 'I am a firm African'. She compared her beliefs to those of Africans. 'I desire to get on with the utter Bushman', she declared, 'and never sneer or laugh at his native form of religion, a pantheism which I confess is a form of my own religion'.

This identity was also an expression of her own philosophy of polygenesism and separate development. Arguing for the promo-

tion of women's traditional sphere and African traditional life
(although not always consistent in the definition of either), she
said the 'African is a feminine race' – misunderstood by a
dominant culture. The most candid revelation of these feelings
was to Nathan, with whom she was unhappily in love:

I will import to you, in strict confidence, for if it were known it would
damage me badly, my opinion on the African. He is *not* 'half devil and
half child', anymore than he is 'our benighted brother' and all that sort
of thing. He is a woman . . . I know those nigs because I am a woman, a
woman of a masculine race but a woman still.

Kingsley became increasingly dissatisfied with the isolation of her
outspoken position, and the lack of support from disunited
traders, and complained to Holt of loneliness. She secretly applied
to nurse in South Africa, hoping to cover the Boer War for the
Morning Post and travel northwards across the Orange River and
far away from European settlements to her 'beloved South West
Coast'. Letting only a few friends know of her imminent
departure, she ended her final lecture at the Imperial Institute
with the words 'Fare ye well, for I am homeward bound'. On
arriving at the Cape at the end of March 1900, the medical conditions horrified her, and soon she was absorbed in the immediate
needs of hospital work. 'All this work here, the stench, the washing, the enemas, the bed pans, the blood, is my world', she wrote
to Alice Stopford Green, 'not London Society, politics, that gallery
into which I so strangely wandered – into which I don't care a
hairpin if I never wander again'. Within two months the typhoid
fever that was daily killing four to five of her patients struck Mary,
and on 3 June she died. She was buried, at her own request, at
sea. Full military and naval honours accompanied the funeral.

Commentators on Mary Kingsley's life and work have often
accredited her with laying the political foundations for the introduction of indirect rule in Northern Nigeria. But it is in the
informal sector, and not Colonial Office policy-making, that we
must look for her political legacy. Morel drew upon her inspiration, and continually agitated against Colonial Office politics, later
leading the Congo Reform Movement, an informal pressure group
relying on press coverage and public speaking in the Kingsley
style. Alice Stopford Green, inheritor of Kingsley's behind-the-
scenes politicking, formed the African Society in her memory, as
a forum for the exchange of information between traders,
academics, and officials involved in West African affairs. John
Holt said, 'Miss Kingsley discovered me and made me think'.

For Further Reading:

Mary Kingsley, *Travels in West Africa* (London, 1897; reprinted Virago, 1982); Catherine Barnes Stevenson, 'Female Anger and African Politics: the Case of Two Victorian "Lady Travellers"', *Turn-of-the-Century Woman* (1985); K. D. Nworah, 'The Liverpool Sect and British West African Politics 1895–1915' in *African Affairs* (1971); A. Olorunfemi, 'The Liquor Traffic Dilemma in British West Africa: The Southern Nigerian Example 1895–1918' in *International Journal of African Historical Studies* (1984). The most recent biography of Kingsley is Katherine Frank, *A Voyager Out* (Houghton and Mifflin, 1986). See also my recently-published *Spinsters Abroad* (Basil Blackwell, 1989)

18

Attic Attitudes
Leighton and Aesthetic Philosophy

Stephen Jones

Opposite: Olympian Jove or the head waiter? Lord Leighton in a watercolour by Tissot, 1873. (Royal Borough of Kensington and Chelsea; Leighton House Museum)

THE SUBJECTS HISTORIANS are interested in inevitably reflect the changing aesthetic viewpoints of their contemporaries, and nowhere is this truer than in looking at the forms and values of Victorian art. Forty years ago the work of Frederic, Lord Leighton (1830–96) and the Aesthetic Movement with which he was associated and of which he was a pioneer was neglected in saleroom and museum alike.

Today all this has changed but, as Stephen Jones in his portrait of the artist argues here, we are still insufficiently aware of the role Leighton played in opening out Victorian aesthetics to the influence of nineteenth-century Europe. It was a role that went far further than merely trying to recreate 'Grecian chic' for the nineteenth century, and it entitles Leighton to be seen as a splendid representative of the cosmopolitan values and vitality that were to transform late-Victorian art, in preparation for the impact of *art nouveau*.

It is very difficult today to make a leap of the imagination and encounter nineteenth-century painting as 'modern art'. To contemporary eyes, however, Rossetti, Millais and Watts were just as much innovators as more revolutionary figures such as Whistler and, in France, the Impressionist painters. This distortion of perspective is inevitable given hindsight, for we know today which horses to back in the race towards Modernism.

Of the Victorian giants, Frederic, Lord Leighton, has suffered most; first, like all of them, from neglect, and subsequently from misunderstanding. The PreRaphaelite Brotherhood regained critical acclaim in the 1950s, and became modern icons in the 1960s, when psychedelic clothes and mysticism found an echo in the canvases of Burne-Jones and Holman Hunt. Since then serious and detailed analysis of their work has progressed steadily. At the same time painters of the Aesthetic Movement, and the applied arts of that taste, have experienced a revival. Recently Leighton and Alma-Tadema have triumphed in the auction rooms. But all too often these names are bracketed together without any recognition of the fundamental differences between the two artists.

Leighton's huge personal success in his lifetime, and establishment role as President of the Royal Academy, have served to obscure his artistic intentions and create a degree of hostility to the man, once described by the writer Vernon Lee as 'a mixture of the Olympian Jove and a head waiter'. Born to private wealth and privilege, nurtured in foreign watering-places and continental academies, Leighton seemed to some contemporaries a hothouse flower of dilettantism. Such judgements, then and now, obscure the curious and important place he occupies in English painting.

Nineteenth-century British art tends on the whole to be parochial, even amateur in its sources. Of the original Pre-Raphaelite Brotherhood only Madox Brown had studied on the continent, while Rossetti was largely self-taught. The intellectual and emotional power behind the PreRaphaelites was considerable, but its horizons were relatively narrow. This is even more true of lesser artists. The Royal Academy, against which Rossetti and his friends reacted, was a stultifying place. Interestingly Leighton, the great academic painter, found it equally uncongenial when he settled in London in 1859.

Though fully documented, particularly by Richard and Leonée Ormond in their monograph, Leighton's close youthful association with Rossetti, Holman Hunt and Ruskin, all aesthetic radicals in the early 1860s, is often overlooked. He had been trained in Frankfurt at the Städelsches Kunstinstitut, a centre of Nazarene painting. The archaic and self-consciously medievalising taste of the Nazarenes was sympathetic with the PreRaphaelite philosophy. However, Leighton had gone on to work in Rome and Florence, and subsequently had studied in Paris. Early drawings show how close a study he made of the Renaissance masters. By the time he arrived in Paris he had synthesised the sinuous linearity of Florentine draughtsmanship with a rich Venetian sense of colour. Technically he had armed himself more fully than any artist of his generation.

Paris must have been the definitive aesthetic experience for the young painter. Here he met Ingres, whose influence is clear in Leighton's *Paolo and Francesca*. He also met Delacroix and Gérôme. This was the Paris of George du Maurier's *Trilby*, and here Leighton also encountered Val Prinsep and Edward Poynter, both to be lifelong friends and colleagues. During this period, three years from 1855 and 1858, the classical taste he adopted and championed in England was all around him. The *'Pompier'* school of art, so-called from the resemblance between classical and Parisian firemen's helmets, was in vogue, and the high finish and Hellenic subjects of the period had their effect on Leighton. In 1858 he returned for a last winter in Rome, before settling in London. Thus he arrived back in England in 1859, the same year in which continental aesthetic taste appeared in London in the paintings of James McNeil Whistler. Whistler and Leighton had known each other in Paris; despite an inevitable element of competition be-

tween two such dandies, the fundamental differences in their personalities paradoxically enabled them to become good friends.

Whistler left Paris after his work was rejected by the *Salon*. He brought with him to London advanced ideas of the purposes and philosophy of art. *At the Piano*, painted in 1859, and *Harmony in Green and Rose: The Music Room*, are typical of his work at this time. That he and Leighton were artistic allies is clear from du Maurier's letter to Thomas Armstrong, dating from spring 1861. Work on *The Music Room* had been protracted by the need to repaint the head of the seated girl, after Leighton 'told him it was out of harmony'. Both artists were clearly primarily concerned with the abstract values of their pictures at this time.

Leighton's counterpart to Whistler's experiments in harmony was his somewhat difficult and cerebral canvas *Lieder Ohne Worte*, painted 1860–1. Here Leighton shows himself surprisingly sympathetic to the nascent Aesthetic Movement. The picture was painted to evoke a mood of contemplation and repose. It combines elements of Hellenic detail with curious pots and vessels which clearly owe something to the designs of Christopher Dresser. Critical reaction from friends and enemies was mixed. Rossetti, writing to William Allingham, considered *Lieder Ohne Worte* to be Leighton's only 'very good' Academy picture that year. Leighton could not persuade Ruskin even to look at the picture when he came to breakfast, the critic insisting instead on viewing Leighton's minutely detailed studies from nature. Both reactions are significant. Rossetti found in Leighton's picture an echo of his own opiate fantasy images of women. Ruskin, delighted by Leighton's technical dexterity in delineating exactly a lemon tree, had no time for any work of art which did not follow his own direction to 'Go to nature in all singleness of heart, selecting nothing, rejecting nothing'.

Leighton himself seems to have been uncertain as to his direction at this time. Flattered by the powerful Ruskin, cheered by the support of Rossetti and Millais when the Royal Academy presented a unitedly hostile front, Leighton must have been encouraged to throw in his lot with the rebels. However, he could not subscribe to their philosophy of truth to nature. Any superficial resemblances between Leighton's early Renaissance subjects

---

Overleaf: 'Lieder ohne Worte', painted by Leighton in 1860–61 to evoke 'a mood of contemplation and repose'. (The Tate Gallery)

and pictures such as, say, Millais' austerely realistic exercise *Loren-zo and Isabella*, are due to such incidentals as literary sources, rather than to a profound unity of aesthetic purpose.

From 1866, when Leighton sent to the Academy his painting of *The Syracusan Bride*, his path was clearly set towards classical art. However, it is a classicism owing more to the tenets of Aestheticism than to archaeology. The painting is inspired by lines from the second Idyll of Theocritus, in which the procession is described as an ancient custom, rendered colourful by the attendant wild animals. Leighton has applied the lessons of his years of study with lavish yet exact effect. The half-length figures occupying the immediate foreground are painted with an enamelled French academic finish. The procession itself, drawn with sculptural effect, is coloured with a Venetian richness. The far distance, where a vivid Mediterranean landscape is sketched, has the immediacy of Corot's studies. But the heart of the composition remains the rhythmic succession of figures, draped in the manner of Phidias' sculptures, which passes across the marble stage. Once this painting appeared at the Royal Academy, Leighton had marked out his ground.

Some critics have seized on Leighton's Hellenism and savaged his works on the grounds that he achieved no more than a hopelessly diluted evocation of never-never-land Grecian chic. In fact he was interested in something altogether less easy, and something altogether more modern. If one looks again at *Lieder Ohne Worte* his preoccupations become clear. That picture, as noted, contains various pots of strange, almost futuristic design. Leighton knew the work of Christopher Dresser (a botanist and polemicist of reformed ornament) and of Owen Jones (architect and author of the *Grammar of Ornament*), and both in this picture and elsewhere he clearly supported their plea for a new reformed grammar or ornament, to be based on conventionalised representations of natural forms. Such stylisations appealed to Leighton and appear in the doors, ceilings and chimney-pieces of his home in Holland Park, designed in conjunction with George Aitchson in 1864–6. The collection of Islamic tiles formed by Leighton in the 1860s and 1870s reflects this preoccupation with abstract patterning, and shows that Leighton's Hellenism is of a modern and essentially innovative form.

In his wide-ranging book, *The Victorians and Ancient Greece*, Richard Jenkyns points out that the theories of Dresser and Jones were in direct opposition to those of Ruskin and his followers.

Ruskin wanted variety and immediacy, while all classical forms of ornament rely for effect on repetition and abstraction. Leighton, whose sympathy with PreRaphaelite theories fell far short of his friendship with that circle, was moving throughout the 1860s towards formalism and economy. He applied the same principles to his art.

Jenkyns, later in the same book, attacks Leighton on the grounds that his paintings are the posturings of a self-proclaimed 'old master' and that the figures are weighed down with masses of drapery, bearing no relation either to Greek prototypes or reality. In contrast, he cites Alma-Tadema as a painter whose archaeological interests enhanced his pictures. A single comparison will illustrate the error of Jenkyns' argument. In 1868, two years after Leighton painted *The Syracusan Bride*, Alma-Tadema exhibited *Phidias and the Parthenon*, a reconstruction of the scene of Phidias showing to Pericles, Aspasia, Alcibiades, Socrates and others the newly installed Parthenon marbles. Accurate as the period detail is, this canvas is as arid as a school textbook. The subject is anecdotal, even sentimental. Leighton's picture, in contrast, says more about Phidias' real contribution to the history of art in technical and formal terms than Alma-Tadema's ever can.

Edgecumbe Staley, writing in 1906, after Leighton's death, and at a time when the artist's work was already part of a completed chapter in art history, hailed Leighton as 'The High Priest of Eclectic Beauty'. Behind the rhetoric there lies a useful perception. Leighton, often seen as an austerely isolated figure, was in fact remarkably in touch with a wide variety of schools and enterprises among his contemporaries. His continental friendships included Giovanni Costa (the Etruscan school landscapist) in Italy, Gérôme in Paris, as well as close professional and personal friendships with artists as diverse as Millais, Burne-Jones, Whistler and Walter Crane.

Leighton's inexhaustible delight in new work kept him as closely in touch with new developments as did his teaching in the Royal Academy schools, which continued until his election as President of the Academy in 1878. The following year he made his first Presidential address. Continued biennially until 1893, these addresses, though nowhere near in the immortal class of his predecessor, Reynolds, serve as an interesting commentary on his work. They are also an insight into the sensibilities of a man who was clearly at heart a passionate aesthete.

Leighton addresses the whole issue of how one should produce modern works of art. In his first address to the Academy, made in 1879, he identifies the central dilemma of style: the Victorian artist being faced with almost limitless choice:

Unconscious work has become and will be henceforth all but impossible; the critical intelligence stands by the imagination of her work, and Fancy no longer walks alone . . .

Stripped of its rhetorical frills, this statement is an acute recognition of the intellectual problem of nineteenth-century art. This age was, for the first time in the history of art, a self-conscious age. The problem is exacerbated by the modern indifference to fine and applied art:

The whole current of human life setting resolutely in a direction opposed to artistic production: no love of beauty, no sense of the outward dignity and comeliness of things . . .

In later lectures Leighton develops his theme, examining the art and culture of the past, in search of an answer to the modern dilemma, feeding in fact off the experience of the past to provide a solution for the future. For Leighton the high point of art, when a perfect balance was achieved between political, cultural and artistic imperatives, was Periclean Athens. His theories at this point become somewhat muddied by considerations of racial characteristics. But the theme which remains clear in all this is his conviction that in ancient Greece the ethical and aesthetic foundations of art were mutually supportive. This places him clearly in the opposite camp from Ruskin:

As artistic production springs from aesthetic and not from ethnic impulses within the artist, so the character of that production is independent of his moral attitude and unaffected by it.

Thus, while civilisations may be more or less conducive to great art, the moral or spiritual state of the artist does not affect his work. Leighton at the same time distanced himself from the strong PreRaphaelite influences still at work in the British art world, claiming that the modern tendency towards 'a more intimate fidelity to nature in its outward aspects' has led to 'an excessive absorption of the attention in the most superficial aspect of things'.

Leighton offers instead a philosophy of the ideal, based on the central conviction that:

Primarily the source of all art whatsoever . . . is the consciousness of emotion in the presence of the natural phenomena of Life and Nature . . .

This 'conscious emotion, a momentary intensification of life', is
very similar to Walter Pater's exhortation made in the first edition
of his influential volume *Studies in the Renaissance*, to experience
constantly new sensations, to seek to 'burn with that hard, gem-
like flame', in the most famous words of the whole Aesthetic
Movement. Leighton advocates, like Pater, a life lived through the
senses. It is however, no mere encouragement to sensuality, but
a serious and austere appeal to artists to dedicate themselves to
sensation at its most fine, for:

Whatever noble fire is in our own hearts will burn also in our work,
whatever purity is ours will chasten and exalt it.

Pater's volume had first been published in 1873. Its influence on
young students and artists was so great that the author felt
obliged to withdraw from the second edition his famous exhortation, finding that his appeal for a life of the senses had been
widely misread as an enthusiastic advocacy of sensuality. Pater
and Leighton were both in fact singularly austere men. Neither
had any time for the excesses of passionate Brompton, as recorded
by du Maurier in the pages of *Punch*. Yet both were indirectly
responsible for stoking the fires of overheated Aesthetic emotion.

Leighton therefore should be seen in the context of the
developing Aesthetic Movement, a prototypical figure, and hero
to many of the young men and women studying art in the 1870s
and 1880s. He remained acutely sensitive, as he grew older, to
the innovations to be found in the works of young artists. Notable
among his percipient judgements is his early advocacy of John
Singer Sargent. Sargent arrived in London from Paris, trailing
clouds of controversy following the public scandal of his portrait
of *Madame X*. In 1887 he exhibited at the Royal Academy his
remarkable symphony of light and colour *Carnation, Lily, Lily,
Rose*, a picture which Leighton admired, using his casting vote to
ensure that it was acquired for the Chantrey Bequest. The painting
is untypical of the Sargent of popular imagination: an informal,
luscious indulgence in sensuous observation. It clearly struck
a chord for Leighton, although far removed from his own
work.

Significantly, Leighton was asked, along with another unlikely
contributor, Henry James, to allow something of his work to appear in the first issue of *The Yellow Book* in 1894. Even to aesthetes

of the latest and most extreme complexion, Leighton remained a seminal figure. It was Aubrey Beardsley who invited Leighton to contribute to *The Yellow Book*. Leighton owned one of Beardsley's drawings, as well as Charles Rickett's *Oedipus and the Sphinx*.

A significant final vignette of Leighton in the character of passionate aesthete and Hellenophile dates from the last months of his life. Racked by the angina which would shortly kill him, he travelled vainly in search of rest and recuperation in the Mediterranean. With him was Pater's newly published *Greek Studies* which he read with enthusiasm.

His intellectual interests were wider, probably, than those of any of his colleagues. When he died the roll-call of his library, sold at Christie's, embraced the whole of European literature, fine art, architecture and archaeology. It is salutary to consider the range of learning that underpinned Leighton's art. His values were rooted in a tradition of which he felt himself only the latest emanation. In one sense he was wrong, for the tradition of figurative art which he represented and continued was to end shortly after his death. In another sense he was right, for his last works exhibit a sense of line and natural form prophetic of *art nouveau*.

Thus, both in his work and in his taste Leighton was also strangely a precursor of what was to follow. The most significant lesson perhaps in Leighton's thought and career is that high Victorian art is founded on aesthetic considerations far more complex than is often admitted.

Easy generalisations about sentimentality do nothing to explain the vital and robust aesthetic controversies which took place in the second half of the nineteenth century. One clue to the source of this strength is the conviction maintained not only by Leighton but by most leading artists and designers, that art mattered. Beauty was perceived as an essential nourishment for all men. Thus art was as important as hospitals and sewers in the betterment of the human lot. This high idealism applied especially to Leighton, with his Phidian preoccupations; but one sees it also in the retreat of PreRaphaelitism into medieval romance. Even Morris' socialism predicated an imaginary modern world of guilds and good craftmanship, where beauty conquers industrialisation. The Aesthetic Movement, though clearly definable within a circle of artists and designers, had a far more prevalent influence than at first glance appears.

For Further Reading:

Frederic, Lord Leighton, *Addresses delivered to . . . the Royal Academy* (Kegan Paul, 1897); Léonée and Richard Ormond, *Lord Leighton* (Yale University Press, 1975); Richard Jenkyns, *The Victorians and Ancient Greece* (Blackwell, 1980); Frank M. Turner, *The Greek Heritage in Victorian Britain* (Yale University Press, 1981).

19

'Commanding the Heart'
Edward Carpenter and Friends

Sheila Rowbotham

Opposite: Male bonding: Edward Carpenter (centre) with a group of his closest associates, George Merrill (seated below) and (right) George Hunkin. (Sheffield City Art Gallery)

AS ASA BRIGGS HAS OBSERVED, the unity of the Victorian period is an artificial one – and by the end of it a powerful body of ideas were challenging the cosy *pater familias* traditionalism that has come to be caricatured as Victorian values. From the late 1870s onwards, trade unionism, socialism and the ideas of state intervention and improvement began to influence and provoke establishment culture. At the same time individuals and groups forced the pace of cultural and social change and challenge in a way that recalls the heady days of the 1960s – Walter Pater's Aesthetic Movement to whom writers such as Swinburne and Oscar Wilde were attracted, the Arts and Crafts groupings around Ashbee and William Morris, often associated with Utopianism, hovering uneasily between a 'drop-out' approach and confronting the establishment order head-on.

Perhaps the most iconoclastic challenge that could be offered was that to traditional family and sexual relationships. It was provided by the radical writer, lecturer and social activist, Edward Carpenter (1844–1926). His endorsement of the 'love that dare not speak its name' and openly homosexual lifestyle made him a founding father of the twentieth-century gay liberation movement, but his role as a link-man for consciousness-raising in socialist, feminist and alternative movements in the late Victorian period was, as Sheila Rowbotham reminds us here, no less crucial also.

Edward Carpenter described the 'Victorian Age' as:

. . . a period in which not only commercialism in public life, but cant in religion, pure materialism in science, futility in social conventions, the worship of stocks and shares, the starving of the human heart, the denial of the human body and its needs, huddling concealment of the body in clothes, the 'impure hush' in matters of sex, class-division, contempt of manual labour, and the cruel barring of women from every natural and useful expression of their lives, were carried to an extremity of folly difficult for us to realise.

This observation made by Edward Carpenter in 1914, indicates his own late-Victorian rebellion which had begun as a young upper-middle-class clerical fellow at Cambridge with religious and social doubts. Influenced by the romantic poets and Walt Whitman he had inclined to the radical nationalism of Mazzini. In the early 1870s he had wrestled with the problem of unearned wealth and debated how to respond to the Paris Commune.

He left Cambridge to find a resolution in social action by working as an itinerant lecturer in the new University Extension Movement in the north which sought to heal class divisions through higher education. Behind this change of course was a yearning for a Whitmanite union with 'the people'.

While in Sheffield, Carpenter was influenced by local radicals who still carried a vision of communitarianism. Joseph Sharpe, a wandering harpist, ex-Chartist and free-thinker, was still tramping the country lanes, communing with the stars and making music at local fairs. Jonathan Taylor from a Chartist family was an outdoor speaker on radical issues like free education. There was a group of secularists who met in the Owenite Hall of Science, with a plan to live communally. They received financial help from John Ruskin to settle at St George's farm, Totley, and Carpenter lived there briefly before moving to Millthorpe.

The influence of Buddhism and Thoreau in the early 1880s strengthened Carpenter's desire to break with materialism and the social conventions of his class. He wanted to be at one with nature and find a more democratic communion with his fellows. His ethical concern about inequality and poverty crystallised into socialism, which included for him a wide-ranging cultural rebellion. In this period he made contact with other young middle-class men and women who were in revolt against various aspects of their times. From King's College, Cambridge, G. Lowes Dickinson dithered between mysticism and commitment to the unemployed. 'Goldie' found the reality of manual labour which Carpenter admired difficult, writing woefully to his college friend Charles Ashbee from a country cottage at Farnham, 'I cannot milk a cow'. Ashbee worked in the settlement at Toynbee Hall and then formed a Guild of Handicraft. He was to conflict with William Morris because he saw artistry and craft as more important than revolution. Henry and Kate Salt were both socialists, and Henry a keen vegetarian. Kate Salt was influenced by the ideas of the 'new woman', as were the writer Olive Schreiner and Edith Lees, a lesbian who later married Havelock Ellis, the sex psychologist who was also in Carpenter's unconventional circle.

Ellis was one of the founders of the grouping called 'The Fellowship of the New Life' in the early 1880s. According to its constitution the Fellowship was to be based on the 'subordination of material things to spiritual' and aimed at 'the cultivation of a perfect character in each and all'. Through discussion, simple living, manual labour and religious communion, members hoped

to lay the basis of a new life. By 1884 a split had developed. According to Bernard Shaw, a leading protagonist:

Certain members of that circle . . . [felt] that the revolution would have to wait an unreasonably long time if postponed until they personally attained perfection.

While the Fellowship emphasised personal and spiritual change, the more material dissidents, including Shaw, split to form the Fabian Society, 'one to sit among the dandelions the other to organise the docks'. Characteristically, Carpenter maintained contact with both factions: his peculiar capacity to overcome the tensions inherent in the pursuit of personal and social liberation made him a pervasive influence in a series of progressive causes from naturalism to an 'anti-smoke' campaign against pollution in Sheffield. He combined Eastern mysticism and homosexual liberation with struggles against unemployment and support of the militant 'new unionism' of unskilled and semi-skilled workers. Lowes Dickinson records in his memoir, asking Carpenter how he did it, to which 'EC' breezily replied that, 'he liked to hang out his red flag from the ground floor and then go up above to see how it looked'.

In 1886 forty-four people signed the Sheffield Socialists' Manifesto. They are a mixed group; apart from Carpenter, they included ex-Chartists, secularists and members of the Totley communal farm. Among them was George Hukin, a razor grinder, and George Adams, an insurance salesman who became a gardener on Carpenter's smallholding at Millthorpe. They had contact with a loose network of socialists which was beginning to form nationally. Carpenter provided money for the first Marxist paper in Britain, *Justice*. William Morris came to speak along with Annie Besant, who had been a secularist and supporter of birth control and had become a socialist propagandist. Havelock Ellis visited the Sheffield socialists' café and drank tea, presumably pondering the simple life and personal perfection. The anarchists, Prince Kropotkin and Charlotte Wilson, also visited the Sheffield socialist club. Raymond Unwin came over from Chesterfield to speak on ancient history and communism. He had worked in Charles Rowley's Manchester settlement, Ancoats, and was to become a planner associated with the garden city movement. Other visitors included Tom Maguire, a young socialist photographer

---

Opposite: An aesthetic distaste of the materialist priorities of the society is reflected in Evelyn de Morgan's painting of 'The Worship of Mammon'. (De Morgan Foundation, Bridgeman Art Library)

friend of Alf Mattison, an engineer. They were both active in the gas workers' strike in Leeds which marked the end of liberal trades unionism in the city. Maguire's ballads *Machine Room Chants* testify to his personal affection for the tailoresses and other women workers.

There were propaganda outings to the neighbouring villages where Maguire's wit and humour were great assets. Isabella Ford, a socialist feminist of Leeds Quaker stock, accompanied them. She also was an organiser in the upsurge of 'new unionism'. The same political interconnections between socialism, feminism and the 'new unionism' were also present in Bristol where Carpenter had links going back to one of the Totley farmers, W. H. Riley. Helena Born and Miriam Daniell were Bristol converts to socialism from the Women's Liberal Association. They helped organise women cotton operatives who went on strike on October 1889. Every Sunday the strikers, in clean white aprons and with shawls over their heads, marched to the churches and chapels.

A young classics teacher, Katherine St John Conway, was so moved that she went next day to the Bristol socialists' coffee house. They gave her Carpenter's *England's Ideal* and she read it far into the night:

As I went back to my Clifton lodgings I vaguely realised that every value life had previously held for me had been changed as if by some mysterious alchemy. I was ashamed of the privileges and elaborate refinements of which I had previously been so proud. The joy of companionship, the glory of life lost and found, the 'age long peerless cause' had been revealed to me, dimming all others.

It was not uncommon for socialists to describe the changes in their consciousness in terms akin to religious conversion. The idea that socialism required an inner transformation of the spirit and new relationships between people as well as external changes was a quite common assumption in the 1880s and 1890s. Tom Maguire died young of poverty and alcohol. Before his death he noted how difficult it was to alter internal responses:

People call themselves Socialists but what they are is just ordinary men with Socialist opinions hung round; they haven't got it inside them. It's hard, very hard; we get mixed up in disputes among ourselves and can't keep a straight line for the great thing, even if we all of us know what that is.

Miriam Daniell and Helena Born introduced women's liberation ideas to the Bristol socialists. Like Carpenter they tried to live the alternative lifestyle as well as talk about their socialist beliefs. Helen Tufts wrote in her panegyric 'Whitman's Ideal Democracy' in 1902:

This set an example of practical simplicity in household matters showing aesthetic possibilities in colour and ingenious and artistic adaptation which was a revelation to their neighbours. With their own hands they tinted the walls of their rooms and waxed the uncarpeted floors, while from the most commonplace materials they improvised many articles of furniture and decoration, combining both beauty and utility.

The aim was the democratisation of everyday life without the dependence on the manual labour of others.

Personal democracy was also the theme of Katherine St John Conway's letter to the rather bohemian socialist Bruce Glasier (later to become a leading figure in the Labour Party). She asked her love:

What does a poet think of a woman with ink on her finger and a hole in her stocking? What would he say to two *thick* ankles? . . . What would he say to a woman who would sooner eat bread and butter and drink milk or buy fruit than cook it . . . Again, what would a poet say to a woman who *liked* earning money and enjoyed the thought of being a breadwinner as well as wife that the husband might *never* have to sell a hair of himself.

Bruce Glasier proved compliant and they married according to Scottish common law by declaration before two witnesses.

These advanced young women in Carpenter's circle read and commented on his lectures on sexual liberation, published in 1896 as *Love's Coming of Age*. Carpenter maintained that women needed communism, for only a non-competitive society which was not ruled by profit could support them as mothers without necessitating dependence on men. He urged women to declare themselves 'free' and break with conventional mores. It was characteristic of Carpenter to assert freedom as an act of will. Though he conflicted with the local Sheffield anarchists he shared some aspects of their faith in propaganda by deed. One of the flaws in this personal politics of liberation was that it disregarded real vulnerabilities.

Carpenter's comments on the inadequacies of the Victorian middle-class man in *Love's Coming of Age* are both mischievous and compassionate. He describes how the boy at public school was 'well pounded into shape, kneaded and baked' for the 'upper crust'. Gliding into a career he settled into 'beefy self-satisfaction' without developing 'affection and tenderness of feeling':

A man pelts along on his hobby, his business, his career, his latest invention, or what not, forgetful that there is such a thing in the world as the human heart: then all of a sudden he 'falls in love', tumbles headlong in the most ludicrous way, fills the air with his cries, struggles frantically like a fly in treacle, and all the time hasn't the faintest idea whether he has been inveigled into the situation, or whether he got there of his own accord, or what he wants now that he is there.

The description fits some of Shaw's helpless male characters caught by spider-like women of dauntless emotional energy.

Carpenter's combination of Whitmanite ideals of comradeship and union with nature combined with romanticism in a more passionate and responsive concept of masculinity. He yearned for a democratic bonding without guilt.

Just as the Socialist Society began he developed a painful love for the razor grinder George Hukin, but had to reconcile himself to Hukin's marriage. In *Philolaus to Diocles* Carpenter reflected:

And sweeter far to suffer is it, dear one, being sometimes absent,
Than (if indeed 'twere possible) to feel the opposite pain
Of too much nearness, and love dying so
Down to mere slackness.

Instead:

The harp is finely strung;
The tender tension animates the string.

He found loving companionship with George Merrill from 1891. Merrill came from the Sheffield slums. He had already had some experience of upper-class men through chance homosexual encounters. His union with Carpenter was deep and proved lifelong. They were contrasting characters, Carpenter self-conscious, vain and fastidious, Merrill rough and openly bawdy, happy in male company and inclined to drink a lot. Some of Carpenter's friends regarded Merrill as an uncouth intruder. Edith Lees adapted more happily. She described the masculine domesticity created by the two companions:

I remember smiling to myself one night when I sat between Carpenter and his factotum and friend in one. One was mending his shirt, and the other a pair of socks. No incongruity struck one, because Carpenter's idea of life is simplification and real division of work. His belief is that what a woman can do a man can always share. He has realised the truth that no occupation is a sex-monopoly, but a chance for free choice, capability and the division of labour. So that when Carpenter takes his share in the washing-up it seems quite as natural as when he lights a cigarette. When he neither sews nor smokes but plays Chopin a curious realisation comes over one that there is no real difference in the arts of love, music, stocking-mending, or redeeming.

Carpenter's homosexuality was no secret in the socialist movement and his pamphlet *Homogenic Love* was published by Manchester Labour Press. Carpenter was one of the case studies in Havelock Ellis' early work on sex psychology. Like Ellis he hoped that the attempt to understand all forms of sexual desire would prevent unnecessary suffering and shame. However, since the 1885 Act, homosexuality was a criminal offence. In 1895 the Oscar Wilde trial created a moral panic and the publishers of *Love's Coming of Age,* Fisher Unwin, took out the chapter on homosexuality. It was not included until the 1906 edition.

Carpenter's writing on sexual liberation produced a mixed response among socialists. In the Independent Labour Party paper, *Labour Leader,* Lily Bell wrote in 1896, that he was one of the few men who could write about women and sex without patronage:

Most men write with such an air of superiority, such an assumption of masculine authority and right to lay down the law as to what women may or may not do, what may or may not be her proper 'sphere' in life, that I usually take up their articles merely to lay them down with a feeling of impatience and irritation.

Robert Allen Nicoll, who had been a member of the Bristol socialist group, wrote enthusiastically about the emancipatory effect of sandals which an Indian friend of Carpenter's had taught him how to make. 'One begins to own one's own body at last', Nicoll remarked from the West Coast of America in 1894. Two years later he told Carpenter of a '. . . clear feeling . . . I could distinguish myself as something apart from and superior to my brain and intellect. There swept thro' [sic] me a power of mastery over my body – not an attitude of rejection but of self-realisation – something I have long known and believed but never up till now realised.' He added, 'I want to realise my body and all its faculties'. Nicoll longed for a glorious comradeship, a band of brothers, men and women each with their art who could co-operate. With a surfeit of radical optimism he declared, 'No longer can priest or anyone cast obloquy on the sexual act or on woman, on the testes or vagina or womb, or the sweetness of coition'.

Robert Allen Nicoll would have confirmed the worst fears of

the Marxist leader of the Social Democratic Federation, H. M.
Hyndman, who dressed formally in tails and top hat and rebuked
Shaw in the 1880s for mixing with Carpenter and his friends:

I do not want the movement to be a depositary of old cranks,
humanitarians, vegetarians, anti-vivisectionists, arty-crafties and all the
rest of them. We are scientific socialists and have no room for sentimen-
talists. They confuse the issue.

Robert Blatchford, editor of the popular socialist paper, *The
Clarion*, was enthusiastic about Carpenter's writing on socialism
and on Indian religion but not about his proposal to write *Love's
Coming of Age*. In 1894 he told Carpenter he did not think our
'parts' should be displayed 'as sexual graces'. He did not find
them beautiful. 'Perhaps I'm a prejudiced old Tory; but the whole
subject is "nasty" to me'. He admitted that sexual relations must
be altered but believed this must come after economic and industrial change. Feeling and prejudice were so strong about
sexuality that 'if Socialists identify themselves with any sweeping
changes in these relations the industrial change will be seriously
retarded.' Blatchford concluded, 'the time is not ripe for Socialists,
as Socialists, to meddle with the sexual question'.

Other late-Victorian rebels busied themselves with many of the
causes which Carpenter espoused – though no one was quite so
all embracing. There were utopian land colonies and communal
houses. Craft guilds promoted aesthetics based on simplicity and
utility. Progressive schools tried to put democratic co-operation
into practice. Settlements of middle-class intellectuals in slum
areas attempted to overcome class divisions. Unwin's designs for
Letchworth brought rural ideals into town planning. Young
women went bicycling in bloomers and vegetarians demanded
respect for animals. Clubs were formed for the frank discussion
of sexuality and the 'Legitimation League' advocated free unions
without marriage. A few brave souls risked ostracism and lived
in free unions. Male novelists, Gissing, Hardy and Moore, created
heroines who were influenced by the 'new woman'. Some
feminists, including Isabella Ford, also began to create a genre
which considered the personal and social dilemmas of women. In
February 1894 the *Daily Chronicle* declared that 'every third novel
published is avowedly a statement of one or other of the "Social
Questions", "the Sex Question" or "the Woman Question"'.

The ferment was more cultural than political, although
Elizabeth Wolstenholme Elmy's Women's Emancipation Union

(1892–9) put forward equality in marriage and equal rights to divorce. The more conventional feminist campaigners focused on education and the suffrage. Millicent Fawcett, for example, regarded Carpenter and his opinions with a distaste equal to Hyndman's. Even the anarchists who were sympathetic to free unions, sexual liberation and co-operative living appeared to have baulked at Carpenter's advocacy of homosexual liberation.

The Oscar Wilde trial in 1895 marked a powerful reaction against sexual and cultural radicalism. In 1898 police seized Havelock Ellis' *Sexual Inversion*, published by the secretary of the Legitimation League. Detective Inspector Sweeney of Scotland Yard claimed police action had prevented 'the growth of a Frankenstein monster wrecking the marriage laws of our country, and perhaps carrying off the general respect of all law'. In fact both marriage and the 'monster' were to prove more resilient than the inspector imagined. However, the tensions within the many-faceted rejection of Victorian establishment values which Edward Carpenter came to represent in the 1880s and 1890s were to become more pronounced in the twentieth century. It proved difficult to hold together the quest for a new life with the external transformation of society. The emphasis on democratising personal relationships was frequently subordinated to less emotionally disorienting social and economic reforms.

Indeed a socialism that dwelt on desire came to be dismissed as naive. Sidney Webb, one of the most influential Fabians, saw only the inadequacies of the ethical and utopian impulse. In 1892 he sought to win over Katherine St John Conway:

. . . the more I study the problems of England's industrial organisation, the more I am persuaded of the need of thorough personal study by all Socialists of the *facts* of modern industry rather than the *aspirations* of Socialists.

The Fabian influence was more in accord with the practical problems Labour was to face in office. But there were losses as well as gains. E. M. Forster, who knew Carpenter through their mutual friend, G. Lowes Dickinson, regretted the marginalising of freedom and love. He compared Carpenter's vision of the union of manual work and fresh air to William Morris' writing about Utopia in *News from Nowhere* in a collection edited by Gilbert Beith on Edward Carpenter in 1931:

The labour movement took another course and advanced by committee meetings and statistics towards state-owned factories attached to state supervised recreation grounds. Edward's heart beat no warmer at such joys. He felt no enthusiasm over municipal baths and municipally provided bathing drawers. What he wanted was *News from Nowhere* and the place that is still nowhere, wildness, the rapture of unpolluted streams, sunrise and sunset over the moon, and in the midst of these the working people whom he loved, passionately in touch with one another and with the natural glories around them. Perhaps labour will listen to him in the end. 'Who shall command the heart?' as he wrote himself.

It is well to remember there are several potentialities in human nature, not one, and though it is possible to organise, organise, organise, which is all that political parties do at present, it is also possible to obey the heart's commands. If labour ever changes its course, he will come into his own, and if, as he maintained, his spirit continues to haunt the places and people he loved he will pass a happy little day in the midst of his immortal bliss.

He noted rather sadly that Carpenter would be 'remembered for his courage and candour about sex, particularly about homosexuality; for his hatred of snobbery while snobbery was still fashionable; for his support for Labour before Labour wore dress-clothes and for his cult of simplicity'.

Victorian values continue to find echoes in our own times. Through their midst steps a white-bearded gentleman in a Walt Whitman hat murmuring about the needs of the body and the heart, checking nuclear fall-out levels and enquiring whether – in the words of his socialist song – it is yet time for England to arise?

For Further Reading:

Edward Carpenter, *My Days and Dreams* (George Allen and Unwin, 1916); Ruth First and Ann Scott, *Olive Schreiner* (André Deutsch, 1980); Stanley Pierson, *Marxism and the Origins of British Socialism* (Cornell University Press, 1973); Sheila Rowbotham and Jeff Weeks, *Socialism and the New Life, The Personal and Sexual Politics of Edward Carpenter and Havelock Ellis* (Pluto, 1977); David Rubinstein, *Before the Suffragettes: Women's Emancipation in the 1890s* (The Harvester Press, 1986); E. P. Thompson, 'Homage to Tom Maguire', in Asa Briggs and John Saville (eds.), *Essays in Labour History* (Macmillan, 1960).

20
The Quest for Englishness

Paul Rich

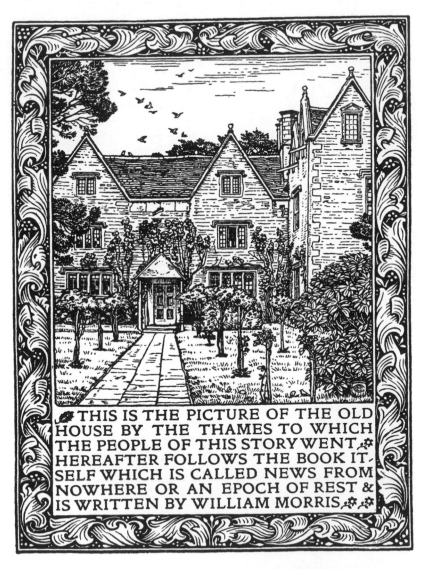

THIS IS THE PICTURE OF THE OLD
HOUSE BY THE THAMES TO WHICH
THE PEOPLE OF THIS STORY WENT
HEREAFTER FOLLOWS THE BOOK IT-
SELF WHICH IS CALLED NEWS FROM
NOWHERE OR AN EPOCH OF REST &
IS WRITTEN BY WILLIAM MORRIS

The frontispiece of News from Nowhere – Morris' utopian account of a future society in which the values of a mythical medievalism held sway, unencumbered by urban capitalism and spiced with sexual liberation and primitive communism. (HT Archives)

'WHAT DO THEY KNOW OF ENGLAND, who only England know?' As the Victorian era wore on, the question of national identity was one that came to be asked with increasing pertinency. The piecemeal acquisition of colonies around the world, and the languid support of them and their trading networks from Whitehall, hardened into a positive and aggressive expansionism and a sense of imperial destiny which channelled and exploited the emotions of the masses. A turning-point in the imperial sentiment was perhaps the failure of Gladstone's Liberal government to sustain the dreams of Christian civilisation of General Gordon in the Sudan; his death at the hands of the Mahdi's insurgents in Khartoum in January 1885 outraged public opinion and turned the GOM ('Grand Old Man') into the MOG ('Murderer of Gordon').

At the same time, however, unease about the crudities of the modern age and scepticism about the amorality of industrial living – sentiments that had earlier fuelled aesthetic phenomena such as the Gothic and Pre-Raphaelite movements – spurred an increasing urgency among intellectuals to find England's 'roots'. Paul Rich examines the manifestations of this in the eulogies of 'Merrie England', and in a heightened racial awareness in the writings of the late-Victorian and Edwardian period.

Nationalism in English Society has not been a subject that has especially interested historians until comparatively recently. This is perhaps in part a legacy of the Whig domination of English historiography and the emphasis on Parliament and good government to the exclusion of political doctrine, which has often been seen as more of a bogey in continental European political history. The attainment of political stability by the mid-Victorian era has thus usually been perceived as a result of the insulation of English politics from the turbulence of European nationalism and a preoccupation with other issues surrounding the moral responses to industrialisation and urbanisation.

Even in its heyday, though, the 'condition of England' question in the nineteenth century assumed a form of unique cultural and political entity entitled 'England'. There was, in fact, in a considerable body of Victorian thought a conscious 'idea' of England that may not have reached the ideological precision of European nationalist visionaries such as Mazzini, but which nevertheless exerted a hold over both educated and informed opinion and more popular sentiments.

Unlike many of its European counterparts, England lacked a

nationalist intelligentsia and by the 1880s much of the energy
of intellectual opinion passed increasingly into a wider imperial
enthusiasm that came to be termed (after a book by Sir Charles
Dilke published in 1867) 'Great Britain'. Many historians of the
latter part of the century have thus chosen to emphasise the
growth in imperial sentiment behind England's mission and to
show how more parochial and inward-looking versions of English
patriotism tended to become eclipsed by a more expansionist jingoism that eventually culminated in the 'mafficking' mobs of the
Anglo-Boer War of 1899–1902.

If imperialism, however, came to define a considerable variety
of English national ideals from the 1880s onwards, it was by no
means a complete or all-embracing phenomenon. Carried to its
logical conclusion, empire would have superseded any sense of
English nationalism through the attainment of some wider imperial entity. This, indeed, was the theme of much imperialist
historiography in the tradition of J. R. Seeley's *The Expansion of
England* (1883) which emphasised an historical process which absorbed English development into a transcontinental and imperial
one. It was, though, an ideal which by no means commanded
universal assent for, as the historian Edward A. Freeman warned
his colleagues in *Macmillan's Magazine* in 1885, 'the soberest of us
will be driven to turn Jingoes and sing "Rule Britannia" if we are
asked that Great Britain shall sink to become one canton or three
cantons of Greater Britain'. Imperial federation seemed to threaten
English national identity at a time when economic and industrial
changes increasingly divorced the population from its rural roots.
Thus, while the imperial idea and the pursuit of some form of
'Anglo-Saxon' alliance with fellow white English-speaking
societies in Australia, America and South Africa appealed to some
imperial enthusiasts in the years up to the Boer War, there were
already signs of an important cultural and intellectual reaction
towards an identification with the native English landscape and
culture.

Some recent cultural history by such scholars as Herbert
Sussman and Martin Weiner has begun to look more closely at
indigenous cultural forces within nineteenth-century English
society which resisted a ready identification with economic expansion and urban industrialisation. In contrast with the emphasis in
imperial historiography on the 1880s, the 'scramble for Africa' and
the mobilisation of pro-imperial opinion by the yellow press, this
'economic backwardness' school has sought to explain contem-

porary problems of British economic decline by looking to the progressive failure of nineteenth-century capitalism in a society which was the first to undergo an industrial revolution. For this school, the decade of the 1850s following the Great Exhibition of 1851 was crucial to the emergence of an intellectual climate that was increasingly critical of the ravages of industrialisation and the brutalisation of an urban working class. If earlier writers like Carlyle had been willing to accept both city life and the disciplines of the Protestant work ethic, from the middle of the century onwards there began to surface a moral crusade against industrialism in such novels as Dickens' *Hard Times* (1854), Ruskin's *Unto This Last* and the radical attacks on capitalism from such figures as William Morris, H. M. Hyndman and Edward Carpenter.

More recently, though, Alun Hawkins has argued (in an essay 'The Discovery of Rural England' in the important collection edited by Robert Colls and Philip Dodd, *Englishness: Politics and Culture*), that the formation of the English rural ideal occurred somewhat later in the 1880s as a south England cultural myth that accompanied the submerging of the industrial middle class in the commercial bourgeoisie of the south and London. The earlier Gothic ideal in architecture began to be displaced by a more self-conscious moral pastoralism and a search for the life and culture of villages. In many respects, this was a retreat towards the ideal of 'merrie England' and a pre-industrial and medieval culture in which human relationships had not yet been complicated by the cash nexus or the demands of profit. It was, also, the assertion of a sense of English cultural and national identity at a time when this appeared to be threatened by more cosmopolitan forces within industry or empire building. It is thus to this movement in the late nineteenth century, especially after 1880, that we should look for the roots of the English national idea.

The moral reaction to Victorian industrialism was significant for its identification with an English national ideal rooted in a mythic past. As Mark Girouard has shown in an important analysis of Victorian culture, there was a general cult of medieval and courtly romance in nineteenth-century England following in the wake of the romantic historical novels of Sir Walter Scott. It was possible for such ideals to be fitted into a mission of building an imperial 'Greater Britain' overseas, and indeed many imperial novels emphasised the chivalric aspects of colonial adventurers and the need to protect white womanhood from the dangers of black savages. The movement for union in the South African colonies after the Boer War called itself *The Round Table* and held Saxon style 'moots' in order to emphasise its links with England's supposed Anglo-Saxon past. But the chivalric theme related rather more directly to the visible symbols of Britain's (or more especially England's) past – especially with the growing interest in Tudor history and the exploits of the Elizabethan merchant adventurers such as Raleigh, Drake and Hawkins.

By the 1880s, however, there developed, alongside the external imperial adventurer ideal, an indigenous 'merrie England' myth which embraced both a moral critique of capitalist industrialism and a search into England's distant past. The movement was especially stimulated by the publication in 1885 of the novel by the naturalist Richard Jefferies, *After London*, in which the capital city and urban civilisation are seen as having been swept away and a return made to a medieval social order in close harmony with nature. In this book, London, in fact, has disappeared into a black, poisonous lake, and the hero of the story ends up marrying and planning to settle down in a fortified castle. The book had a considerable impact and William Morris read it aloud to his friends in his Oxford rooms. Morris' own *News From Nowhere* (1890) was written in a similar idiom – the hero dreams of a future golden age in which a medieval society has returned to England and where human sensibilities, especially sexual ones, are allowed free play in a communist society liberated from the restrictions of urban capitalist living. Here was an alternative kind of adventure which sought to avoid the rapacious exploits of Victorian imperialism.

The mythical nature of this medievalism was undoubtedly important for a generation whose religious certainties had been undermined by the advent of Darwinism and who felt insecure in a rapidly urbanising world: between 1801 and 1901 the population of England and Wales grew by 24 million, 80 per cent of whom lived in towns. Furthermore, the development of capitalist agriculture on the land produced rapid mechanical and technological changes in which the old rural population became increasingly divided along class lines. By the 1880s it became apparent that much of the older rural way of life was disappearing. It thus seemed especially important to many writers to anchor what was happening within some kind of historical tradition; Jefferies, however, for all the power of *After London*, was out of tune with this historical consciousness preferring to pursue a more mystical nature religion which tried to deny the dominant evolutionist faith of the age. His important autobiography, *The Story of My Heart* (1883), which was taken seriously by a number of his contemporaries, urged that there was 'no evolution any more than there is design in nature. By standing face to face with nature, and not from books, I have convinced myself that there is no design and no evolution. What there is, what was the course, how and why, is not yet known.'

Such mysticism had its attractions for a minority opinion in British society and filtered down into movements like theosophy in the early years of the twentieth century. But for an age attracted by science, more concrete explanations were demanded and the search for English roots became bound up with attempts at producing a 'science' of race. In many cases, theories of the racial origins of the English people tended to reinforce views concerning their 'Saxon' or 'Teutonic' origin for, as English Whig historians such as E. A. Freeman and J. R. Green had reminded their readers, the origins of English parliamentary liberties were seen to lie in the forests of North Germany.

This obsession with historical continuity and the notion of the English as the racial 'survivors' of earlier demographic migrations were confirmed by the biologist and Darwinian anthropologist, Thomas Henry Huxley, in a paper on 'British Ethnology' in 1871. Huxley saw Britain as made up of only two main races, the dark-skinned 'Melanochroi' and the light-skinned 'Xanthochroi' which he saw as continuous from the time of Tacitus' observations during the Roman occupation. This distinction broadly resembled the traditional 'Celtic' and 'Teutonic' classification of racial types in British society, with the Celts resident mainly in the north and west and the Teutons scattered over other parts of the British Isles.

The interest in race in the 1860s and 1870s reflected a wider European interest in national identities at a time when countries such as Italy and Germany obtained national unification. The pseudo-science of anthropometry began to become increasingly popular as the measurement of skulls and the heads of living people seemed to provide a method for establishing patterns of 'racial' continuity on scientific grounds. In 1884 the mathematician and founder of the pseudo-science of eugenics, Sir Francis Galton (a cousin of Charles Darwin), measured some 9,000 people at an International Health Exhibition in South Kensington, and though there remained fierce disputes among physical anthropologists as to the exact criteria by which anthropometric 'types' might be established, the notion that there were scientific and biological entities called 'races' pervaded a considerable proportion of the literature on England and English national identity.

The effect of this Darwinian anthropology lay especially in its reinforcing the idea of the *distinctiveness* of races. Earlier writers, like Ralph Waldo Emerson in *English Traits* (1854), had emphasised English racial ancestry, but had also written of the intermixture of such elements as 'Celt' and 'Saxon'. In general Emerson had seen English nationality as a southern English phenomenon, based mainly on the character of the English governing class:

It excludes Ireland, and Scotland, and Wales, and reduces itself at last to London, that is, to those who come and go thither. The portraits that hang on the walls in the Academy Exhibition at London, the figures in *Punch's* drawings of the public men, or of the club houses, the prints in the shop windows, are distinctive English, not American, no, nor Scotch, nor Irish: but 'tis a very restricted nationality. As you go north into the manufacturing and agricultural districts, *and go to the population that never travels*, as you go into Yorkshire, as you enter Scotland, the world's Englishman is no longer found. [Author's italics.]

By the 1870s and 1880s, there was a growing recognition of both the urbanisation and mobility of a population who had hitherto 'never travelled'. The emphasis thus shifted towards the significance of old racial types as survivals from a rural past and landscape that was under growing threat. The naturalist and novelist W. H. Hudson, for example, was an acute observer of supposed racial types in his travels through southern England in the latter part of the century. Like Jefferies, Hudson hated the 'strangeness' of cities; coming from a childhood background in Argentina his observations were goaded in some degree by a search by the colonial 'outsider' for roots and identity in British society. Hudson sought to apply Huxley's classification to the English people, seeing for example those in Berkshire, Oxfordshire and the Midlands as the 'common modified Saxon type'. In Hampshire, however, the presence of 'small, narrow headed men of black hair' indicated a race of 'Iberian' descent who stretched back to the neolithic period. 'Like the small existing herds of indigenous white cattle', he concluded, 'they have preserved their peculiar physical character down to the present time by remaining mixed with the blue-eyed people.'

This was a mode of race classification that had become absorbed within a wider pastoral movement in English nature-writing by an essentially urban-based group writing about the countryside and its people without being an essential part of it. The rural English racial survivals thus in many respects resembled other ancient features of the landscape, such as pre-historic burial mounds and dolmens which began to attract a growing archaeological interest. These were areas, though, not merely of professional and scientific curiosity but visible symbols of ancient time-spans in an age increasingly conscious of differing rates and modes of historical change. Stonehenge, for instance, had long held a fascination for observers of England and, for Emerson, it appeared to confirm the ancient pastoral lineage of the rural shepherds of Wiltshire, for:

On the top of a mountain, the old temple would not be more impressive. Far and wide a few shepherds with their flocks sprinkled the plain, and a bagman drove along the road. It looked as if the wide margin given in this crowded isle to this primeval temple was accorded by the veneration of the British race to the old egg out of which all their ecclesiastical structures and history had proceeded.

The ancient stone blocks seemed a tangible link with a pre-Christian and pagan past and it was fitting that Thomas Hardy should set the arrest of his heroine Tess, in *Tess of the d'Urbervilles* (1892), descendant of a decadent line of aristocrats, in the ruins as she lay asleep on a large stone as if ready for sacrifice. The ancient megalith was evidence of an even longer span of human history in England compared to the span of identifiably 'English' history stretching back to medieval knights and lords, and the more immediate span of rapid economic change in the Victorian countryside which threatened to disconnect the age from its past.

The late-nineteenth-century travel and nature writers were thus already subconsciously aware of a tendency that J. H. Plumb came to call the 'death of the past'. The effort to forge out of the visible symbols of the past a national culture which bore some direct relationship to the past was thus a conscious effort at pre-empting this possibility of loss. Hudson, for example, felt the ruins of the ancient Roman town of Silchester in *Afoot in England* epitomised both the tranquillity of the English countryside and its ancient history as well as providing an historical link for its present-day neighbours:

The perfect sense of satisfaction, of restfulness, of peace, experienced here is very perfect; but in the wilderness, where man has never been, or has at all events left no trace of his former presence, there is even a mysterious sense of loneliness, of desolation, underlying our pleasures of nature. Here it seems good to know, or to imagine, that the men I occasionally meet in my solitary rambles, and that I see in the scattered rustic villages hard by, are of the same race, and possibly the descendants of the people who occupied the spot in the remote past – Iberian and Celt, and Roman and Saxon and Dane.

The English landscape thus appeared as quintessentially a tended and tranquil 'middle landscape', which Leo Marx has designated as the ideal compromise between the lonely and remote 'wilderness' and the urbanised landscape of the city. It provided for Hudson a means of psychological identification after his earlier isolated residence on the Argentinian pampas, and at the same time it denoted the continuation of at least some of the older rustic order in the new machine age.

The ideological significance of this suburban middle landscape ideal lay in the fact that it tended to relegate the more radical attacks on English gentility to the peripheries of political debate in this period. A number of writers in the tradition of William Morris' Arts and Crafts movement sought a more direct return to nature and communal living outside the mainstreams of society. Edward Carpenter, for example, established a rural commune at Millthorpe outside Sheffield and in a number of books attacked middle-class pretensions tó gentility. Championing the ideas of Thoreau and Kropotkin, Carpenter actively sought a return to a simpler rural life where there was to be found the true sources of 'social brotherhood' and 'honesty'. He berated the seaside homes of the south coast *rentier* bourgeoisie and the 'polite villa residences' which 'like unwholesome toadstools dot and disfigure the whole of this great land', for these "noble" mansions of organised idleness were built upon the bent back of poverty and lifelong hopeless unremitting toil'.

However, in his struggle against the claims of bourgeois gentility in the makeup of what he termed the 'national conscience', Carpenter confronted a basic dilemma; that, by the 1880s the English peasantry no longer existed as a cohesive social and cultural entity. Unlike that of Ireland, English peasant culture by the late nineteenth century remained a mere memory, and Carpenter was drawn more towards a comparison with simpler societies overseas. In *Civilisation: Its Causes and Cure* (1889) he thus reinvoked the idea of the romantic savage as he contrasted the seemingly corrupt English urban society with the apparent

cohesion of 'savage society'. '. . . the social life of the wilder races
. . .', he wrote, 'within its limits is more harmonious and compact
than that of the more civilised nations. The members of the tribe
are not organically at warfare with each other; society is not
divided into classes which prey upon each other; nor is it consumed by parasites. There is more true social unity, less of
disease.'

But such romantic ideas were out of keeping with the mood
engendered by late-nineteenth-century imperial expansion, which
tended to exacerbate more racist notions of black and brown racial
inferiority in combination with Darwinian conceptions of evolutionary struggle and 'survival of the fittest'. With the growing
interest in colonial adventure fiction such as that of G. A. Henty
and Rider Haggard, 'savage' societies were not ones to be emulated as ideal social models but rather to be 'civilised' and, as far
as possible, 'uplifted'. By the late 1890s, though, a number of
liberal critics of imperialism such as J. A. Hobson and L. T. Hob-
house did become increasingly worried by the manner in which
imperialism and jingoism had found a base in the 'villa toryism'
of the suburban middle and lower middle class. The incorporation
of some aspects of the rural and pastoral ideal in the suburbanisa-
tion of late-Victorian England seemed to have forged a new
aggressive national consciousness which masked internal social
and economic differences. For a writer like H. G. Wells, who was
familiar with the developments in scientific thought, this emerging intellectual trend behind the popular 'social imperialism' was
one that filled him with concern: his time traveller, for instance,
in the scientific romance *The Time Machine* (1894) enters a future
England in which class differentiation has followed evolutionary
lines leading to two separate 'races' which, in terminology
reminiscent of T. H. Huxley, Wells called the Eloi and Morlocks.
The supposedly peaceful and tranquil agrarian order of the Eloi
above ground is at a high price as the small hairy Morlocks living
beneath ground have been thoroughly brutalised in the same
manner as sections of the English working class. The Morlocks
physically feed off the Eloi, whose culture is decadent too, as
literacy and books have been abandoned.

Wells' writing at this time continued to reflect an underlying
anxiety about the nature of imperial conquest, which he saw in
more universal terms than the conventional ideal of white Anglo-
Saxon domination of black races. His novel *The War of the Worlds*
(1898), for example, can be read at one level as an attempt to

awaken the Victorian reading public to the experience of colonial conquest as the Martian invaders of a placid rural England take on many of the trappings of British colonial intruders in Africa.

The domination of the heroic and chivalric in English historical consciousness by the end of the century was such that the warnings of writers like Wells tended to be understood by only a few. If there was a lesson to be learnt from the construction of the English national past it was generally one that emphasised the making of an imperial nation by both military conquest and the blending of racial stocks. The Darwinian writer Grant Allen, whom Wells later held to have been an important influence on his own thought, depicted in a popular survey of English county history, *Country and Town in England* (1901), a pattern of racial settlement derived from the work of the physical anthropologists and archaeologists. Dorset was still an area of semi-Celtic survivors of the old Dorsetae tribe at the time of the Roman conquest, while Sussex was 'one of the most purely Teutonic counties in England'. As with most imperial history, this was a pattern dictated by boundaries and frontiers and Berkshire marked:

. . . the final great northern extension of the West Saxon power, when the English colonists began to cross the ridge of the North Downs and descend into the valleys of the Kennet and the Thames. The White Horse formed the standard of the invading Teutons, as it still does both of Hanover, whence they came, and of Kent, where, perhaps, they first landed in Britain.

Such interest in English racial 'survivals' continued to preoccupy the 'experts' in archaeology and anthropology until at least the end of the First World War, and would be introduced to a newer generation by such authorities as H. J. Fleure and Harold Peake. But already, by the end of the Anglo-Boer War of 1899–1902, the mood was one of growing disenchantment with imperialism, and the resurgence of liberalism in Edwardian England led to a search for more indigenous English values to the exclusion of the wider colonial empire. Indeed, W. H. Kent in the liberal *Westminster Review* argued in February 1902 that 'patriotism' and 'imperialism' were 'two incompatible and mutually destructive ideas', and argued for an 'enlightened and practical patriotism' which concentrated on the tasks of domestic social reform.

In the years after the Liberal election victory against the Conservatives in 1906, G. K. Chesterton and a number of anti-imperial writers began to popularise many of the conceptions of England

and Englishness which had been developed over the previous two or three decades, though not always with the same enthusiasm for English racial ancestry, which Chesterton tended to decry as bogus pseudo-science. The movement united the appeals of English history and rural values in an attempt to undermine the pretensions to imperial grandiosity, though it was largely un-successful in demolishing the dominant school of Whig history at Oxford and Cambridge which was so important for turning out new recruits to the colonial service and India Office. Chesterton's *History of England* was written without a single date, and his weekly column in *The Illustrated London News* was accepted by him on condition that he steered clear of political topics. As both jour-nalist and critic, Chesterton was never treated with too much seriousness by his fellow intellectuals, and his eminence came to be tarnished too with charges of anti-semitism, despite his denials to the contrary. Nevertheless, Chesterton's voluminous output marked a certain intellectual celebration of Englishness, smallness, and parochialism, and he became most popularly known as a writer championing certain recognisable codes of common sense.

For a number of writers over the following generation or more, the experience of the First World War marked an indelible hiatus in the English national experience, destroying forever the seem-ingly placid and tranquil world before 1914. The memory of long hot summer days in green English villages, in which tea served during a cricket match and fish could be caught in cool, un-polluted streams running through quiet meadows, became the stuff and substance of novels, short stories and poetry. 'The past is a foreign country', L. P. Hartley wrote in his celebrated novel *The Go-Between* in 1953, 'they do things differently there'. The sense of loss and regret that this nostalgic memory entails belies the degree of continuity in English thought concerning the ap-parently rural and pastoral qualities of national identity. In one sense, loss had always been a central theme in the English rustic ideal and in *The Heart of England* (1907) Edward Thomas lamented the decayed image of suburban streets as he left the town for the countryside, for 'an artist who wished to depict the Fall, and some sympathy with it in the face of a ruined Eden, might have had little to do but copy an acre of the surviving fields'.

The nostalgic and sad English pastoral ideal proved, in fact, all too successful in surviving the modernity of the twentieth century and two world wars. By the 1920s the Conservative Prime Mini-ster Stanley Baldwin cultivated the image of a country gentleman (later to be copied by Harold Macmillan in the early 1960s) and a new motor-car age began to discover the delights of the English terrain on the summer tour. H. V. Morton's popular *In Search of England* (1927) ensured the continuation of the myth for a new generation of more mobile tourists by carefully skirting the industrial towns and urban heartland for an older England since 'the village and the English countryside are the germs of all we are and all we have become: our manufacturing cities belong to the last century and a half; our villages stand with their roots in the heptarchy.'

The cultural roots of English resistance to industrialisation may thus be found at a considerably later date than the mid-Victorian period, for it was only in the last quarter of the Victorian age and in the Edwardian one following it that a strong movement to cultivate the nostalgic, pastoral ideal emerged in the context of growing political crisis accompanying imperial expansion. Though the empire continued as a commonwealth into the 1960s and 1970s, a more nationalist age in recent years has seen a partial restoration of many of the earlier themes discussed in this article. Movements for the restoration of 'real' ale, bread and cheese have proved very popular, there is a growing resistance to factory farming, while such pagan symbols as Stonehenge have become an arena for an annual summer struggle with authority. This movement back to the English landscape, furthermore, significantly echoes a theme in English national identity evident before the comparatively recent extensive popularisation of the monarchy, which occurred only in the age of radio and television, from the 1930s onwards. The degree of entrenchment in both popular consciousness and the English cultural tradition, therefore, suggests that it is stronger than a mere compensation for loss of great power status as has been the case with the royal family. To this extent, the English pastoral ideal has proved to be both an enduring and somewhat inscrutable quality of modern English culture, one that historians can ill afford to ignore.

For Further Reading:

Mark Girouard, *The Return to Camelot: Chivalry and the English Gentleman* (Yale University Press, 1981); Martin Weiner, *English Culture and the Decline of the Industrial Spirit* (Cambridge University Press, 1980); Herbert L. Sussman, *Victorians and the*

Machine (Harvard University Press, 1968); Raymond Williams, *The Country and the City* (Chatto and Windus, 1973); John Coates, *Chesterton and the Edwardian Cultural Crisis* (Hull University Press, 1984); W. J. Keith, *The Rural Tradition* (The Harvester Press, 1975).

21

Diamonds are Forever?
Kipling's Imperialism

Denis Judd

Opposite: Family of nations?: the West Indian Rifles in the great procession to St Paul's, June 22nd, 1897, highpoint of the Jubilee hype, but open to question from the Empire's most patriotic poet. (Hulton-Getty Collection)

THE LITERARY FIGURES of the late Victorian period – even when as disparate as Joseph Conrad and Oscar Wilde – have in common a sense of
restlessness and challenge often borne out of a sense of fin de siècle
brittleness about a social fabric and structure grown complacent over the
long years of Victoria's reign. It might then seem strange to bracket
them with undoubtedly the most popular writer of late Victorian and
Edwardian Britain – arguably the man who came closest to embodying
the authentic voice of *hoi polloi* both in the middle and working classes
of that society – Rudyard Kipling (1865–1936).

Yet Kipling's writing, from his essays of *mores* East and West in *Plain
Tales from the Hills*, the traumas of cruelty in childhood in a story like
'Baa Baa Black Sheep' or the praise of the 'poor bloody infantry' against
bone-headed superiors that emerges in his *Barrack-Room Ballads*, is shot
through with an ambivalence that indicates a character far more complex
than the mere jingoistic laureate of imperialism which he is often caricatured as.

Denis Judd here examines a defining moment in that ambivalence:
Kipling's response, via his poem *Recessional* penned for the occasion, to
the event which seemed to sum up the zenith of Empire – the celebrations for Queen Victoria's Diamond Jubilee in June 1897.

A hundred years ago, between June 19th and 24th, 1897,
Britain and the British Empire celebrated the sixtieth anniversary of Queen Victoria's accession to the throne. The Diamond
Jubilee celebrations were chiefly staged in order to affirm the
achievements of the British people and to glorify the British Empire. During the June festivities the public, both in Britain and
throughout the Empire, were able to feast on a rich diet of ceremonial and display, speech-making and official processions, chief
of which was the royal procession to St Paul's Cathedral for the
Thanksgiving Service in the imperial capital on June 22nd. The
festivities were generally marked by an outpouring of over-heated
patriotic sentiment, by lavish spending on receptions, balls, street
parties and shows, by military and naval displays, and by flags,
bunting and glittering illuminations in the streets.

Commenting on the Diamond Jubilee, *The Times* wrote that
'History may be searched, and searched in vain, to discover so
wonderful an exhibition of allegiance and brotherhood among so
many myriads of men'. Sir Arthur Sullivan composed the 'Jubilee
Hymn'. The Poet Laureate, Alfred Austin, proffered some medio-
cre, celebratory verse.

The *Daily Graphic* claimed that the Jubilee

... to the foreigner ... has been a revelation. He has been enabled to realise for the first time the stability of English institutions, the immensity of the British Empire, and, finally, the strength of the bonds by which the family of nations owing allegiance to the British Crown is united.

In France, *Le Figaro* told its readers that Rome itself had been 'equalled, if not surpassed, by the Power which in Canada, Australia, India, in the China Seas, in Egypt, Central and Southern Africa, in the Atlantic and in the Mediterranean rules the peoples and governs their interests'. From Berlin the *Kreuz Zeitung*, perhaps a shade regretfully, described the Empire as 'practically unassailable'.

Of the sparkling, elaborate and undeniably impressive royal procession of June 22nd, Mark Twain astutely observed that it was Queen Victoria, gravely acknowledging the tumultuous acclamation of her people from her carriage, who was the 'real procession' and 'all the rest ... embroidery'. G. W. Steevens, in the newly established *Daily Mail*, described the procession lyrically as 'a living gazetteer of the British Empire'. He went on:

A plain, stupid, uninspired people, they call us, and yet ... each one of us – you and I, and that man in his shirt-sleeves at the corner – is a working part of this world-shaping force. How small you must feel in the face of this stupendous whole, and yet how great to be a unit in it!.

Not that the response to the Diamond Jubilee celebrations was uniformly favourable. The Labour politician Keir Hardie, looking ahead to the great royal procession, wrote: 'Millions will go out on Tuesday next to see the Queen. What they will see will be an old lady of very commonplace aspect. That of itself will set some a-thinking. Royalty, to be a success, should keep off the streets.' The future Fabian and socialist reformer Beatrice Webb recorded in her diary somewhat disdainfully, 'imperialism in the air, all classes drunk with the sight-seeing and hysterical loyalty'. Among active trade unionists, left-wing Liberals, certain Nonconformist sects, Irish nationalists, pacifists and libertarians could also be found misgivings and, sometimes, downright hostility to the self-congratulatory outpouring of imperial and patriotic sentiment.

Unexpectedly, perhaps, misgivings were also articulated by Rudyard Kipling, one of the most popular and widely read writers of late-Victorian Britain, but also a man widely regarded as a stalwart imperialist, unshakeably loyal and patriotic.

Kipling had been passed over for the post of Poet Laureate shortly after the formation of Lord Salisbury's Conservative and Unionist government in the summer of 1895. Although both Salisbury and his nephew, Arthur James Balfour, had expressed a strong preference for Kipling, discreet enquiries revealed his antipathy to official recognition. It is also possible that the queen had vetoed his candidature having taken offence at his sprightly, not entirely respectful poem, 'The Widow at Windsor'. At any rate, according to Sir Ian Malcolm's judgement, 'That ass Austin' was named as Poet Laureate on January 1st, 1896, in spite of Salisbury's preference for Kipling, 'though he blows his own trumpet rather loud sometimes'.

Despite Austin's appointment and the common contempt which many felt for the new Laureate's literary powers, Kipling at first resisted a number of suggestions that he should compose an ode to mark the occasion of the Jubilee. The editor of *The Times*, however, persistently lobbied him. As Kipling ruefully recalled: 'The Times began sending telegrams so I shut myself in a room ... I found just one line I liked – "Lest we forget" – and wrote the poem around that.'

On June 22nd, Jubilee Day, Kipling set aside his draft for some new nursery stories, as well as the early version of the 'White Man's Burden', so that he could work on a poem based on the line 'Lest we forget'. That evening he walked, with his wife Carrie, from their Sussex home to hear the pealing of church bells and to watch the chain of bonfires light up along the south coast, the flames leaping 'on dune and headland', as his poem 'Recessional' was later to put it.

The Jubilee ode had still not been completed by July 16th; indeed a house-guest staying with the Kiplings, Sallie Norton, given permission to rummage through the contents of Kipling's wastepaper basket, pulled out the draft of the poem on the Diamond Jubilee, entitled 'After'. Miss Norton's protest at the notion of destroying the poem was reinforced by others in the household, and eventually Kipling sat down to revise it. He reduced its length from seven to five stanzas, and the final version was dispatched to *The Times*'s office that evening by special messenger.

On July 17th *The Times* published the re-titled poem 'Recessional' in its middle pages. The poem was an instant triumph, greeted with a storm of praise, and amply confirming Kipling's reputation as the greatest popular poet of the day. His gratification at his success was compounded a month later when his only son was born, and named John after his grandfather.

Four stanzas of the poem 'Recessional' are worth quoting in full:

> God of our fathers, known of old,
> Lord of our far-flung battle-line,
> Beneath whose awful Hand we hold
> Dominion over palm and pine –
> Lord God of Hosts, be with us yet,
> Lest we forget – lest we forget!
>
> The tumult and the shouting die;
> The Captains and the Kings depart;
> Still stands thine ancient sacrifice,
> An humble and a contrite heart.
> Lord God of Hosts, be with us yet,
> Lest we forget – lest we forget!
>
> Far-called, our navies melt away;
> On dune and headland sinks the fire:
> Lo, all our pomp of yesterday
> Is one with Nineveh and Tyre!
> Judge of the Nations, spare us yet,
> Lest we forget – lest we forget!
>
> If, drunk with sight of power, we loose
> Wild tongues that have not Thee in awe,
> Such boastings as the Gentiles use,
> Or lesser breeds without the Law –
> Lord God of Hosts, be with us yet,
> Lest we forget – lest we forget!

Kipling had used an almost magical formula in the writing of these verses. The lines are stirring yet disturbing, containing a series of measured and sober warnings against patriotic and imperial excess within a framework of thoughtful introspection. Far from indulging in a literary form of imperial and patriotic flag-waving, Kipling plainly identified one of the deep, but barely acknowledged, explanations as to why the nation, and to some extent the Empire, had apparently thrown itself so wholeheartedly into the Jubilee extravaganza.

Behind the bold, brash and frequently self-congratulatory front that the Diamond Jubilee celebrations presented to the world lurked, in almost unquantifiable measure, pessimism and insecurity. Although many of Britain's leaders and opinion-makers chose not to articulate it, there was a deep-seated anxiety as to what the future held both for the nation and the Empire, especially during the imminent, and unknowable, new century.

Britain seemed beset by a host of problems, pressing in from all sides. On the world stage a revitalised France provided an obstacle, or at least an irritant, in a number of areas of British interest. The arrival on the scene of recently united and now actively colonising nations like Germany and Italy had disturbed the old imperial order and put Britain under new and unwelcome pressures. The serious threat posed to British manufacturing and commercial supremacy by the rapidly expanding capacities of both Germany and the US provided further challenges, highlighting the British failure adequately to modernise and reinvest in their industrial base, and a reminder – to those who chose to see it – that the British economy was only carried into surplus on an annual trading basis by the success of 'invisible' exports.

In addition, the late-Victorians were troubled by a number of challenges, many of them unwelcome, to the old domestic order. From within, British society was faced with a new, more militant, mass trade unionism, with the 'new' man as well as the 'new' woman – who was soon to press for enfranchisement as well as full equality before the law, with the persistence of Irish nationalism, with the perils apparently posed by the growth of domestic socialism and much else besides. Certain 'British' standards, long taken for granted, seemed to be slipping: the public fretted over the adulteration and processing of foodstuffs and the dilution of beer; while such incidents as the conviction of Oscar Wilde in 1895 for homosexual activities had convinced many that the nation, the 'race', was on the slippery downward slope of decadence and decline.

It was these, and a host of other unformed and barely acknowledged anxieties, that made Kipling's great Jubilee poem appear so relevant and timely. The very real prospect of Britain's loss of its naval supremacy was, by itself, sufficient cause for concern: 'far-called, our navies melt away', Kipling had written. The apparently irresistible rise of the US as a great naval power, and Imperial Germany's naval ambitions, soon to be made plain by the passing of the 1898 Navy Law in the Reichstag, could only mean that the days of Royal Naval supremacy were, if not numbered, then soon to be seriously challenged. The nightmare of the loss of naval supremacy would return like an unwanted phantom to haunt the British imagination in the years before the outbreak of war in 1914, most painfully during the 'navy scare' of 1909. It is no accident that this nightmare was soon to be given menacing fictional form in what is commonly regarded as the first British spy novel, Erskine Childers's best-selling *The Riddle of the Sands*, published in 1903.

If Britain failed to respond to these, and similar challenges, then surely chronic and irreversible decline would follow. As Kipling wrote:

> On dune and headland sinks the fire:
> Lo, all our pomp of yesterday
> Is one with Nineveh and Tyre!

The poem contains other strong images. Britain's battle-line is 'far-flung', her navies are 'far-called'. The anxieties over the stretching of national resources to breaking point were thus strikingly illustrated and reinforced, and were to be promptly addressed shortly after the turn of the century by the Fisher naval reforms, the Anglo-Japanese alliance and the ententes with France and Russia. Until then, however, the bonfires which Kipling and his wife had seen in Sussex blazing on Jubilee Day, might well prove to be temporary and over-optimistic symbols: 'On dune and headland sinks the fire'. The perils of uninhibited and thoughtless celebration, which manifested themselves with such intensity and frequency throughout Britain and the Empire, needed to be put into sharp perspective:

> If, drunk with sight of power, we loose
> Wild tongues that have not Thee in awe,
> Such boastings as the Gentiles use,
> Or lesser breeds without the Law –
> Lord God of Hosts, be with us yet,
> Lest we forget – lest we forget!

Kipling, secure in his reputation as an imperialist and a patriot, had issued 'a call to humility and a warning that the proudest empire is ephemeral as a day's pageant'. The 'lesser breeds without the law' were not necessarily, as was so quickly assumed by critics of the poem, the black or brown citizens of Britain's empire. The poet is surely here referring both to foreigners and to those British citizens and subjects, no matter what their origin or ethnicity, who were unable or unwilling to see what needed to be done in the national interest and what perils and spectres lurked in the shadows. It was not merely the easily distracted, superficially educated and politically immature mass of the British public that Kipling was berating, it was also the 'flannelled fools at the wicket', and the 'muddied oafs at the goal' – more

likely to be the products of the public schools than of the poorly
funded and chaotically organised state education system.

Kipling was deluged with praise after the publication of
'Recessional'. His literary agent, A. S. Watt, hastened

... to offer you congratulations on the appearance ... of your magnificent poem. It strikes the right note with regard to the Jubilee Celebration
and will recall the nation to the source of its real strength. You are the
only rightful heir to the mantles of Shakespeare, Milton, and Tennyson,
and the laureate *de facto!* I tried to read 'God of our fathers' aloud this
morning at home but I broke down.

His cousin by marriage, J. W. Mackail, an intellectual and a paci-
fist, wrote: '... in our household, at least, your poem in *The Times*
of this morning was read with tumult of acclaim. I cannot tell
you how glad I am of it ... There are all the signs of England
saving up for the most tremendous smash ever recorded in history if she does not look to her goings'. In reply, Kipling wrote:

Seeing what manner of armed barbarians we are surrounded with, we're
about the only power with a glimmer of civilisation in us ... This is no
ideal world but a nest of burglars, alas; and we must protect ourselves
against being burgled. All the same, we have no need to shout and yell
and ramp about strength because that is a waste of power, and because
other nations can do the advertising better than we can. The big smash
is coming one of these days, sure enough, but I think we shall pull
through, not without credit. It will be the common people – the 3rd class
carriages – that'll save us.

If Britain's need for vigilance and self-renewal, most usefully
manifested in the maintenance at whatever cost of her naval supremacy, was one of the great themes of Kipling's poetry as the
century drew to a close, there was another one that both commanded attention and fitted neatly, hand in glove, with the first
preoccupation.

The year after the publication of 'Recessional', Kipling had
finally composed 'The White Man's Burden'. The message of the
poem was apparently straightforward and, at first sight, surprising. It was that the United States should shoulder, with Britain,
the responsibility for the spread of Anglo-Saxon civilisation. The
United States' comprehensive defeat of Spain during the war of
1898–99 had led to the acquisition of a formal American empire
in the Caribbean and the Pacific. Kipling appealed to the American
people, as he saw it – the other great half of the English-speaking

race and true 'white men' as well – to share Britain's global civilising mission.

The verses were composed 'to the rhythm of a hymn-tune, and the language was again biblical'. The poem was full of striking and unexpected imagery:

> Take up the White Man's burden –
> Send forth the best ye breed –
> Go bind your sons to exile
> To serve your captive's need

Americans who, like the British, Kipling took instinctively to understand both the limitations and the benefits of 'the Law' (and among whom were large numbers of 'gentiles', on the poet's analysis), were thus encouraged to endure the tribulations of imperial rule and to put up with the ingratitude of their subject peoples. They must

> . . . wait in heavy harness
> On fluttered folk and wild –
> Your new-caught, sullen peoples,
> Half devil and half child.

The drudgery of imperial rule would offer, in Kipling's opinion, little by way of material reward or even any clearly identifiable token of gratitude. It might, moreover, all end in catastrophe, or at least in sterile failure:

> Take up the White Man's burden –
> And reap his old reward:
> The blame of those ye better,
> The hate of those ye guard . . .
>
> And when your goal is nearest
> The end for others sought,
> Watch Sloth and heathen Folly
> Bring all your hope to nought.

Although these inducements were hardly sufficient in themselves to send thousands of young American men in quest of administrative service overseas, leading American statesmen were pleased enough. Theodore Roosevelt, the recently elected governor of New York State and destined to be President, thought the verses 'rather poor poetry, but good sense from the expansionist stand-point'. Henry Cabot Lodge told Roosevelt in turn: 'I like it. I think it is better poetry than you say.'

Taken together, the poems 'Recessional' and 'The White Man's Burden' contained a compelling diagnosis not merely of Britain's current ills but of the possible remedies for the malady. If 'Recessional' had urged sober restraint, introspection and a sensible set of national priorities, 'The White Man's Burden' pointed the way to a resolution of British difficulties through a process of détente and co-operation with the United States – manifestation of the Special Relationship well before the phrase had been invented.

In this respect at least, Britain's policy markers and Rudyard Kipling marched in step. Unwilling to accept the inevitability of its own decline, Britain was making a calculated attempt to bring the New World to the rescue of the Old. During the late 1890s this discreet, sometimes invisible policy was in full swing. It was underpinned by the fact that, overall, Britain's world interests were not seriously in conflict with those of the United States. On those occasions where conflict seemed likely, for example over the Venezuelan boundary dispute with British Guiana, over the Hay–Pauncefote Panama Canal Treaty and over the demarcation of the Alaskan border with Canada, Britain simply sold out on each occasion to the demands of the United States. This was nothing short of appeasement – on a scale that very few contemporaries were able, or willing, to recognise.

The wheels of Anglo-American co-operation and collaboration were also oiled by the surprisingly substantial level of social interaction between leading British and American families. The most obvious example of this lay in the marriages contracted between high-profile British men and American women – many of them from wealthy US families. It is significant that Kipling was one of those Britons to marry an American, his wife Carrie being the daughter of a well-to-do family based in Vermont in New England. Among contemporary British statesmen who chose American brides were the Liberal Lewis Harcourt, the Duke of Manchester, Lord Randolph Churchill, Lord Curzon and Joseph Chamberlain. Chamberlain had already gone on record in 1887 proclaiming: 'I refuse to think or to speak of the USA as a foreign nation. We are all of the same race and blood . . . Our past is theirs – their future is ours . . . I urge upon you our common origin, our relationship . . . We are branches of one family.' Such sentiments were reinforced by the often complex but enduring connections that linked one side of the Atlantic to the other and involved the commercial spheres of banking, insurance and trade, as well as the ready acknowledgement of a shared linguistic, political, cultural and legal inheritance.

Judged, then, on the evidence of the years 1897 to 1899, and chiefly his two poems, 'Recessional' and 'The White Man's Burden', an impression of Kipling can be formed sharply at odds with the commonly accepted stereotype of imperial tub-thumper and vulgar patriot. Kipling was a character far more complex, and in some ways perverse, than many suppose. That he composed much bumping, jangling verse mimicking the idiosyncratic and debased English of the common soldier should mislead no one. Kipling was no mere acolyte of Britannia, no superficial and loud-mouthed camp follower. He saw quite clearly the failings of Britain's self-pronounced imperial mission and did not shrink from proposing remedies. His criticisms were, of course, intended to avert disaster and to consolidate and perhaps enhance British global power. His strictures were, in this sense, self-serving. Behind the manifest popularity of much of his work, however, lay a shrewd and accurate analysis of what needed to be done.

Kipling was, indeed, a dangerous enemy of those who either actively wished to destroy the British Empire or were indifferent to its prospective demise, but not in the way that is generally imagined.

For Further Reading:

Lord Birkenhead, *Rudyard Kipling* (Weidenfeld and Nicolson, 1978); C. Carrington, *Rudyard Kipling; his life and works* (Penguin, 1986); C. Chapman and P. Roben, (eds.) *Debrett's Queen Victoria's Jubilees, 1887 and 1897* (Debrett's Peerage, 1977); R. Kipling, *Rudyard Kipling's Verse; the definitive edition* (Macmillan, 1949); J. Morris, *Pax Britannica: the Climax of an Empire* (Penguin, 1979).

Notes on Contributors

Caroline Arscott is Lecturer in History of Art at the Courtauld Institute.

Dea Birkett is a freelance writer. Her books include *Spinsters Abroad* (Basil Blackwell, 1989) and *Mary Kingsley: Imperial Adventuress* (Macmillan, 1992).

Ian Cambell Bradley is a writer and broadcaster. His books include *Enlightened Entrepreneurs* (Weidenfeld & Nicholson, 1987) and *Abide with Me: The World of Victorian Hymns* (SCM Press, 1997).

Asa Briggs (Lord Briggs of Lewes) was formerly Provost of Worcester College, Oxford. Longman has published his immensely influential *The Age of Improvement, 1783–1867*, and, more recently, *Modern Europe 1789–1889* (written with Patricia Clavin).

Philip Collins is Emeritus Professor of English at the University of Leicester. His books include *Charles Dickens* (Routledge, 1993) and, co-edited with Edward Giuland, *The Annotated Dickens* (Orbis, 1986).

Trevor Fisher is the author of *Scandal: The Sexual Politics of Late Victorian Britain* (Alan Sutton, 1995).

Derek Fraser was formerly Professor of History at the University of California, Los Angeles and is author of *The Evolution of the British Welfare State* (Macmillan, 1984).

Brian Harrison is Professor of Modern History at the University of Oxford, and Fellow and Tutor in Modern History and Politics at Corpus Christi College, Oxford. His books include *Drink and the Victorians* (Keele University Press, 1994) and *The Transformation of British Politics 1860–1995* (Oxford University Press, 1996).

Charles Harvey is Professor of Business History and Management and Director of the School of Management at Royal Holloway, University of London and is the author (along with Jon Press) of *William Morris: Design and Enterprise in Victorian Britain* (Manchester University Press, 1991), *The Life and Work of William Morris* (London, 1996) and *Databases in Historical Research: Theory, Methods and Applications* (Macmillan, 1996).

The late *Stephen Jones* was Director of Spencer House and formerly
  Editor of Publications, The National Art Collections Fund, and
  author of *The Eighteenth Century* (Cambridge University Press,
  1985).
Denis Judd is Professor of History at the University of North Lon-
  don. His books include *Empire: the British Imperial Experience
  from 1765 to the Present* (Fontana Press, 1997).
Gordon Marsden was formerly Editor of *History Today*, and is now
  Member of Parliament for Blackpool South.
Colin Matthew is Professor of Modern History at the University of
  Oxford, and Fellow and Tutor in Modern History at St Hugh's
  College, Oxford. He is currently seconded to the New Diction-
  ary of National Biography, 1992–7. He is Editor of *The Gladstone
  Diaries* (Oxford University Press, Volume IX, 1986) and of *Brief
  Lives: 150 Intimate Biographies of the Famous by the Famous* (Oxford
  University Press, 1997).
Edward Norman is Canon Treasurer of York Minster and Honor-
  ary Professor of History at the University of York. His books
  inlcude *The English Catholic Church in the Nineteenth Century*
  (Oxford University Press, 1984) and *The House of God: Church
  Architecture, Style and History* (Thames and Hudson, 1990).
Jon Press is Professor of History at Bath College of Higher Educa-
  tion, and is the author (along with Charles Harvey) of *William
  Morris: Design and Enterprise in Victorian Britain* (Manchester
  University Press, 1991), *The Life and Work of William Morris*
  (London, 1996) and *Databases in Historical Research: Theory, Methods
  and Applications* (Macmillan, 1996).
Paul Rich is Principal Lecturer in the Department of Politics, Uni-
  versity of Luton, and author of *Race and Empire in British Politics*
  (Cambridge University Press, 1985).
Sheila Rowbotham is Senior Research Fellow in the Department of
  Sociology at Manchester University, and author of *A Century of
  Women* (Viking Penguin, 1997).
Anne Summers is a Curator of Manuscripts at the British Library,
  and author of *Angels and Citizens: British Women as Military
  Nurses, 1854–1914* (Routledge, 1988) and *How to Find Source
  Material* (British Library, 1996).
Robert Thorne formerly worked as an historian for English Herit-
  age's London Division, and is now Senior Associate at Alan
  Baxter & Associates, Structural Engineers. He is co-author of
  Birmingham Pubs 1890–1939 (Alan Sutton, 1986) and *Change at
  King's Cross* (1990).

John Tosh is Professor of History at the University of North London, and author of *The Pursuit of History* (Longman, 2nd Edn 1991). With Michael Roper, he has edited *Manful Associations: Masculinities in Britain since 1800* (Routledge, 1991).

Janet Wolff was formerly Reader in the Sociology of Culture at the University of Leeds, and is now based at the University of Rochester, New York. Her books include *Aesthetics and the Sociology of Art* (Macmillan, 1993), *The Social Production of Art* (Macmillan, 1993) and, as co-editor, *Culture of Capital: Essays on the Nineteenth-Century Middle Class* (Manchester University Press, 1988).

Nigel Yates is Honorary Fellow in Church History at the University of Wales Lampeter. His books include *The Oxford Movement and Anglican Ritualism* (1983) for the Historical Association, and *Crown and Mitre: Religion and Society in Northern Europe since the Reformation*, written with W. M. Jacob (Boydell Press, 1993).

Robert M. Young is Professor of Psychotherapy and Psychoanalytic Studies at the University of Sheffield. His books include *Darwin's Metaphor: Nature's Place in Victorian Culture* (Cambridge University Press, 1985), and he is Editor of the journal *Science as Culture*.

Index

Caird, Mona, 85
Cambridge, 244, 245
Cambridge Camden Society, 68
Carlyle, Thomas, 39, 72, 105–6,
204, 259
Carnegie, Andrew, 108, 180
Carpenter, Edward, 15, **243–54**,
259, 264–5
Catholicism *see* Anglo-Catholicism;
Roman Catholicism
Chamberlain, Joseph, 12, **165–77**,
220, 221, 224, 225, 280
Charles, Prince of Wales, 3–4
Chartism, 104, 168, 192, 194, 245,
247; Lovett and, 19–33
Chesterton, G. K., 11, 266–7
Childers, Erskine, 277
children: and bourgeois cult of
home, 78, 80, 81, 82–4; child
labour, 99; child prostitution,
159–60, 161–2; in Dickens'
novels, 56
Christian Socialists, 189–200
Christmas, 11, 52, 55, 56, 78, 79
Church of England, 10, 81, 169,
171; and Christian Socialists,
191, 195–6; and medievalism,
66, 67, 68, 70–2, 73–5; and
nursing reform, 142, 143, 144–7
Church and Stage Guild, 198
Cobbett, William, 57, 69, 72
Cobden, Richard, 30, 104
Colchester, 157–8
Collings, Jesse, 170
Collins, John, 24, 26, 29
Collins, Wilkie, 53
Combe, George, 25, 32
Congregationalism, 89–100, 169
Conservative Party, 157–8
Contagious Diseases Acts, 153,
154–9, 160, 163
Conway, Katherine St John, 248,
249, 253
Cook, William, 173
countryside, attitudes to, 45, 97,
259, 260, 262–8

Craik, Mrs, 112–13
Crane, Walter, 212, 237
Crimean War, 140, 141, 145, 154
Criminal Law Amendment Bill,
160–2

Dale, Robert, 169
Daniell, Miriam, 248–9
Darwin, Charles, 103, 110, 180,
186
Darwinism, 260, 261, 262, 265, 266
Dawson, George, 169
deaconess movement, 143
decorative arts, 201–13
Diamond Jubilee (1897), 7, 16,
271–81
Dickens, Charles, 11, 37, **47–62**,
97, 143, 259
Dickinson, G. Lowes, 245, 247,
253
Disraeli, Benjamin (Lord
Beaconsfield), 4, 73, 130, 131
divorce, 82, 85
Dixon, George, 170, 171
Dresser, Christopher, 235, 236

Economist, The, 183
education, 99, 170, 171, 183; adult
education, 192–3, 245; under
Gladstone, 134, 136; Godwin on,
125; Headlam on, 192, 199, 200;
Lovett and, 19–33; public
schools, 84, 85; Smiles on,
111–12
Eliot, George (Mary Ann Evans),
49–50, 58, 183
Ellis, Havelock, 15, 245, 247, 251,
253
Ellis, Sarah, 80
Elmy, Elizabeth Wolstenholme,
252–3
Emerson, Ralph Waldo, 80, 104,
106, 262, 263
'Englishness', 4, 15, 56–7, 58,
112–13, **255–69**
Enlightenment, influence of, 21, 23